Empowering Marketing and Sales with HubSpot

Take your business to a new level with HubSpot's inbound marketing, SEO, analytics, and sales tools

Resa Gooding

BIRMINGHAM—MUMBAI

Empowering Marketing and Sales with HubSpot

Copyright © 2022 Packt Publishing

Associate Group Product Manager: Alok Dhuri
Senior Editor: Rohit Singh
Content Development Editor: Kinnari Chohan
Technical Editor: Maran Fernandes
Copy Editor: Safis Editing
Project Coordinator: Manisha Singh
Proofreader: Safis Editing
Indexer: Hemangini Bari
Production Designer: Shyam Sundar Korumilli
Marketing Coordinator: Rayyan Khan

First published: June 2022

Production reference: 1230622

Published by Packt Publishing Ltd.
Livery Place
35 Livery Street
Birmingham
B3 2PB, UK.

ISBN 978-1-83898-714-5

www.packt.com

To my mother, Reva Gooding, for the selflessness and sacrifices made in order to build the foundation upon which I stand today. To my father, Oscar Gooding, for teaching me how to embrace life's challenges and see the best in everyone always. To my life partner, Yossi Efraim, for his unwavering support and constant love throughout this journey and to our four amazing kids – Itamar, Gilad, Ofry and Eytan – who continue to be my source of inspiration each and every day.

– Resa Gooding

Contributors

About the author

Resa Gooding is a HubSpot Certified Trainer and an expert in multiple digital marketing disciplines, including marketing automation and closed-loop reporting. Resa is the co-founder and ex-CMO of Cacao Media, a HubSpot-certified Diamond Partner Agency that was acquired by ScaleOps in 2022. Using CRM and marketing automation processes set up by Resa and her team, paired with digital marketing best practices, organizations were able to spend more time closing deals instead of being bogged down by administrative tasks or misaligned processes.

I would like to thank my past employees, clients, and contractors, without whom this book would not have been possible. I would also like to particularly thank Brian Halligan and Dharmesh Shah for creating a company that has impacted millions of lives and particularly mine by giving me a platform to build not just a successful business but an outstanding life.

About the reviewers

Mike Tatum has dedicated his career to using a life cycle marketing strategy and marketing automation to create profitable and engaging customer journeys from initial discovery to reactivation. He's a HubSpot Marketing Hub expert who was a featured speaker at HubSpot's INBOUND conference in 2021, as well as an active member of HubSpot's Revenue Council. He currently is the director of life cycle marketing at Athletic Greens and consults with businesses looking to get the most out of HubSpot.

Lyndon Brathwaite is the founder and lead consultant at OPAAT-SWY Consulting Ltd. He started his career as a sales representative in 2003 and gradually moved through the sales ranks throughout the years. He held the position of sales manager at Massy Technologies InfoCom, before moving on to start the first sales enablement agency in the English-speaking Caribbean.

Driven by a mantra of change, create, different, and achieve, Lyndon is best known for inspiring his teams to find different ways of being the best version of themselves and achieving the things they want in life by making the changes needed for success.

Lyndon has been able to achieve certain milestones within his short but impressive 4-year journey as an entrepreneur. His stints include being co-founder of a second sales development company in Trinidad and Tobago, hosting three sales conferences between 2019 and 2021, becoming a solutions provider with HubSpot in 2019, and speaking internationally at HubSpot's major **INBOUND** conference in 2020.

Esther Ohayon has been in key roles in sales and marketing for years, but she believes that tracking the customer journey is more critical now than ever. Marketing must find and nurture the ideal customer with the most effective content, and sales must prove their solution is the best option for their clients. HubSpot keeps track of all the data so that businesses can run smoothly and grow steadily.

Specializing in brand development and digital marketing with a distinct leaning toward sales and customer service, she always tries to put the customer at the center. She is curious about what customers really want and how to deliver that message in the most valuable way to them.

Table of Contents

3

Using HubSpot for Managing Sales Processes Effectively

4
Empowering Your Sales Team through HubSpot

Part 2: Scaling Your Business with HubSpot

5
Increasing Online Visibility Using HubSpot's SEO Tool

8

Conducting a Portal Audit

9

Converting Your Visitors to Customers

10

Revive Your Database with HubSpot Email Marketing Tools

11

Proving That Your Efforts Worked Using the Reports

Part 3: Is HubSpot Right for Your Business?

12

Inbound or Outbound – Which Is Better for Your Business?

13

Leveraging the Benefits of the Marketing Flywheel

14

Using HubSpot for All Types of Businesses

Assessments

Index

Other Books You May Enjoy

Preface

Rated as the top-performing **customer relationship management (CRM)** platform by G2 Spring 2022 CRM Grid, HubSpot continues to help companies win on customer experience. A cloud-based CRM platform built from the ground up, not by acquisition, HubSpot has become a single source of truth for businesses to deliver a best-in-class customer experience.

With four main hubs – a marketing hub, a sales hub, a service hub, an operations hub, and CRM – as well as over 1,000 integrations available through its App Marketplace, HubSpot reduces friction from your customer experience. It seamlessly combines content, messaging, automation, reporting, and data all in one unified platform, making it easier for your teams to adapt and speed up their efficiency in order to improve the buyer's experience.

With this amount of functionality, it can be sometimes overwhelming to know where to begin, and even though HubSpot offers a wealth of resources through its academy, blogs, website, and even natively in the portal, there is nothing like an old-fashioned manual to walk you through the steps from A to Z. For this reason, this book was written.

This book is not meant to be a duplication of the vast output of resources of HubSpot that are readily available to all users; instead, it aims to serve as a guide to help marketing and sales teams understand where to begin, what to focus on, and what best practices to consider when implementing various tools. In addition, the last section aims to help you understand whether HubSpot is right for your business and also discusses some of the terminology used over the years, such as funnel, flywheel, and RevOps, that increased the demand for CRM platforms as companies aimed to scale.

It is important to point out that although we previously mentioned that HubSpot has four main hubs, including CRM, this book specifically focuses on the marketing and sales hubs and CRM. You can choose to focus on any of the chapters you wish or read all of them if you want to learn some best practices or simply double-check any of your previous setups or campaigns.

We do hope that you are able to implement some of the recommendations mentioned throughout the chapters, and we encourage you to share any lessons or tips learned in your reviews or feedback on the book.

Who this book is for

This HubSpot marketing book is for sales and marketing professionals, business owners, and entrepreneurs who want to use HubSpot for scaling their sales and marketing activities. A basic understanding of key marketing terms is required to get started with this book.

What this book covers

Chapter 1, Overview of HubSpot – What You MUST Know, explores how to get started in Hubspot and navigate the system. You will get step-by-step walkthroughs of how to set up the various parts of HubSpot correctly and become a system administrator.

Chapter 2, Generating Quick Wins with HubSpot in the First 30 days, explains how to combine the most basic features in HubSpot to generate quick wins in the first 30 days of setting up the platform.

Chapter 3, Using HubSpot for Managing Sales Processes Effectively, shows you how to manage their sales process using HubSpot. From reading this chapter, you will be able to understand which contacts in your database are real prospects and have the potential to close as a customer, and to closely identify which stage in the sales process they are currently in and what's needed to take them to the next stage.

Chapter 4, Empowering Your Sales Team Through HubSpot, explains how to manage Hubspot CRM and Sales Hub for sales teams and managers. You will learn how to use Hubspot tools to create meetings, tasks, and functions only designed for sales.

Chapter 5, Increasing Online Visibility Using HubSpot's SEO Tool, demonstrates how to use the HubSpot SEO tool to get found online.

Chapter 6, Getting Known Through Social Media on HubSpot, explores how to use the social media tool within HubSpot to listen, monitor, and engage appropriately with your target audience.

Chapter 7, Expanding Your Reach with Paid Ads Managed in HubSpot, shows you how to master integrating adverts (LinkedIn, Google Ads, and Facebook) with HubSpot and use this information to drive these visitors further down the funnel.

Chapter 8, Conducting a Portal Audit, examines some of the missed opportunities the marketing and sales team forego when using HubSpot, resulting in poor reporting and understanding of business activities.

Chapter 9, Converting Your Visitors to Customers, explains how to create landing pages, forms, and workflow strategies and nurture programs to engage with your leads and customers. This section will help you create a marketing funnel using Hubspot's lead capture and engagement tools.

Chapter 10, Revive Your Database with HubSpot's Email Marketing Tools, shares tips and best practices for creating emails and sending. You will gain knowledge on templates, sending options, functionalities, and best practices for writing and sending emails in Hubspot.

Chapter 11, Proving That Your Efforts Worked Using These Reports, explores how to create reporting and tracking within Hubspot and identify key trends in your data. You will learn to build custom reports, dashboards, and notifications to keep on top of company marketing goals.

Chapter 12, Inbound or Outbound – Which Is Better for Your Business?, deciphers the benefits of inbound versus outbound and whether the two can co-exist in today's businesses.

Chapter 13, Leveraging the Benefits of the Marketing Flywheel, explains why the marketing flywheel replaced the marketing funnel and how it helps marketers produce more successful campaigns and businesses reach their targets faster.

Chapter 14, Using HubSpot for All Types of Businesses, explains how to use HubSpot for every type of business, such as manufacturing, agriculture, technology, SaaS, and e-commerce.

To get the most out of this book

To get the most out of this book, it is highly recommended to have either a HubSpot Marketing Hub Professional license, a Sales Professional license, or a combination of both. You will also need super admin access to your portal in order to perform many of the tasks outlined in the chapters. You should also have some understanding of digital marketing concepts, such as **search engine optimization** (**SEO**), social media, paid ads, or email marketing, as well as some knowledge of sales operations and processes.

Software/hardware covered in the book	Operating system requirements
HubSpot	Windows, macOS, or Linux

If you are focusing on the marketing tools discussed in this book, note that you will need to also have admin access to your social media platforms and paid ad platforms – for example, Facebook, LinkedIn, and Google Ads. For the initial setup, having access to the backend of your website and domain provider is necessary. However, if in doubt about how to manage these platforms, it is recommended to work with your IT provider to avoid any issues.

After reading this book, please share any improvements or successes achieved via your preferred social media channels using the #hubspotlessons hashtag so that other readers can benefit as well.

Download the color images

We also provide a PDF file that has color images of the screenshots and diagrams used in this book. You can download it here: https://static.packt-cdn.com/downloads/9781838987145_ColorImages.pdf.

Conventions used

There are a number of text conventions used throughout this book.

Code in text: Indicates code words in the text, database table names, folder names, filenames, file extensions, pathnames, dummy URLs, user input, and Twitter handles. Here is an example: "Set the Invite subject, which can have a personal token or company token in it, so it can read Meeting with [Your Name] + [Company Name / Contact Name]."

Bold: Indicates a new term, an important word, or words that you see onscreen. For instance, words in menus or dialog boxes appear in **bold**. Here is an example: "The quotation tool is a paid feature of HubSpot Sales Professional and can be found by navigating to the top menu and clicking on **Sales | Quotes**."

> **Tips or Important Notes**
> Appear like this.

Get in touch

Feedback from our readers is always welcome.

General feedback: If you have questions about any aspect of this book, email us at customercare@packtpub.com and mention the book title in the subject of your message.

Errata: Although we have taken every care to ensure the accuracy of our content, mistakes do happen. If you have found a mistake in this book, we would be grateful if you would report this to us. Please visit www.packtpub.com/support/errata and fill in the form.

Piracy: If you come across any illegal copies of our works in any form on the internet, we would be grateful if you would provide us with the location address or website name. Please contact us at `copyright@packt.com` with a link to the material.

If you are interested in becoming an author: If there is a topic that you have expertise in and you are interested in either writing or contributing to a book, please visit `authors.packtpub.com`.

Share Your Thoughts

Once you've read *Empowering Marketing and Sales with HubSpot*, we'd love to hear your thoughts! Scan the QR code below to go straight to the Amazon review page for this book and share your feedback.

`https://packt.link/r/1838987142`

Your review is important to us and the tech community and will help us make sure we're delivering excellent quality content.

Part 1: HubSpot – Starting Off HubSpot

If you've decided that HubSpot is the **Customer Relationship Management (CRM)** platform for scaling your business, then you've come to the right place. This section aims to help you understand the fundamental requirements for setting up your portal correctly, how to see a return on your investment within 30 days, and ensure your sales teams are empowered to close more deals. Although it is highly recommended to read through all of the chapters for any tips or best practices you may not have previously considered, feel free to skip to any of the chapters that you think would be most useful to you at this time.

This part contains the following chapters:

- *Chapter 1, Overview of HubSpot – What You MUST Know*
- *Chapter 2, Generating Quick Wins with HubSpot in the First 30 Days*
- *Chapter 3, Using HubSpot for Managing Sales Processes Effectively*
- *Chapter 4, Empowering Your Sales Team Through HubSpot*

1
Overview of HubSpot – What you MUST Know

HubSpot is a mega platform on its own and it's easy to get lost in all the guidelines suggested when setting up your portal. But whether you have a free HubSpot account or a paid account, some basic features must be set up for your portal to operate correctly.

In this chapter, we will break this down for you. The goal is not to do everything at first but to do what's absolutely necessary to get you started. Many features are not covered in this chapter—such as the chatbot tool, the Ads tool, and so on—but they will be covered in later chapters throughout the book. For now, we will keep it stupid simple so that by the end of this chapter, you will have your HubSpot portal ready to send out your first campaign with your company's branding, ensure your emails reach the recipient's inbox and not their spam folder, have multiple channels to engage with your prospects—such as social media, email, and website—as well as track the **return on investment** (**ROI**) of your efforts.

Here is a list of topics we will cover in this chapter. You will learn the value each of these steps will bring to you so that you can decide whether it is important for you to do them or not during your setup or simply skip to sections you may have overlooked in the initial setup so that you can return to fix them:

- **Setting your brand colors and logo**: This step allows you to ensure all landing pages, emails, and so on appear with your company's logo, address, and brand colors.

- **Connecting your website to HubSpot**: This step allows you to collect information on how individual visitors engage with the content on your site so that you ensure you are giving them relevant and engaging content at exactly the right point of their journey.

- **Connecting Google Analytics to HubSpot**: Google Analytics is the most robust platform for tracking how visitors engage with your website. However, it only gives you general data, not specific individual data. Connecting Google Analytics to HubSpot allows you to use HubSpot analytics to show not just how many people came to your site and which pages were the most visited but exactly **who** those individuals were once they had been converted as a lead in your HubSpot portal.

- **Filtering out personal traffic**: In order to have a true reflection of the ROI of your campaigns, you must filter out visits from you, your team, and anyone else who is not a potential customer but may interact with your site regularly—for example, vendors, and so on.

- **Setting up your subdomains—landing pages and blog**: Many companies overlook this step, but it is important if you plan to use HubSpot to host your landing pages and/or blog. Without doing this step, your **Uniform Resource Locator (URL)** will be HubSpot-branded, instead of having your own domain branding.

- **Verifying your email domain**: In order to send marketing emails via HubSpot from your own company's domain, it is important to verify your domain with HubSpot. This is essential to ensure your emails don't land in the recipient's spam folder.

- **Connecting your social media accounts**: HubSpot's social media tool is more than just a scheduling tool. Connecting your social media accounts— LinkedIn, Facebook, Instagram, and Twitter—with HubSpot not only allows you to manage multiple profiles at once on various platforms but also helps you monitor what people are saying about you and see exactly which of your contacts are more engaged on social media. This helps you prepare specific campaigns for them via social media.

- **Deciding which integrations are necessary during setup**: HubSpot has a vast marketplace of third-party platforms that can integrate seamlessly into your portal—for example, Zoom for sending meeting links or hosting your webinars, Slack for sending notifications to your sales teams, or Salesforce if you are using this platform as your **customer relationship management (CRM)** system. These are just a few integrations that can be useful during setup, and in a later chapter, we will take you through these setups and more.

- **Importing your contacts into HubSpot**: Now that everything is set up, the next important step is to import your contacts so that you can begin executing some campaigns and tracking the engagement of your contacts.

- **Incorporating planning and strategy**: As mentioned in the introduction, the main part of this book is about showing the best practices of what works for other companies. HubSpot has set the trend for us by providing all the templates they use combined with other industry best practices in order to execute various marketing tactics such as webinars, gated content, email nurtures, and so much more. This tool gives you the framework for planning and executing your campaigns.

- **Analyzing ROI and performance**: Today, everything that is done in digital marketing is measurable. This section shows you how to set up performance tracking dashboards covering areas such as contacts by lead source, deals by lead source, contacts by industry, deal forecast, deal velocity, and much more.

Technical requirements

Before we get into the details of the setup, be sure you have the following items:

- Super Admin access to HubSpot

- Admin access to your WordPress installation

- (Editor or Reader permission to your website gives insufficient privileges and won't allow you to download the HubSpot plugin.)

- Admin access to your Google Analytics account

- Admin access to the platform where you purchased your domain—for instance, GoDaddy, Namecheap, Bluehost, and so on

- Admin access to your social media accounts—LinkedIn, Facebook, Twitter, Instagram

- Company logos and brand guidelines

So, let's begin!

Setting your brand colors and logo

In your HubSpot portal, under **Account Defaults**, click on **Branding** and then **My Brand Kit**, and upload your logo and favicon, as seen in the following screenshot:

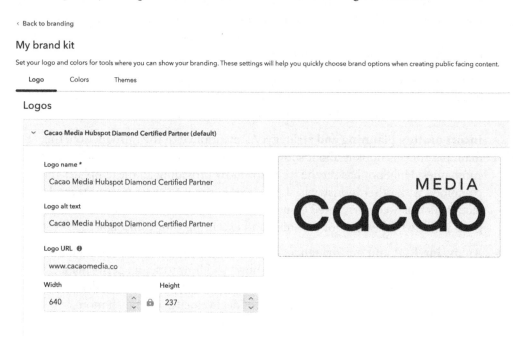

Figure 1.1 – Adding your branding assets to HubSpot

These logos appear on your landing pages as well as the URL of your pages, so your brand will always be recognized as users engage with your content.

Be sure to also update the **Logo alt text** section with the name of your company so that search engines have another way to index your company.

Your brand is an integral part of your marketing message as it provides a constant recall to your audience via subliminal signals to the brain that reminds people who you are. So, every chance you get to include your logos in your message should be taken.

Connecting your website to HubSpot

The most common **content management system (CMS)** used for hosting websites is WordPress. If you are using WordPress, HubSpot has a plugin that, once downloaded, allows you to connect your website to HubSpot. Follow these steps for a successful integration between your website and HubSpot. First, we need to install the HubSpot WordPress plugin.

Follow these steps to connect WordPress to HubSpot using the HubSpot plugin:

1. Log in to your WordPress dashboard.

2. Scroll down to **Plugins**.

3. Click on **Plugins**, as shown in the following screenshot:

Figure 1.2 – WordPress plugins

4. Click **Add New Plugin**.

5. Search for the **HubSpot All-in-One Marketing – Forms, Popups, Live Chat** plugin, as shown in the following screenshot:

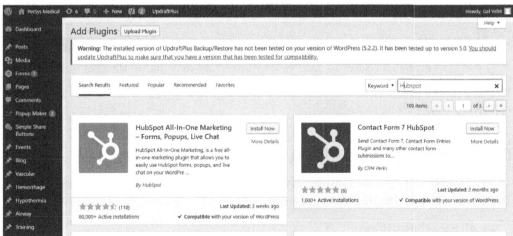

Figure 1.3 – HubSpot plugin

6. Click on **Install Now**. Once the installation is finished, click on **Activate**.

Once your installation is successfully completed, you will be redirected to a confirmation page, as shown in the following screenshot:

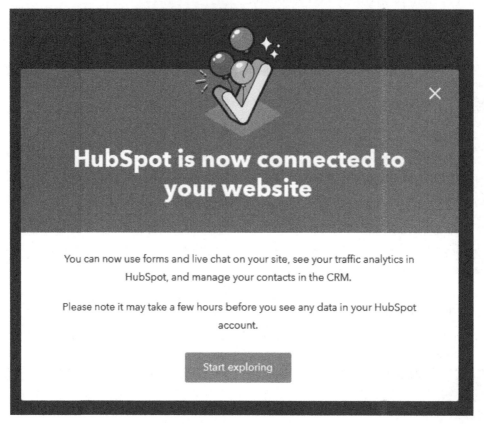

Figure 1.4 – Success screen: your website is now connected to HubSpot

With these actions completed, you have now installed the HubSpot WordPress plugin and connected your website to it.

Connecting Google Analytics to HubSpot

There are several options to consider when adding your Google Analytics tracking code. You can add tracking to the following areas:

- All pages on all domains
- All pages on a specific domain
- A specific blog
- A specific page

The easiest and most recommended approach is the first option—adding tracking to all pages on all domains.

To do this, perform the following steps:

1. Go to **Settings** on the top navigation bar of your HubSpot portal.

2. Then, scroll down to the last section on the side menu, **Tools**.

3. Click on **Website**, then **Pages** on the left navigation sidebar.

4. For the **Choose a domain to edit its settings** option, choose **Default settings for all domains**.

5. Choose **Integrations** on the menu that appears below it.

6. Then, check the **Integrate with Google Analytics** box and enter your Google Analytics tracking code, as shown in the following screenshot:

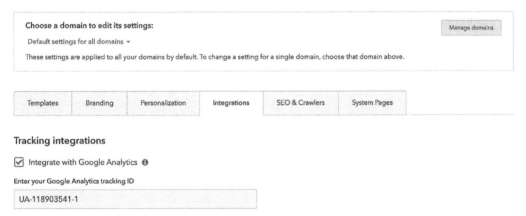

Figure 1.5 – Installing the Google Analytics tracking code

> **Note**
>
> It is important to note that if you have a cookie consent policy operating on your site (which is required by law today in most countries), the Google Analytics script will not load until a user has accepted, and if a visitor does not accept this policy, then Google Analytics will not be tracked for them. This functions only on HubSpot-hosted pages. HubSpot cannot control the Google Analytics script on externally hosted pages.

Filtering out personal traffic

To ensure your analytics are a true reflection of your visitors' behavior, add **Internet Protocol (IP)** addresses or domains you wish to exclude from your traffic. Do this by following these steps:

1. Go to **Settings**, then on the left navigation bar look for **Tracking & Analytics** and then **Tracking Code**.

2. Click on the **Advanced Tracking** tab.

3. Scroll down until you see the **IP Addresses to Exclude** and **From these referrers** sections. Here, you can place the IP addresses of your partners, employees' home addresses, various office locations, and so on. Just ask the person from each one of the locations to google My IP Address and send you the coded sequence of numbers that will appear.

4. You can also exclude traffic from competitors or irrelevant companies you find visiting your site often by adding their domains to the **From these referrers** section, as illustrated in the following screenshot:

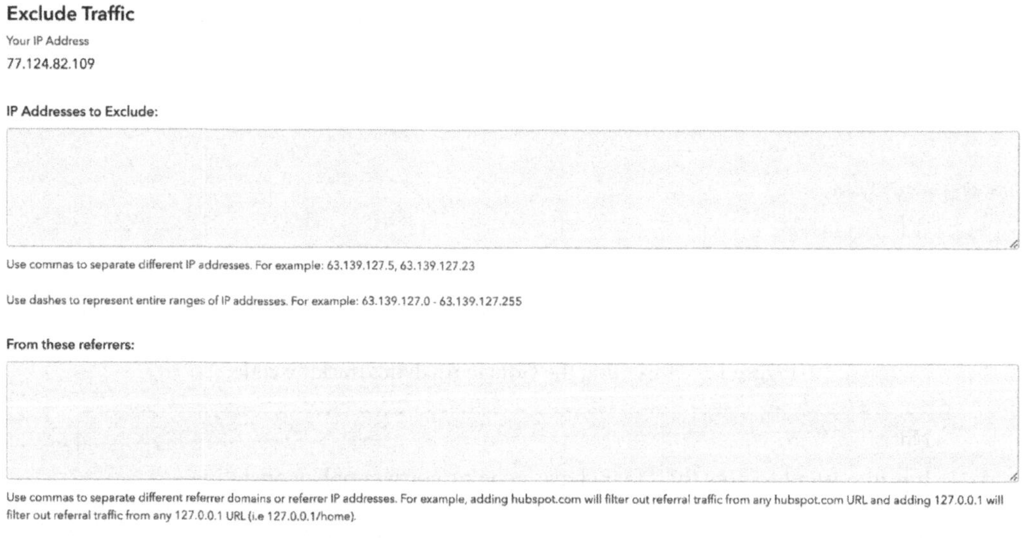

Exclude Traffic

Your IP Address
77.124.82.109

IP Addresses to Exclude:

Use commas to separate different IP addresses. For example: 63.139.127.5, 63.139.127.23

Use dashes to represent entire ranges of IP addresses. For example: 63.139.127.0 - 63.139.127.255

From these referrers:

Use commas to separate different referrer domains or referrer IP addresses. For example, adding hubspot.com will filter out referral traffic from any hubspot.com URL and adding 127.0.0.1 will filter out referral traffic from any 127.0.0.1 URL (i.e 127.0.0.1/home).

Figure 1.6 – Exclude Traffic screen

Now that traffic from visitors who aren't potential prospects—such as your team, vendors, or management—is filtered out from your analytics, you will have a truer reflection of your efforts.

Setting up your subdomains – landing pages and blog

The next most important thing to set up is making your subdomains for your landing pages and blog visible.

As mentioned at the beginning of this chapter, if you do not connect your landing pages and blog to your main domain, then you will effectively be hosting them on a HubSpot domain. This erodes your brand recognition as the URL that will be visible will look something like this: `[HubSpot ID].hs-sites.com`.

Connecting these pages to your main domain helps ensure that only your URL is visible. It will look something like this: `go.[url name]` or `info.[url name]`. Note that you cannot use your original domain because this is already hosting your website. Since HubSpot is another CMS hosting your content, you cannot effectively host two CMS sites on the same domain. For this reason, you need to create what is referred to as a subdomain. You can choose anything you wish for the prefix of your subdomain, such as marketing, pages, and so on.

We will now set up your subdomains. Before doing that, ensure you have Admin access to the platform from which you bought the domain. The most common platforms are GoDaddy, Namecheap, and Bluehost. If in doubt, ask your **information technology** (**IT**) department.

Once you have the login credentials, log in to the site, keep the page open, and in a different tab, go to your HubSpot portal and follow these steps:

1. Navigate to **Settings**, then scroll down to the **Tools** subsection.
2. In this section, click on **Website** and then **Domains and URLs**.
3. Click on **Domains** in the submenu.

4.   A new section appears. Click **Connect a domain**, which takes you to the following screen:

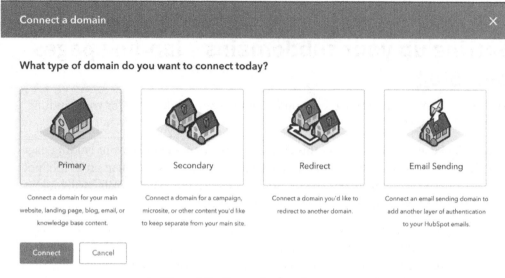

Figure 1.7 – Connect a domain screen

5.   When the box shown in *Figure 1.7* appears, choose the type of domain you wish to connect.

6.   Primary domains are the main subdomain that will host content such as landing pages or blogs. It can be info.[your company name].com or marketing.[your company name].com. For example, for my business, I use info.cacaomedia.co.

7.   Secondary domains are alternative domains to your primary domain that can be used for subcategories of different content—for instance, events, workshops, and so on. For example, this domain can be events.[your company name].com.

8.   Redirect domains are used when you would like to redirect content from a site that is already hosting your content but you would like to update the URL currently being used.

9. Email sending is connected in order to send emails from HubSpot using your existing email addresses.

    It is recommended at this first stage of your setup to connect the primary and email-sending domains.

10. Another page then appears, prompting you to select which types of assets you are creating today. As your website and blog are most likely hosted on another platform such as WordPress, you will want to choose **Landing pages** and **Email** at this stage, as shown in the following screenshot. Then, click **Next**:

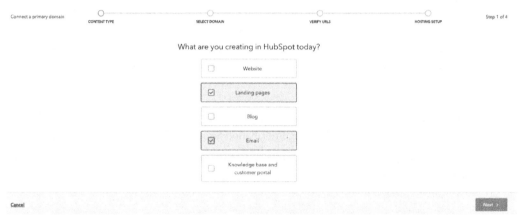

Figure 1.8 – Choosing content type

11. In the next section that appears, enter your root domain—for instance, mysite.com, and click **Next**, as illustrated in the following screenshot:

Figure 1.9 – Entering your root domain

12. Enter information for your subdomain (`info.`), brand domain (your company name), top-level domain (`.com`), and primary language (**English**), as illustrated in the following screenshot:

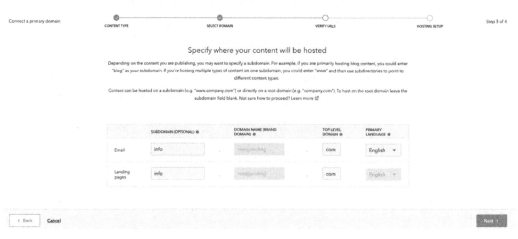

Figure 1.10 – Entering information for your subdomain

13. Next, you will be taken to a screen to verify that these are the URLs you wish to use, as shown here:

Figure 1.11 – Verifying your URLs

14. After clicking **Next**, you are then redirected to another page that asks you to set up your hosting. If you are using GoDaddy, for instance, you can simply choose the **Authorize with GoDaddy** option, as shown in the following screenshot:

Figure 1.12 – Setting up your host

15. You will then be redirected to GoDaddy to confirm access. Click **Connect**, as shown in the following screenshot. Remember that you must be logged in as **Admin** to GoDaddy for these changes to take effect:

Figure 1.13 – Confirming access with GoDaddy

16. Once the domains are connected, the following screen will appear, confirming the connection:

Your domain was successfully connected!

Note that DNS changes can sometimes take up to 72 hours to take effect worldwide. If users are unable to view your site after 72 hours, ask them to clear their browser's cache and try again. You can also use www.whatsmydns.net to check a domain name's current IP address and DNS record information against multiple name servers located in different parts of the world.

Figure 1.14 – Domain connection is successful

If your domain is hosted by another provider, you will need to manually log in to your hosting provider and look for **DNS Settings**, then **Manage DNS**, and update the **Canonical Name (CNAME)** record. Here are the steps to take if you need to do a manual setup of your domain connection.

First, choose the **No, I'll set it up manually** option when you get to the screen shown here:

Figure 1.15 – Choosing the manual option to connect your domains to HubSpot

You will then arrive at the following screen, with four steps to follow. Check the boxes for each of these steps when you have completed the actions. Then, copy the **Domain Name System** (**DNS**) records as directed to your domain hosting provider. If you are unsure where your domain is hosted, speak to the IT administrator within your company:

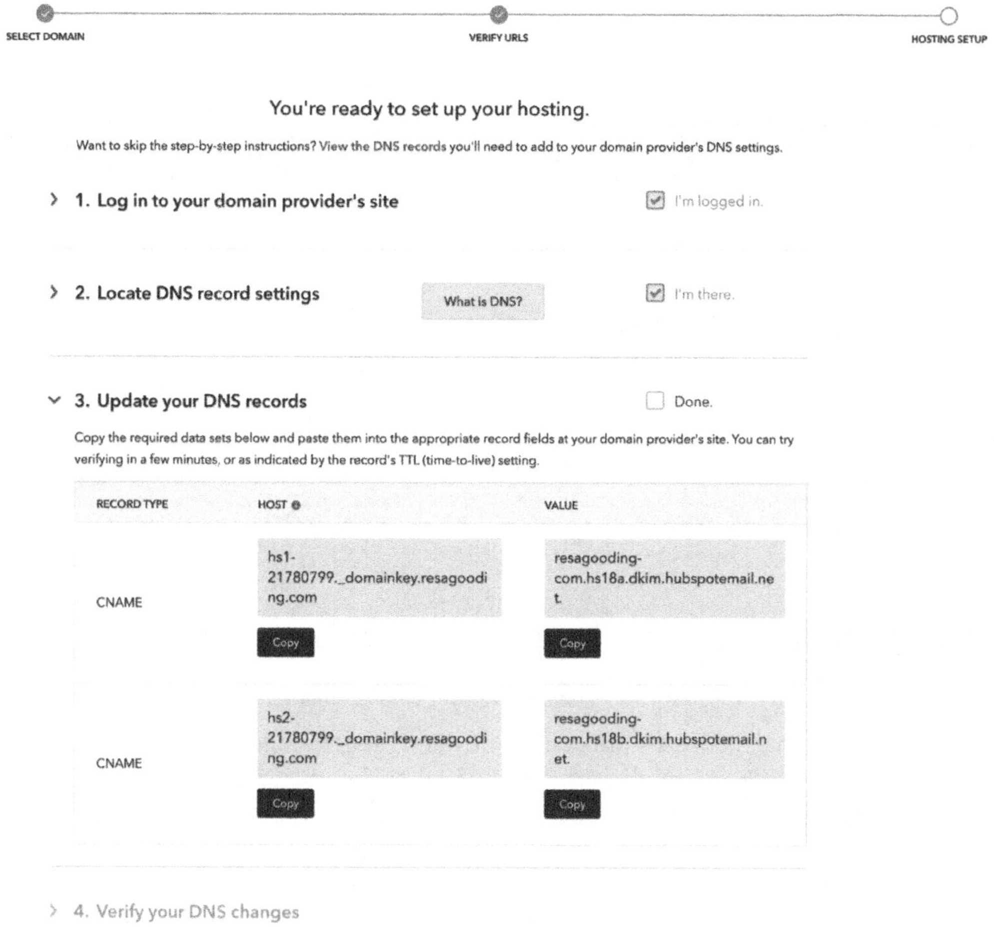

Figure 1.16 – Updating your DNS records

Once these steps are completed, whenever you publish a landing page, it will be hosted under your company's URL and not HubSpot's URL. Now, let's look at the steps to connect your email domain.

Verifying your email domain

This step is crucial as it verifies your domain so that it improves the chances of your email landing in the recipient's inbox instead of their spam folder. Follow these steps to verify your email domain:

1. In your portal, go to **Settings | Tools | Website | Domains and URLs**. Click on **Domains** in the submenu and then **Connect a Domain**. When the box shown in the following screenshot appears, select **Email Sending** and then **Connect**:

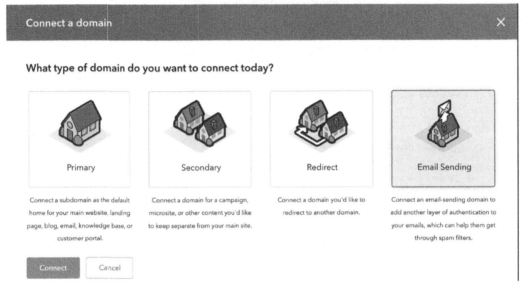

Figure 1.17 – Connecting your email domain

2. Choose any email address—preferably one that is generic, such as info@ yourwebsite.com—and insert it in the box, as shown in *Figure 1.18*. Note that it is recommended to connect a generic domain such as info@yourwebsite.com and not an actual user email address since this address may not be valid once the employee leaves, and this will cause this connection to break:

SELECT DOMAIN   VERIFY URLS   HOSTING SETUP

Type one of the email addresses that you
use to send marketing emails:

events@resagooding.com

Figure 1.18 – Entering a generic email address in this box

3. Even though this screen is asking you to verify emails will be sent out from this email address, note that you will have the ability to add many more email senders to your portal. So, simply click on **Next** to continue to the next screen, as illustrated in the following screenshot:

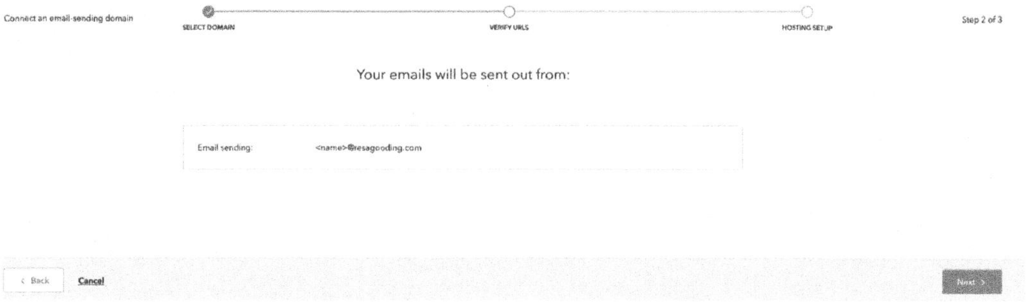

Figure 1.19 – Verifying the email sender

4. Now, you will arrive at the following screen, which by now is quite familiar. This is where you will either authorize GoDaddy to connect your domains or choose to do this manually. Similar to setting up your landing page, follow the preceding steps until you have reached the confirmation screen that shows your email is connected:

Figure 1.20 – Connecting to your hosting provider

This brings us to the end of one of the most technical setups in HubSpot—ensuring your domains are connected to HubSpot. Once it's completed correctly, you will see the following screen, confirming with a green light that your domains are connected:

Primary domains

| Landing pages | info.resagooding.com
● Connected | Edit ▾ |
| Email (web version) | info.resagooding.com
● Connected | Edit ▾ |

SSL is turned on by default to help your SEO, make your site more secure, and build trust with your visitors. ●

Secondary domains

Connect a domain for a campaign, microsite, or other content you'd like to keep separate from your main site.

Connect a secondary domain

Redirected domains

Connect a domain you'd like to redirect to a primary or secondary domain.

Connect a redirect domain

Email sending domains (DKIM)

| Email (sending) | resagooding.com
● Connected | Disconnect |

Figure 1.21 – Confirmation that all domains are connected

I cannot stress enough how important this step is. Without completing these actions, you will not be able to use HubSpot for hosting landing-page content or sending emails. But understanding that not everyone wishes to dabble in such technical details, be sure to ask your IT administrator for help if you don't feel confident in doing these steps.

Important Note

HubSpot is an inbound platform, which means they strictly advise against contacting people who have not opted in to hearing from you or given you some form of consent to email them—for example, having met them at a trade show or conference. You therefore should desist from purchasing lists of cold emailing contacts who have never heard from you. If this is an important part of your strategy, it is highly suggested to use another type of email platform to prevent you from compromising your HubSpot portal.

Connecting your social media accounts

Social media is a crucial channel for businesses to engage with potential and existing customers, but it can also be a time-consuming activity. With HubSpot, marketers now have a social media tool that can help them effectively manage their company's social accounts and give better insights into which contacts in their database prefer interacting on social media. Let's get you connected.

Follow these steps to connect your social media accounts to HubSpot:

1. Go to **Settings** | **Tools** | **Marketing** | **Social** | **Accounts**.

2. Click on **Connect Accounts**. The following screen will pop up, enabling you to choose which social media accounts you would like to connect. At the time of publishing, the social media accounts illustrated here are what HubSpot currently supports:

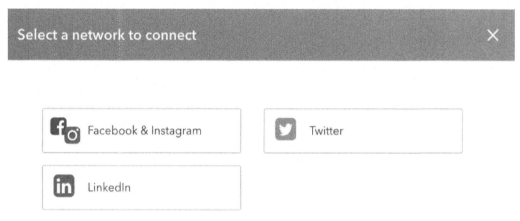

Figure 1.22 – Choosing which social media accounts to connect to HubSpot

3. You must have Admin access to accounts you wish to connect to HubSpot. Then, follow each step that will appear on subsequent screens to connect the accounts.

4. Once your social media accounts are connected, you can choose the scheduling format you'd like by clicking on the **Publishing** tab, as shown next. Here, you can choose the times you wish to publish each day, as well as choose the intervals at which each post should be published:

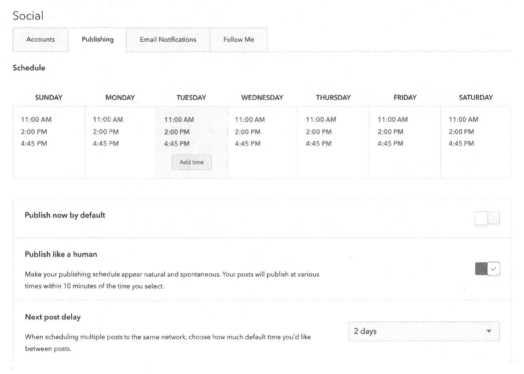

Figure 1.23 – Publishing schedule

5. Next, you can set up how often you would like to receive notifications and updates about your social media activity by clicking on **Email Notifications**, as illustrated in the following screenshot:

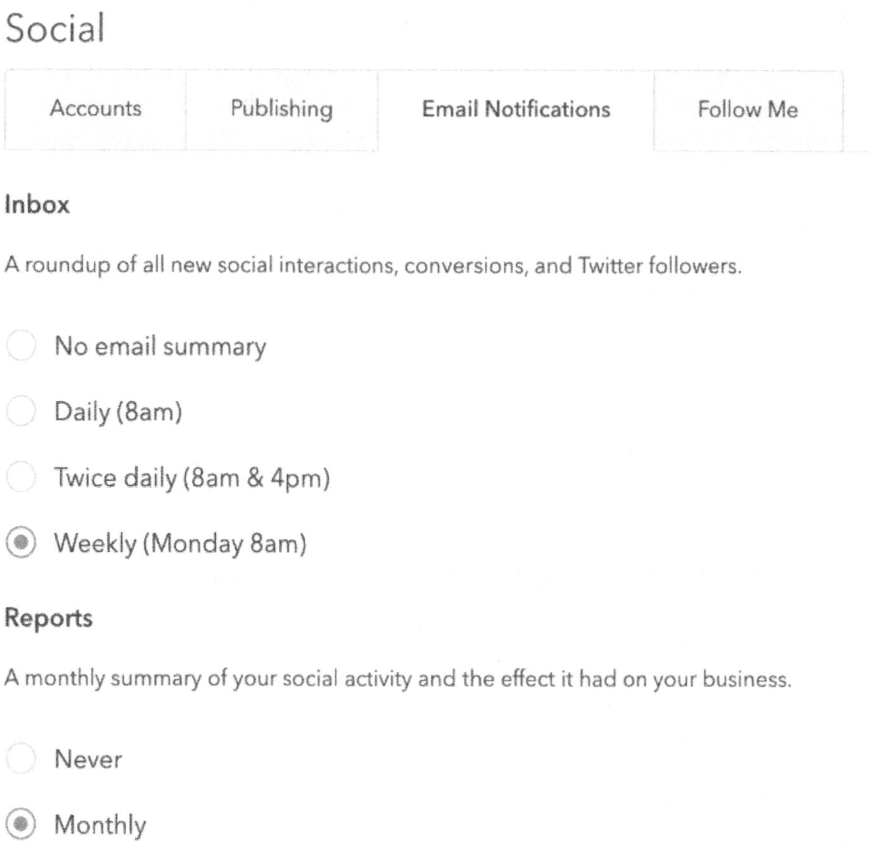

Social

| Accounts | Publishing | Email Notifications | Follow Me |

Inbox

A roundup of all new social interactions, conversions, and Twitter followers.

○ No email summary

○ Daily (8am)

○ Twice daily (8am & 4pm)

◉ Weekly (Monday 8am)

Reports

A monthly summary of your social activity and the effect it had on your business.

○ Never

◉ Monthly

Figure 1.24 – Email Notifications

HubSpot's social media tool is much more than a scheduling tool. It allows you to monitor conversations happening online about your brand and business, respond to those comments within the HubSpot platform instead of logging in to each social media channel, see exactly which contacts in your database are more interactive on social media than other channels, and measure the engagement you are achieving on each platform. In later chapters, we will show how you can successfully integrate your social media strategy into an existing campaign using HubSpot's social media tools.

Managing contacts and creating lists

The power of HubSpot lies within its CRM. It is your **single source of truth** (**SSOT**). The CRM collects all information about the contacts in your database as the properties are used to gather and store this intelligence. With a very robust CRM in place, you can fuel all other activities that take place in HubSpot—marketing, sales, and service. This section is dedicated to helping you manage the CRM efficiently and correctly.

Understanding properties

Properties are used to store data on certain objects within HubSpot—for example, contacts, companies, deals, and tickets. There are default properties that are built into the HubSpot platform and cannot be edited. A few examples of such properties are **First Name**, **Last Name**, **Email**, and so on, and there are custom properties that every user can decide to build.

Tips for building your own custom properties

Before adding more properties to HubSpot, take time to understand what already exists and—more importantly—how it is configured. Then, examine your business needs and what kind of information you would like to collect about contacts, their companies, your sales process, or your service process, and then create properties accordingly.

Here are a few things to consider when creating your own properties:

1. **Choose for which object a property should be created—contacts, companies, deals, or tickets**: If it is a property that will collect information about an individual, then create it under **Contacts**. If it's about the company, then it should be created under **Companies**. Information about your sales process should be created under **Deals**, while information related to your service process should be captured under **Tickets**. Note that only properties created under the **Contact** object type, as in the following screenshot, can be used in forms. All other properties will only be seen by internal users of HubSpot:

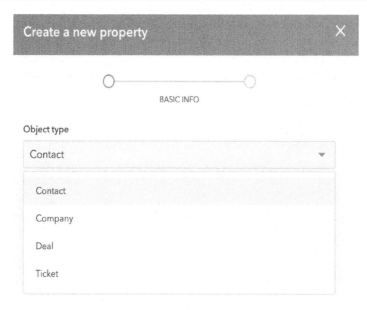

Figure 1.25 – Creating a custom property: choosing an object type

2. **Deciding under which group the property should sit**: Choosing the appropriate group helps you find information easily when you want to use it eventually. For example, under the **Contact** object type, you may want to collect information about a contact's social media profile, so you can add this field under **Social Media Information**. Note that you can also create your own group to fit your business requirements. The following screenshot illustrates how to select a group:

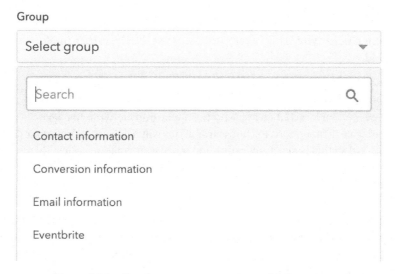

Figure 1.26 – Creating a custom property: selecting a group

3. **Choosing a label and a description**: When choosing a label, consider what you would like users to see when they fill out a form. It should be short, clear, and to the point. The **Description** field can be used to explain to internal users the purpose of the field. The following screenshot illustrates how to choose a label and a description:

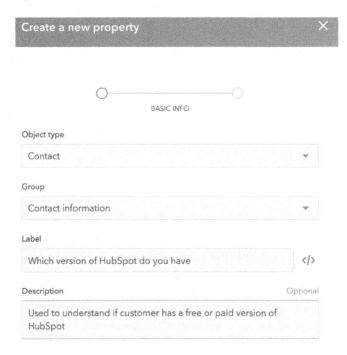

Figure 1.27 – Creating a custom property: choosing a label and description

4. **Selecting a field type**: This is very important as it determines the format of your field.

Important Note

Wherever possible, avoid giving users the opportunity to write free text; instead, give them options to choose from. This will help control how your data is collected so that it makes reporting and other segmentation easier. Therefore, fields such as **Dropdown select**, **Multiple checkboxes**, and **Radio select** should always be considered first.

Note when creating options for these types of fields, an internal value is automatically created that matches the label. You cannot edit this internal value as this is what the system reads to update values in the system. So, if you wish to change a label, you must create a new label and delete the old one.

The following screenshot shows how to select a field type:

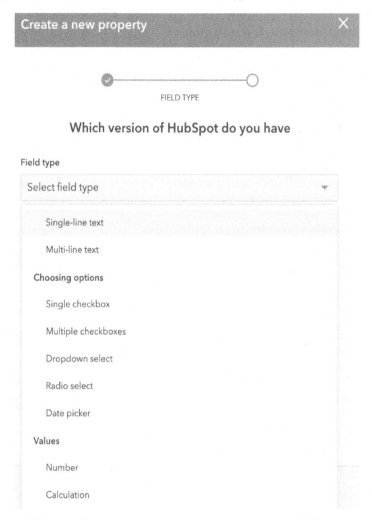

Figure 1.28 – Creating a custom property: selecting a field type

Properties are the backbone of your CRM system as they help you build the information you need about your contacts, but to ensure you are collecting information in a systematic way, it is important that you build properties correctly.

Contact management

Once the necessary fields have been created, you are now able to organize your contacts in a more systematic way to segment your database for better management and activities. Here are a few ways to better manage your contacts.

Filters

Filters are one way to segment your database, giving you a quick view of a segment of your database right from the **Contacts** page, **Companies** page, **Deals** page, or **Tickets** page. Note that these filters cannot be used in anything such as an email list, report, and so on—their purpose is simply for viewing the database. There are many use cases for filters, but some reasons behind why you may want to use filters could include the following:

- To see contacts that belong only to you or a specific contact owner

- To see which contacts are missing information—for instance, **Country** or **First name** field

- To see that contacts from a certain country/region are assigned to the right contact owner

The following screenshot provides an example of this:

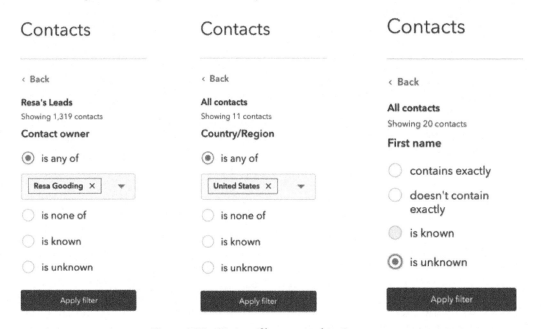

Figure 1.29 – Various filters created in Contacts

You can also save views of your filters and share them with other members of your team for easy access in the future. Simply click **Apply filter**, then **Save filter**, choose a name for the filter, and finally, select the **Share with everyone** option.

Lists

Lists also allow you to segment your database, but the main difference is that they give you more options to choose from. For example, under **Contact Properties**, you can choose from submissions, page views, and so on. This allows you to use these options to segment your database for specific marketing activities, such as the following:

- Nurturing emails based on page views or form submissions

- Enrolling in workflows

- Keeping track of people who sign up for an event when it is integrated into another platform—for example, registrants to a webinar event hosted on Zoom or GoTo Webinar

Note that lists exist in two forms: static and active. Active lists are updated in real time as contacts meet the criteria, as seen in the following screenshot, while static lists are not updated after a list is created:

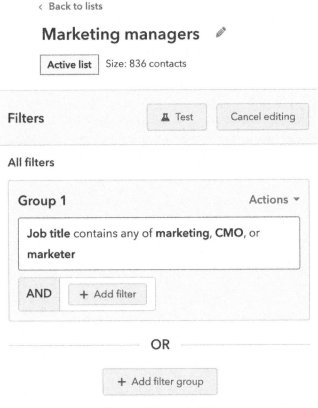

Figure 1.30 – Active list

These lists can then be used to do many things. You can attach them to your email marketing campaigns, use them in workflows when you need to update certain features, or simply use them to keep track of leads being generated from ongoing campaigns.

Exploring tools for every marketer

HubSpot has built many tools that can definitely help marketers strategically organize various parts of your campaigns, as well as digitally "pick the brains" of HubSpot expert marketers as they share with you everything that has worked for them to build such a successful company over the last few decades. There is no denying that when it comes to inbound marketing, these guys are the litmus test to measure against.

Some of the tools we will discuss in this section are listed here:

- **Calendar**
- **Campaigns**
- **SEO**
- **Projects**

You should definitely consider setting these tools up in order to help you plan and execute your campaigns more successfully.

Calendar tool

The HubSpot **Calendar** tool is mostly used for managing your social calendar. You can find it by going to **Marketing | Social**. Then, click on **Manage** and **Calendar**, as shown in the following screenshot:

Figure 1.31 – Calendar tool

At a glance, you can see when social media posts have been published or are due to be published and on which channels. You can also use the calendar for planning your blog-post schedule, email scheduling, landing pages, and event tasks.

The goal is to use the HubSpot calendar tool as your marketing content calendar, giving you a bird's-eye view of the amount of content you have produced over time.

Campaigns tool

This is one tool that is often used incorrectly. To locate it, go to **Marketing | Campaigns**. In HubSpot, a campaign is created only when you have more than one marketing asset or content related to a main theme or event. For example, should you be attending an upcoming conference such as *CES*, then you can open a campaign and associate all marketing assets—such as emails, social media posts, blog posts, landing pages, and so on—with this campaign. You can even add a budget to measure how much money you allocated and spent on this campaign. The goal is then to use campaign analytics to measure which activity or asset generated the most leads or customers. This allows you to know which campaigns were most effective and on which channels you should focus your efforts and resources.

The following screenshot shows an example of the **Campaigns** tool in use:

Figure 1.32 – Campaigns tool

As mentioned before, one of the most common mistakes made is opening a campaign for each marketing tactic, such as a blog post or email. A campaign is meant to show the various channels that brought leads to a specific theme, so opening a campaign for every blog post provides no additional information except how many views were received for each blog post. However, opening a campaign for a topic on which a blog post is written and then associating the blog with the campaign, then sending a social media post promoting the blog to the campaign and an email to subscribers about the blog to the campaign provides more value because you can then measure which asset generates more leads for this topic.

SEO tool

Search engine optimization (**SEO**) is critical for content visibility and conversion. Without good SEO, no one finds your content online, and since HubSpot supports your blog, landing pages, and even your website (if needed), the SEO functionality was added in order to help you plan your content strategy and build search authority.

To get to the **SEO** tool, go to **Marketing | Website | SEO**. In *Chapter 5*, Increasing Online Visibility Using HubSpot's SEO Tool, we deep dive into exactly how to use the **SEO** tool. For now, we would like to simply give you some insights into why you should consider setting it up.

The **SEO** tool works alongside **Google Search Console** (**GSC**). Integrating this free tool with HubSpot's **SEO** tool allows you to bring search data from Google directly into your HubSpot portal for a better understanding of how your content shows up on Google search engines, as seen in the following screenshot:

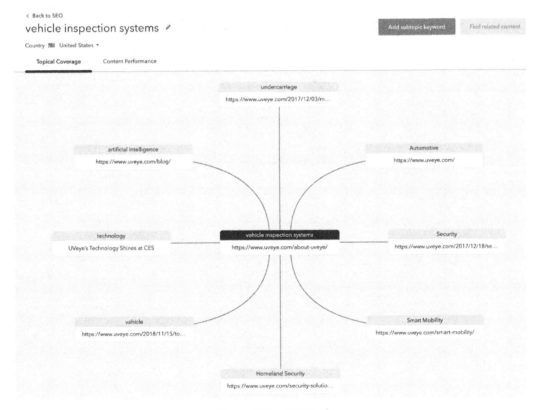

Figure 1.33 – SEO tool

It is important to recognize that green lines indicate that the sub-content is associated with the main pillar page, while a red line indicates that the sub-content is not linked to the main content. To fix this, you will need to go into the sub-content piece and hyperlink a relevant phrase connecting it to the main pillar content. There's more on this in *Chapter 5, Increasing Online Visibility Using HubSpot's SEO Tool.*

Projects tool

This is literally every marketer's hack for appearing as a marketing rockstar. Being the masters of inbound marketing, HubSpot has gifted each portal owner with templates and step-by-step instructions for executing any and every type of digital campaign. Just dream it, then search for it in **Project Templates**, and it appears. To get to this tool, click your company name in the top right-hand corner of your portal, then scroll down to **Projects**, as illustrated in the following screenshot. You will then see **Project Templates** as a submenu, and there, you can search for any type of template you are looking for:

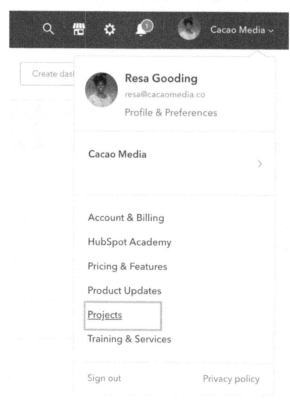

Figure 1.34 – Projects

So, if you are ever unsure where to begin with a webinar campaign or how to set up and launch an e-book, or even how to build reports your manager actually cares about, it can all be found in HubSpot **Project Templates**.

The following screenshot shows some of the things you can do with the **Projects** tool:

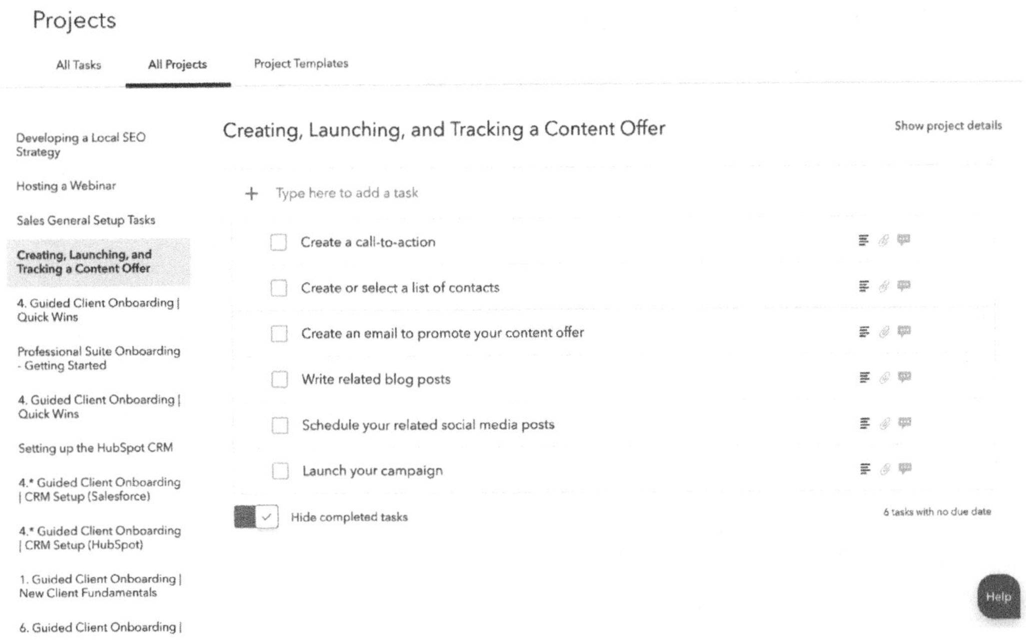

Figure 1.35 – Projects tool

Using these tools can give you the advantage you need to better execute and manage your campaigns as well as to measure their success, so do take some time to familiarize yourself with how they work. We will expand on their usefulness in later chapters.

Analyzing ROI and performance

Back in the day, marketing ROI was extremely hard to measure. How did we ever know that because of a billboard posted on a freeway, *X* amount of leads were generated that converted to *Y* amount of revenue? It was virtually impossible. However, today, with digital marketing, where every click, visit, and page view can be measured, it has become of paramount importance to justify your marketing spend.

HubSpot's **Analytics** tool provides you with built-in reports that are already automatically generated for you within the portal. At your disposal, you have many ready-made reports. Let's take a look at a few of them, as follows:

- **Website Analytics**: This report focuses on your website pages (if they are hosted on HubSpot, landing pages, and blog pages). In the following screenshot, you can see an example of a **Website Analytics** report:

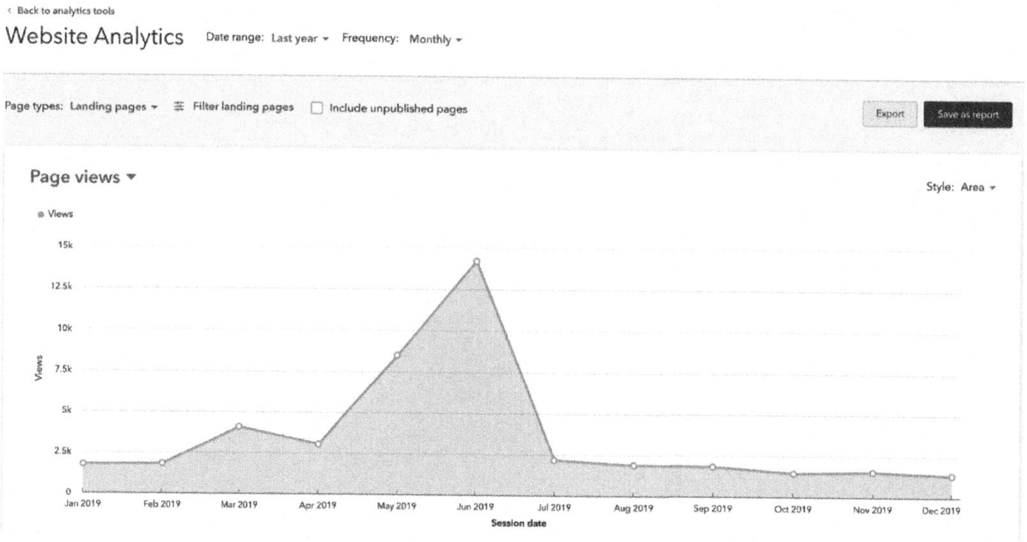

Figure 1.36 – Website Analytics

- **Traffic Analytics**: This report breaks down the various sources of your traffic and gives you a traffic overview of your website pages (even if your website is not hosted on HubSpot) and topic clusters if you are using the **SEO** tool. In the following screenshot, you can see an example of a **Traffic Analytics** report:

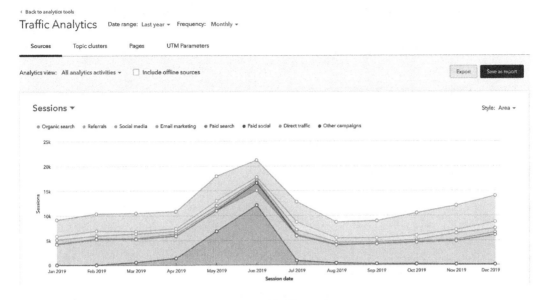

Figure 1.37 – Traffic Analytics

- **Contact Analytics**: This report shows you how many contacts and which contacts came from various sources. In the following screenshot, you can see an example of a **Contact Analytics** report:

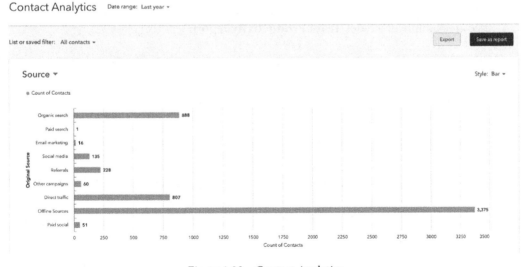

Figure 1.38 – Contact Analytics

- **Campaign Analytics**: This report shows you a summary of which contacts came from individual campaigns. In the following screenshot, you can see an example of a **Campaign Analytics** report:

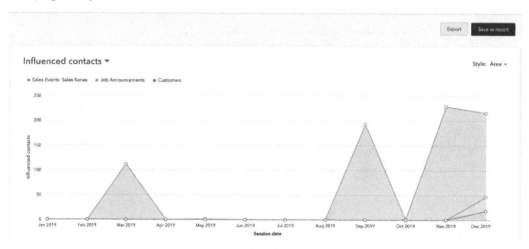

Figure 1.39 – Campaign Analytics

- **Sales Team Productivity**: This report gives exactly what it says—it shows you which team members are closing the most deals, having the most meetings, making the most calls, sending the most emails, and so on. In the following screenshot, you can see an example of a **Sales Team Productivity** report:

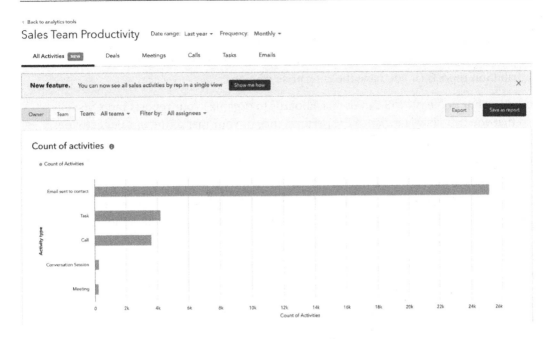

Figure 1.40 – Sales Team Productivity

- **Sales Content Analytics**: This shows you which sales assets are performing the best in terms of templates, documents, and sequences. In the following screenshot, you can see an example of a **Sales Content Analytics** report:

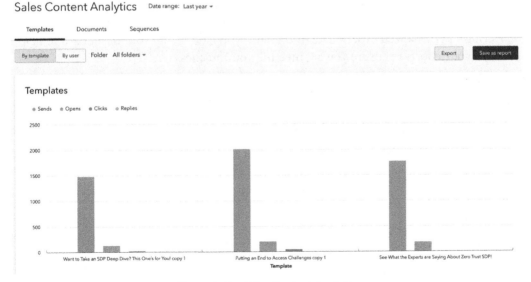

Figure 1.41 – Sales Content Analytics

At the same time, if you don't find a report that you are looking for, you can build your own custom reports using any of the objects available to you, such as contacts, companies, deals, tickets, and even activities. Additionally, you can create funnel reports as well as attribution reports (if you have the enterprise version).

And last but not least, you can use dashboards to organize your reports more visually so that you can view at a glance the performance of your marketing or sales activities, as well as use this format for meeting updates. One of the most valuable features of this dashboard is the ability to send automatic updates to your management team by email so that it takes one more task off your plate.

I know that was a lot to digest, so in *Chapter 11, Proving That Your Efforts Worked Using These*, we have covered everything you will need to know about building reports in HubSpot.

Summary

There's a whole lot more you can do with HubSpot, but I am sure this was more than enough to get you started. The goal of this chapter was simply to give you an overview of what you can expect from the HubSpot portal. We covered the main parts of the platform and gave you a starting point from which to focus your resources and efforts.

Specifically, you have now connected your website to HubSpot to track your visitors' engagement, connected your email domains so that you can now send relevant and engaging content such as newsletters, and nurtured your contacts after they downloaded one of your gated assets from your landing pages. Most importantly, you have now imported your contacts and segmented them as needed so that you can ensure you are delivering a personalized experience. And finally, you have set up your dashboard to help measure your efforts to ensure you are meeting your business goals.

In the next chapter, we will explore in more detail each of the tools and functionalities of HubSpot and show you how to generate some quick wins in the first 30 days of setting up your portal.

Questions

To ensure you understand the value of the steps you've just completed, let's practice some common troubleshooting tactics you can implement if faced with any of these issues. Have a go at answering the following questions:

1. Why do you need to create subdomains for your landing pages or blogs if you are hosting these assets in HubSpot?

2. If one of your team members asks why the company needs to use HubSpot analytics if it already has Google Analytics, how would you respond?

3. If you would like to plan an upcoming webinar campaign but are unsure of all the steps you need to do to ensure this campaign is a success, where can you go for a detailed step-by-step guideline?

Further reading

For more information or instructions on any of the items covered in this chapter, do check out these resources:

- HubSpot's *Knowledge Base*: `https://help.hubspot.com/`
- Contact HubSpot Support: `https://help.hubspot.com/`

2
Generating Quick Wins with HubSpot in the First 30 Days

Now that you have your HubSpot system set up correctly, the next phase is to show the ROI you can get. Inbound marketing generally takes time, but your management and sales teams are anxious to see what the system can really do. So, there is little time to sit back and figure out what your next steps should be or to think about that amazing campaign you would love to implement but would simply take too much time to plan and execute. Your focus now should be to show results, not plans.

HubSpot has a wealth of resources, in HubSpot Academy and the Projects tool, which help to guide you on how to build and execute your campaigns, as well as teaching you valuable skills and ones that you may want to improve upon. I therefore recommend checking out this wealth of resources and, in the meantime, we will show you how to bring quick wins to your organization.

In order to choose a quick-win idea that will be considered successful, it's highly recommended to first align your campaign ideas with your company's goals. Do they want to increase traffic or to improve conversions? Do they want more qualified leads or for the sales teams to speak to more opportunities? Whatever your company's goals are, this chapter provides you with a host of ideas to choose from, all of which can be planned and executed to generate results in less than 30 days.

Here are some of the tips to be covered in this chapter for each of your goals:

- Increasing website traffic by optimizing pages, building internal links, and amplifying social media posts

- Increasing conversions by adding exit popups and chatbots, and optimizing your forms

- Generating more qualified leads by building a lead nurture and retargeting campaign, and creating a webinar series

- Generating more opportunities for sales by giving away a part of your service, offering a free consultation, and re-engaging past sales opportunities

By the end of the chapter, you'll know which campaigns you can set up immediately that will contribute to your company's business goals.

Technical requirements

Before we get into the details of executing any of these quick wins, be sure you have the following items:

- Super admin access to HubSpot

- Access to Google Analytics

- Access to a keyword research tool such as Ubersuggest or Moz

Increasing website traffic

Website traffic is crucial to every company's online strategy. It gives you the opportunity to present your products and services to curious shoppers but, more importantly, acts as a litmus test to determine whether your business is providing real value to your prospects.

By now, you have understood all the pillars for having a good website in terms of design, user experience, and developing useful and consistent content. However, without investing in **search engine optimization** (**SEO**), it's the equivalent of going into a library and finding all the books in a pile on the ground for you to sort through until you find what you are looking for.

In this section, we won't overwhelm you with all that is needed to optimize your site for SEO, but will instead provide you with the strategic steps needed so you can at least be found by relevant prospects of your business. We will first look at how to select which pages to optimize on your site, and then how to find the related phrases or words users may type into a search engine that can bring traffic to your site. Next, we will describe exactly how to optimize your most attractive pages so they can appear in the top results, and finally, how to use internal link building to give your site more authority for search engineers.

SEO is crucial for any business to be found online today. In its simplest terms, SEO is the process by which you improve your company's online content in order to attract organic traffic from a search engine to your results page.

Today, most users default to the Google search engine when doing any online shopping, browsing, or any online activity, but there are many more search engines, such as Bing, Yahoo, and Ask.com. The bottom line is that they all operate the same way – they use algorithms to crawl online content and display relevant and related information in response to a user's query.

Therefore, if you are looking for a quick way to increase your company's website traffic, the most obvious place to begin is SEO. The challenge though is that SEO usually takes time, and if you wish to attain a quick win from this tactic, you must be willing to think outside of the box.

So, here are a few steps to show you how to optimize your website smartly for SEO in order to see results in less than 30 days.

Analyzing the top pages that bring traffic to your website

To get this information, go to your Google Analytics account, select a date range (for instance, the last year or something similar), and then navigate to **Behavior | Overview**. You will see the top website pages that were visited during your selected time period.

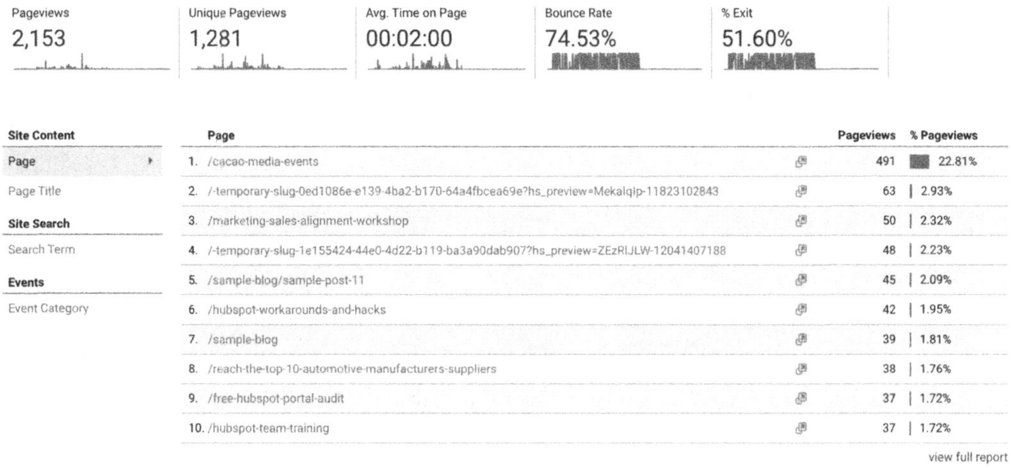

Pageviews	Unique Pageviews	Avg. Time on Page	Bounce Rate	% Exit
2,153	1,281	00:02:00	74.53%	51.60%

Site Content	Page		Pageviews	% Pageviews
Page ▶	1. /cacao-media-events		491	22.81%
Page Title	2. /-temporary-slug-0ed1086e-e139-4ba2-b170-64a4fbcea69e?hs_preview=Mekalqlp-11823102843		63	2.93%
Site Search	3. /marketing-sales-alignment-workshop		50	2.32%
Search Term	4. /-temporary-slug-1e155424-44e0-4d22-b119-ba3a90dab907?hs_preview=ZEzRlJLW-12041407188		48	2.23%
Events	5. /sample-blog/sample-post-11		45	2.09%
Event Category	6. /hubspot-workarounds-and-hacks		42	1.95%
	7. /sample-blog		39	1.81%
	8. /reach-the-top-10-automotive-manufacturers-suppliers		38	1.76%
	9. /free-hubspot-portal-audit		37	1.72%
	10. /hubspot-team-training		37	1.72%

view full report

Figure 2.1 – Top website pages. Source: Google Analytics

Oftentimes, the home page is the landing page as it's often the first page visitors arrive at when they get to your site. But in some cases, you will be pleasantly surprised to see that other pages are attracting relevant traffic.

In the preceding screenshot, the website's events web page attracts the most visitors, so this is a good page to optimize for a quick win.

Doing a keyword research

Now that you have identified the top page you wish to optimize, the next step is to perform a keyword search to identify what the most popular keywords your target audience is searching for are as it relates to your business and, in particular, the context of this page.

There are generally two ways to perform this audit:

- An internal analysis
- An external analysis

To check which keywords your competitors (both direct or indirect) are ranking for, you can take your top three competitors' websites and plug them into an SEO platform, such as Ubersuggest, Ahrefs, or Semrush. In this example, we use Ubersuggest to demonstrate the steps that would be taken in order to do a simple keyword search.

The first step would be to check which keywords bring traffic to a similar event website such as Inbound.com.

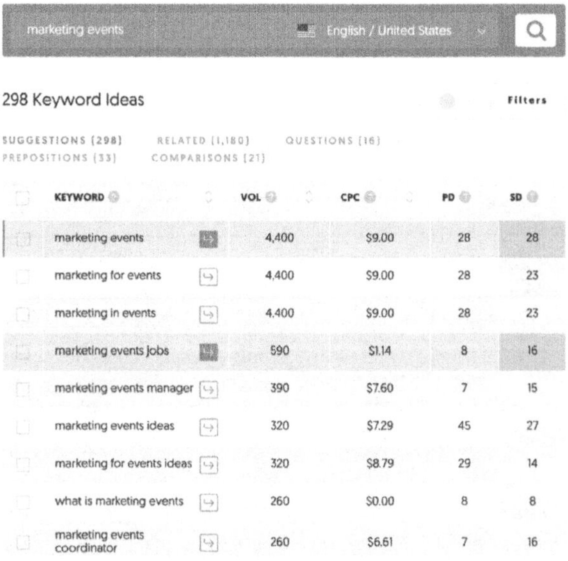

KEYWORD	VOL	CPC	PD	SD
marketing events	4,400	$9.00	28	28
marketing for events	4,400	$9.00	28	23
marketing in events	4,400	$9.00	28	23
marketing events jobs	590	$1.14	8	16
marketing events manager	390	$7.60	7	15
marketing events ideas	320	$7.29	45	27
marketing for events ideas	320	$8.79	29	14
what is marketing events	260	$0.00	8	8
marketing events coordinator	260	$6.61	7	16

Figure 2.2 – Top SEO keywords for Inbound.com. Source: Ubersuggest

Understandably, the top keywords for your competitors are often branded keywords that rank first, as seen in the preceding screenshot. So, extend this search to include keywords you would like to rank. For example, "marketing events" allows you to get a better idea of keywords that you can target.

Optimizing each page with the chosen keyword having a high search volume but low SEO difficulty

Now, taking two to three of these keywords that have high search volume and low **SEO difficulty** (**SD**), you can optimize the page you wish to improve. Note that it's not advised to do keyword stuffing for these pages. Instead, you can add some introductory content to the page and, where it is organically possible, use the keywords you have identified. Note that the more content you have on the page the better, but at the same time, you should never compromise the user experience for higher SEO rankings.

Once you've decided which page to optimize, there are generally five places where you want to insert those strategically chosen keywords on your site. Most of them are found in your content management system's page meta settings. Here are the most common places to add these keywords:

- Page header
- URL
- H1 title(s)
- Meta description
- Content body

By placing your keyword in each of these areas, you're creating a common thread for Google to follow throughout your page that says, "This page is about X."

After discussing optimization, let's look at another method for generating traffic.

Link building

Link building is an industry-wide technique that you can implement but is often ignored. It is simply linking content from one page on your domain to another page. The real hack here though is to take previously created gated content that has either not performed very well or is no longer getting submissions, and then open it as a website page in the form of a pillar page. Finally, ensure that there are links from other related blogs or website pages to this pillar page. The end result is that you increase the authority of your content with search engines.

In HubSpot, there is an easy way to build and track internal links using their SEO feature, as shown in the following diagram:

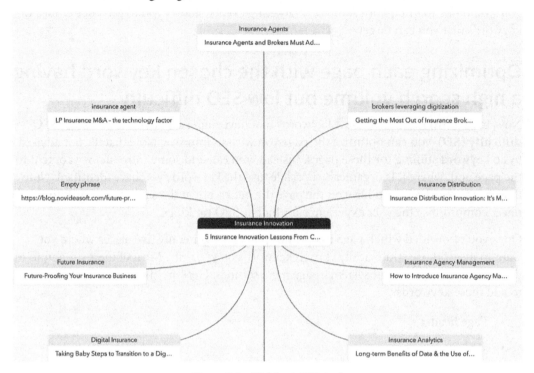

Figure 2.3 – HubSpot SEO tool

The first step is to select a seed keyword and its related content, which can be a pillar page or a landing page. Then, select related keywords, known as *sub-topic keywords*, and their related content such as blog posts or other landing pages. And finally, ensure that there is a link in the related content chosen for the sub-topic keywords to the pillar page.

Completing this internal link-building exercise successfully will help search engines understand your site structure better as they can then give the most important pages more link value than others. In HubSpot, red lines suggest that the link to the pillar content is missing, while green lines signify that the link exists.

Using your team and network to amplify your social media posts

Another tactic you can easily implement to gain more website traffic is to choose some of your best content and get your team and/or network to re-publish these posts. To make these tasks even more motivating, you can create competition among your employees so the posts that generate the most traffic to your site or get the most engagement can be rewarded with a gift card or something similar.

It is important to create unique tracking URLs to give to users, especially influencers, so that you can track which social media posts actually brought traffic to your site. To create these unique tracking URLs, you can use HubSpot's **Tracking URL Builder**. It can be found on the top menu under **Reports | Analytics Tools**.

Figure 2.4 – Analytics Tools in Reports

Then, scroll to the bottom of the page to find the **Tracking URL Builder** option:

Figure 2.5 – Accessing Tracking URL Builder

The following screenshot shows how the tracking URL builder page looks like.

Figure 2.6 – HubSpot's Tracking URL Builder

SEO is typically a long-term game. The algorithms search engines use to identify, classify, and prioritize online content are frequently updated to prevent irrelevant content from showing up when users conduct searches via search engines. But knowing that most sites generally don't take the time to optimize their content for SEO, using any of these three tactics will help you see a significant increase in traffic.

Increasing conversions

Another benefit that can quickly be achieved from implementing HubSpot as part of your martech systems is improving conversions. Some of the ways in which you can achieve this using existing HubSpot tools will be discussed in this section.

Adding exit popups

Exit popups are a popular tactic employed by most sites in an effort to mitigate high bounce rates. It is your last chance to convert a visitor before they leave your site. Some people often find popups to be annoying, but the reality is that statistics show they do indeed work. So, even if you annoy one or two visitors, you might as well take the chance since they were about to leave anyway.

In HubSpot, preparing an exit popup can be done in just a few easy steps:

1. Navigate to the top menu to **Marketing | Lead Capture | Forms**. Click on **Create Form** and then choose **Pop-up Form**, as shown:

Figure 2.7 – Choosing the type of form in order to create an exit popup

2. You can then choose how you'd like the popup to appear: whether it's in the middle of the page, as a dropdown from the top of the site, or entering from the left or right.

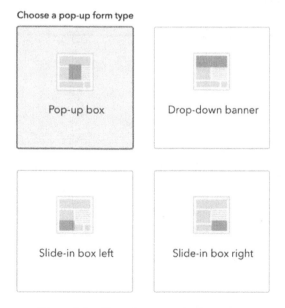

Figure 2.8 – Choosing a pop-up form type

3. Once you've decided what you'd like visitors to receive at this stage, include the text, image (if needed), and **call to action (CTA)** text.

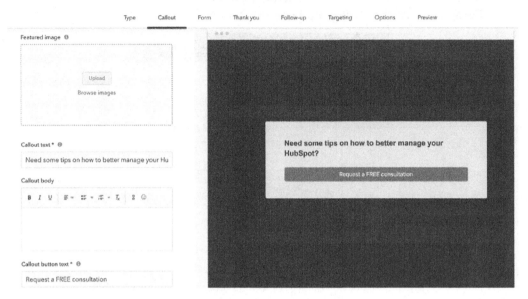

Figure 2.9 – Completing the CTA

4. Customize the CTA to match your brand colors and choose the next page a visitor sees once they click on the CTA.

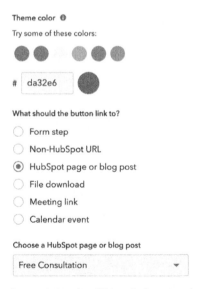

Figure 2.10 – Customizing the CTA and choosing the next action

5. Choose the pages and the targeting group where the popup should be seen. You can exclude some contacts, such as **customers**, who should not see a popup suggesting they sign up for a free consultation.

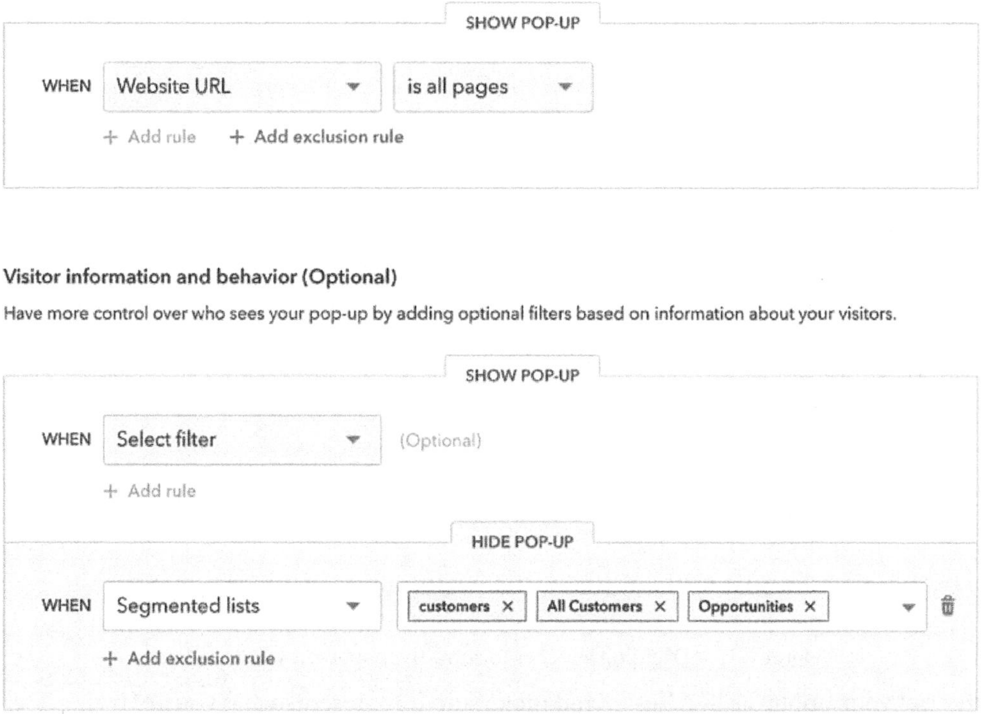

Figure 2.11 – Choosing the pages and to whom the popup should appear

6. Decide whether the popup should be seen on mobile screens as well as how often it should be seen if visitors return to your site. Also, add the recipients who should receive these notifications if someone signs up through the popup.

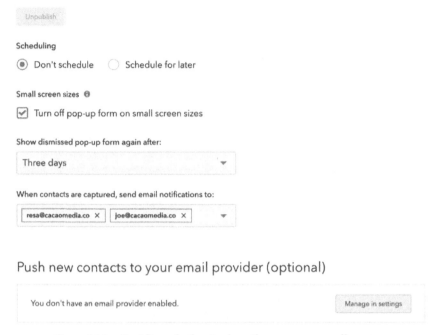

Figure 2.12 – Deciding whether to show the popup on small screens

7. Set your popup as live. Test it and make sure it represents what you are trying to achieve.

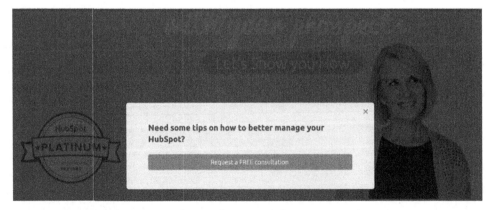

Figure 2.13 – Setting the popup as live on your website

Whether or not people are annoyed by your popups, remember that companies have shown they have worked in recapturing lost leads. So, ignore the naysayers and think outside the box. You can use exit popups to offer content, get sign-ups to your blog or newsletter, offer a discount, present a survey, and implement many more creative tactics in order to capture lead information and improve conversions. The sky's the limit!

Adding a chatbot

Chatbots have become increasingly popular as part of businesses' customer service experience. Customers and prospects alike have come to appreciate their existence according to the *Drift 2018 Chatbot Report* as they provide 24-hour service and an instantaneous customer experience. Unlike their traditional counterparts, such as contact us forms or phone services, both of which rely on someone being available to respond to your prospect's enquiries, chatbots are the ultimate mind-readers that give visitors instant responses.

Within HubSpot, you can easily create a chatbot by following these steps:

1. Map out the experience you would like your visitors to have once they engage with your chatbot.

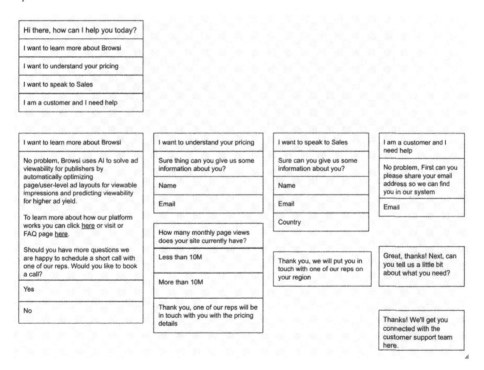

Figure 2.14 – Chatbot map

2. In your HubSpot portal, navigate to the menu and go to **Conversations | Chatflow**. Click on **Create Chatflow** and then choose **Website**.

Figure 2.15 – Choosing a website

3. You will then be prompted to create a **live chat** first before you can create a **bot**. Click on **Add live chat**.

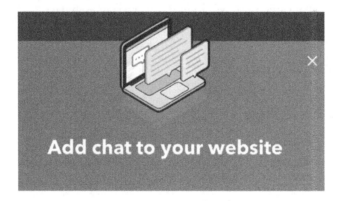

Figure 2.16 – Creating a live chat

4. To create a live chat, we first need to select the users who will appear for the chat and welcome message. At this point, you can also write a custom welcome message.

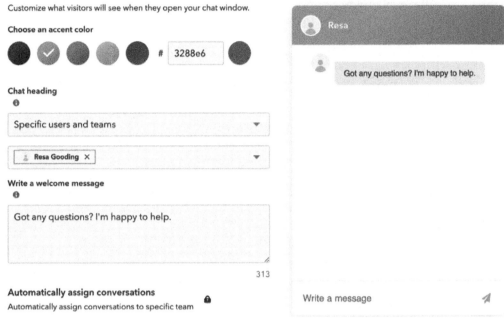

Figure 2.17 – Selecting the user and writing a custom message

5. You also need to select when you would like to be available to chat. I generally recommend choosing the **Based on team member status** option to avoid no one being online even during business hours.

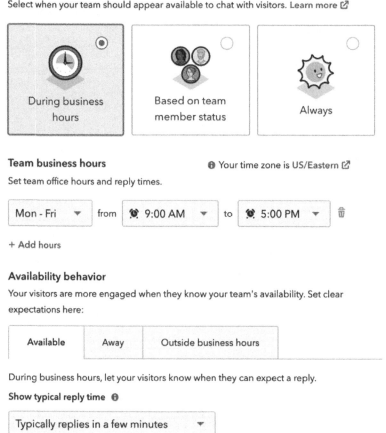

Figure 2.18 – Choosing availability

6. Next, choose which pages the chat should appear on and to which types of visitors it should and should not be shown.

Target

Set rules to decide which web pages your chatflow shows up on. You can also choose to show your chatflow only to specific visitors based on their identity or actions.

Website URL

Target your visitors by choosing the web pages where you'd like your chatflow to appear ❶

Visitor information and behavior (Optional)

Have more control over who sees your chatflow by adding rules based on your visitors' identity or behavior

Figure 2.19 – Choosing which pages and to whom the live chat should be shown

7. Then, choose whether the chat will be shown on both desktop or mobile or just desktop, and what will trigger the chat.

Chat display behavior

Control how the chat widget looks when visitors first access your website. ℹ

Desktop	Mobile

○ Pop open the welcome message as a prompt
◉ Only show the chat launcher
○ Open the chat widget

Chat display triggers

Decide when the chat welcome message should show to your targeted visitors.

☐ On exit intent ℹ

☐ Time on page in seconds = 0

☐ Percentage of the page scrolled = 50% ▾

Want to customize your chat widget?

Manage the accent color, chat placement and more under inbox settings ☑ .

Figure 2.20 – Choosing whether to show the live chat on small screens

8. Finally, set the chat as live.

Start a live chat

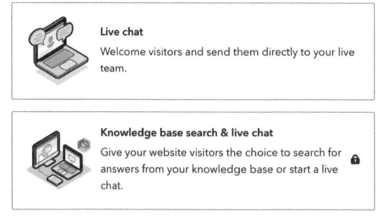

Live chat
Welcome visitors and send them directly to your live team.

Knowledge base search & live chat
Give your website visitors the choice to search for answers from your knowledge base or start a live chat. 🔒

Figure 2.21 – Setting the chat as "live"

9. Once the live chat is created, you can now return to creating your chatbot. Return to the **Chatflow** page, click on **Create a chatflow**, and then choose **Website**.

10. On the next screen, choose the **Qualify leads bot** option and then click on **Next**.

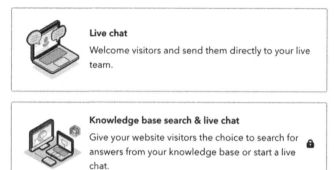

Start a live chat

Live chat

Welcome visitors and send them directly to your live team.

Knowledge base search & live chat

Give your website visitors the choice to search for answers from your knowledge base or start a live chat.

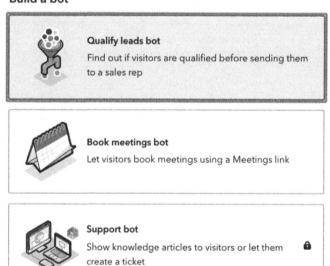

Build a bot

Qualify leads bot

Find out if visitors are qualified before sending them to a sales rep

Book meetings bot

Let visitors book meetings using a Meetings link

Support bot

Show knowledge articles to visitors or let them create a ticket

Figure 2.22 – Choosing Qualify leads bot

11. Build out your bot according to the process you mapped out at the beginning.

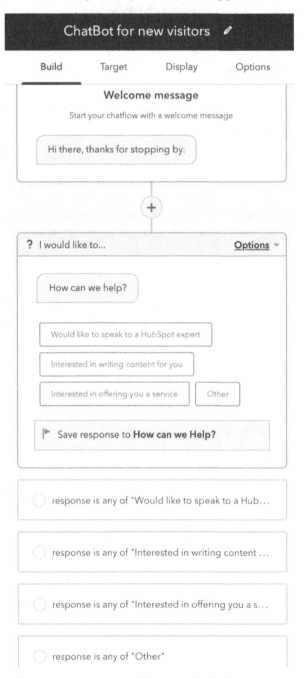

Figure 2.23 – Building out the chatbot

12. Choose which pages will display your chatbot and to whom.

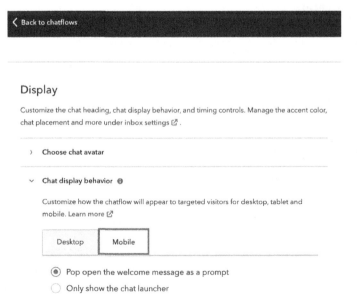

Figure 2.24 – Choosing which pages and to whom the chatbot should be shown

13. Decide which type of device it will be shown on – desktop or mobile – and the triggers that will show it.

Figure 2.25 – Deciding whether to show the chat on small screens and when

14. Then, choose the length of time allowed for delays between messages.

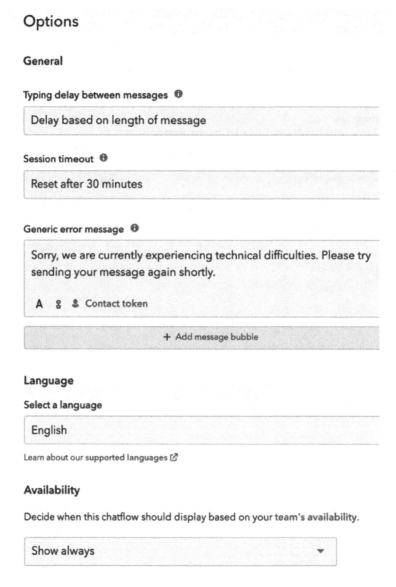

Figure 2.26 – Choosing when the chatbot will end if there is no response

15. Set your bot as live on your website and test it.

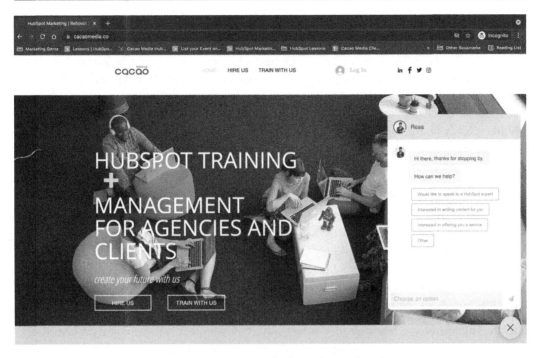

Figure 2.27 – Setting your chatbot as live and testing it

16. View the conversations in your inbox by navigating to **Conversations | Inbox**.

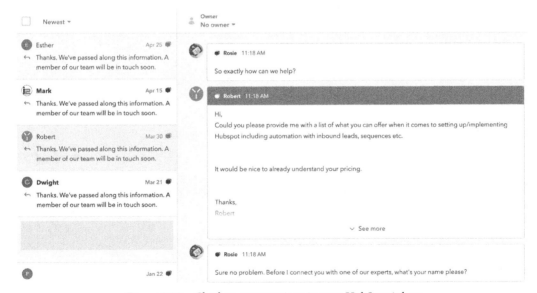

Figure 2.28 – Chatbot conversations in your HubSpot inbox

Whether you decide to do a live chat or chatbot, implementing this feature on your website today is critical as it can greatly improve conversions. Aside from the benefits cited by users while using this feature, companies have also seen great benefits. Some of these benefits include operational cost savings, 24*7 assistance, better customer engagement, personalized messaging – a boost in brand value since they need less manpower to deliver a customer experience – as well as gaining further insights into their customers, which would typically be missed just by trying to interpret their journey on their websites. So, if you don't yet have a chatbot on your site, make it a priority today.

Optimizing your forms

Forms are commonly used in every website as they are one of the easiest ways to capture a lead's information. However, forms are very similar to the questions you may ask when first meeting someone. You should try to be as unobtrusive as possible and, on your first interaction, ask for as few personal details as possible. So, asking for someone's first name, last name, and email is expected, but more than that for the first time can be risky. The next time you meet them, you can ask further questions.

Luckily, HubSpot has a feature called progressive fields on forms to help you do just that. So, instead of asking for details you have already collected, you can now ask more relevant questions to further qualify a contact, as shown:

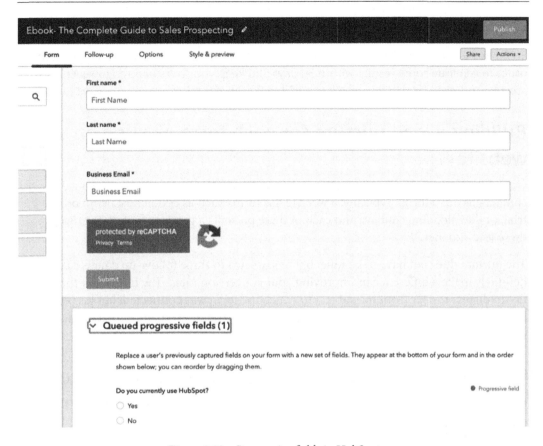

Figure 2.29 – Progressive fields in HubSpot

The type of questions you ask as progressive questions are similar to the types of questions you would ask if you met someone in person more than once. If a visitor is returning to your website, there is no need to ask their name and email address again, as you've already captured this information at the *first meeting*. So now that they have returned for a *second meeting*, you can ask more in-depth questions, such as *Which job role best describes you?* or *Which CRM systems do you use?* Nothing too personal, but questions that can still get you more information that is critical for you in understanding your prospect.

Generating more qualified leads

So far, we've discussed a few one-off tactics that can be employed in less than a week in order to generate some results within 30 days and keep your boss happy. However, there are a few other ideas that can also be considered even if it takes a few more days to set up.

Building a lead nurture for each form existing on your website

One of the most missed (and easiest) opportunities is building a lead nurture once a contact fills out a form. Typically, a website has forms such as contact us, demo or free trial, or downloading content, and each of these presents a gateway for you to engage these leads further.

The nurture does not have to be long, but at least two to three follow-up emails can definitely make a difference in improving your conversion rates. The important thing is not to digress too far from the subject to which the form was connected, but keep the information you are sending as closely related to the original content or request made when the contact submitted the form.

Building a retargeting campaign to further engage and convert contacts emerging from your best-performing channels

A quick review of your website analytics can show you which channels are bringing you the most leads. You may find, for example, that social media brings you quite a few leads or paid media gets you quite a few clicks and contacts. However, generally, you may not have enough information about these leads to deem them worthy of a conversation with sales.

Creating a retargeting campaign allows you to provide additional lead magnets to the contact and give them another opportunity to tell you a bit more about themselves. Using HubSpot's progressive forms feature, you can now submit different questions to the leads who revisit your content besides their first name, last name, and email. This gives you the added benefit of capturing more relevant information that qualifies if they are a good fit for your business or service.

Creating an educational webinar

This quick-win tip is one of my favorites as it can help you achieve two goals in one – generate new leads and improve conversions – by running an educational webinar. With a subscription to Zoom, Go To Webinar, or any of your preferred platforms, a speaker, who can easily be one of your team members, such as your product marketing manager, and some promotional banners ready for organic and paid media, you can have this campaign up and running in less than a week and have the webinar hosted in another 2 weeks.

The reason why I always recommend webinars is that they provide two opportunities to capture leads – one before the webinar goes live so the contacts can join the live stream, or after the webinar takes place when it can be set up as on-demand where contacts can watch at any time they choose.

It also provides countless opportunities for repurposing content as you can then create 30-second video snippets from the full webinar video or write a blog or even produce some other type of content, such as a guide or infographic depending on the content that was shared. So, this is definitely one tip not to be missed.

Generating more opportunities for sales

One of the most popular, but often least effective, forms on a website is the **contact us** form. Every company has one, but unless a prospect is anxious to be in contact with you, most of the time, they will skip this page. So, in this section, we would like to offer a few alternatives to the contact us form that can create some real opportunities for your sales teams.

Giving away part of your service

For service providers, this can be a very useful tactic as you can decide to share for free a part of your process for which you typically charge. For instance, as a marketing agency, a big part of any initial engagement for us is doing an audit of the client's HubSpot portal or marketing strategy. So, deciding to offer this stage for *free* helps us attract many prospects who would like to know how they are doing and to get some free advice.

This tactic though, if pulled off well, can be an opportune time for you to impress prospects with your knowledge. Hence, you shouldn't try to give as little information as possible. Instead, be super helpful as even giving away a few trade secrets such as showing them how to fix certain problems in their portal or strategy will pay off in the end.

Doing this establishes you in their mind as a professional who absolutely knows what they are doing and gives them an opportunity to evaluate what it would be like working with you even before they sign on the dotted line. In many cases, it's a win-win situation for both parties.

Recording "How to" videos for a critical part of your process

Another quick-win strategy for those in the decision stage is to produce some short how-to videos about executing any part of your service or using your product. People have come to rely on Google and YouTube to solve almost every problem they have. So, what may seem easy to you, or obvious, can be mind-blowing for a new user.

To decide on what types of videos you should produce, simply do a search for something related to your product or service, or check on popular chat streams such as Quora and look for questions that appear quite regularly. Then, create a *"How to.."* video showing the solution for that specific pain point.

Even if someone else has created such a video, don't be deterred by this, because the way you may explain something will be completely different from others. In addition, people often check a few explanations in order to see which video gives the clearest explanation.

You can then post this video on YouTube, your social media channels, and your website, and add a CTA to the end of the video, or to the post, for people to contact you should they have further questions.

Offering a free consultation (no strings attached)

Often, users are just looking for advice without the pressure to buy something or to become your client. Converting your contact us page to this type of consulting page positions you as an expert and, at the same time, takes away the fear of commitment.

The most important part of this page is the messaging; making sure users feel comfortable approaching you for advice without feeling like you would ask them for a commitment is important.

To differentiate between contacts who are potential customers and those who are simply looking for a freebie, add some qualifying questions to the forms on this landing page. For example, if you are an agency, you can ask a question such as *Which HubSpot platform do you currently have – Free, Professional, or Enterprise?* If a client chooses the Free version as their answer, this could indicate they may have issues committing to a budget for your service.

Re-engaging past sales opportunities

Many times, leads are lost because of bad timing, the lack of a budget at the time they were engaged, they weren't overly familiar with you, at the time of the interaction you didn't have the product or service they were interested in, or they simply decided to go to a competitor. Whatever the reason, now that some time has passed, one or more of these circumstances may have changed and this can be a great time to reach out to them.

Building a nurture campaign specifically for leads that were considered lost and that addresses one or two of these issues can have surprising results. I would suggest first building a list with each sales rep of contacts that were *Closed Lost*, and then using HubSpot's Sequence tool to send a more personal message from the respective sales reps' emails.

Creating these types of decision-making content and lead nurtures surely helps serve two sides of a coin. First, it gives your sales reps some much-needed opportunities to engage with, and, on the other hand, it allows potential prospects to engage with you and to decide whether they wish to do business with you. So, don't just rely on your **contact us** page to convert visitors, but pay attention to other ways in which you can provide immediate value without commitment for the visitor or long-term investment on your part.

Summary

All in all, investing in a platform such as HubSpot should not be taken lightly, and the sooner you can show and prove that the ROI from this tool allows you to be confident that the investment was worth it, the better. Whether your company needs to attract more traffic to the website, improve conversions, generate more qualified leads, or ensure the sales teams have a steady stream of opportunities to engage, HubSpot has the tools to provide a quick win in less than 30 days.

So, don't get caught in the trap of trying to set up an elaborate campaign that will take time and much-needed resources to implement. You now know that you should instead focus on the low-hanging fruit and see where you can easily generate a quick win to prove that your investment in this platform was worth it.

In the next chapter, we will discuss how to use HubSpot to empower your sales team regardless of whether you plan to use HubSpot to manage your sales process.

Questions

To ensure you understand the value of the steps you've just completed, have a go at answering the following questions:

1. What is one tactic you can use to generate more traffic in less than 30 days?

2. How can you convert your contact us page to a more appealing form that visitors want to fill out?

3. How can you capture more information about your contacts over time without asking a bunch of questions all at once?

Further reading

- HubSpot marketing blog: `https://blog.hubspot.com/marketing`

- HubSpot Academy: `https://academy.hubspot.com/`

- Projects tool (this is located within your individual portal)

3
Using HubSpot for Managing Sales Processes Effectively

First things first, let's put this on the table – your sales process will never be perfect. It simply cannot be as the two main parties involved are often at opposite ends of the spectrum – sales teams wanting the best price to maximize their commissions and customers wanting the lowest price to reduce costs.

That being said, the goals in your sales process should be to gain clarity, achieve transparency, and, most importantly, understand what is the best way to serve your customers in order for them to fuel your business.

These goals are ultimately achieved by establishing a functioning CRM that becomes your company's source of truth for every interaction your sales teams has with potential and existing customers.

In this chapter, we will focus on the following points:

- How to define your sales process

- How to set up your sales process in HubSpot

- Best practices for setting up and managing your sales pipeline in HubSpot

- Automate actions to save your reps time

- How to set up custom views to keep track of potential prospects

Prerequisites

To get the most out of this chapter, it would be helpful to consult with your sales team leaders when building your sales processes and discuss with them the best terminology to use for building the pipeline. Of course, having admin access to your HubSpot portal is a requirement so you can set up the pipeline as needed.

Defining your sales process

Most business sales processes are well...lacking a process. Sales teams often cite the need to do things their own way and rebuke any level of input or system that gives insights into their daily activities. But this is not the main purpose of investing in a CRM or building a sales process. The goal is not to be a "big brother," but instead to implement a set of repeatable steps that each member of your team can take to move a prospect from a lead to a customer. The goal of such a process is to help your reps consistently and successfully close deals with a framework that works.

In addition, setting up a well-defined framework for your sales process in HubSpot gives the following added value to the marketing team:

- It allows Marketing to tie the ROI from campaigns directly to the revenue generated.

- It can be used as a future indicator to approximate the number of customers and the amount of revenue a particular campaign should generate. After all, if you know how many leads should become customers, you can backtrack and figure out how many leads you'll need to hit a certain goal.

- It improves the timing of sales and marketing programs. For example, now you know how long a typical lead should spend in your funnel. That way you can launch new campaigns and know how long it will take to close those deals.

- It helps to identify bottlenecks. Are leads getting stuck at one stage? What can you do to improve? Maybe you need better messages/offers/information at that stage. What literature, tools, or information can you provide to meet the customer's requirements at this step? Or maybe you need to train your reps in a particular area. Or perhaps leads are falling through the cracks! Do you have any ideas for decreasing the time that a prospect will spend at each step?

So how do you get started with building your sales process?

HubSpot has advised that for each step in your sales process, you work with your sales teams and ask the following questions:

- What does the rep need to do to help the prospect move forward?
- What indicates that the rep has completed their role in that phase of the buying process?
- Is there any particular information they need to collect from the prospect?
- Are there certain commitments they need to secure?

Being able to answer these questions provides the foundation for setting up the deal stages required to build the sales pipeline in HubSpot. But before getting into HubSpot, you may need to trim down some of the steps.

Let's look at an example. If you are a B2B tech company selling software to a potential prospect, more often than not, your sales process will look something like this:

1. Identify Prospect
2. Qualify Lead
3. Warm Lead
4. Hot Lead
5. Discovery Call
6. Decision Maker Brought In
7. Define Project/POC
8. Project Approval
9. Evaluation
10. Quote
11. Contract
12. Negotiation
13. Closed Won

The potential problem with some of these stages is that it isn't always clear what actually needs to be done in that respective stage or if every prospect must go through each stage in order to be qualified as a customer. For example, see the following points:

- **Identify Prospect**: Does this mean you know the prospect's name and company or does it mean you have made contact with them?

- **Discovery Call**: Does this mean you have booked a call with the prospect or if the call has been completed?

To overcome this ambiguity, group your sales stages into these buckets:

- **Mandatory**: These are the steps your sales rep must complete in order to identify the prospect as a customer. When examining your current sales process, consider taking out anything that can reasonably be skipped without hurting the customer's long-term success and happiness. In the preceding example, this might be Discovery Call, Contract, or Closed Won.

- **Factual**: Identify which stages in your sales process are tied to a specific action rather than based on a feeling. In other words, when it comes to determining whether a step has been completed, you want a clear-cut yes or no. Looking at our example again, these stages could be Discovery Call, and so we will change this definition to *Discovery Call Booked* to make it clear that at this stage, you at least have something on the calendar with the prospect. We will know whether the discovery call was completed and the prospect moved on to later stages.

- **Inspectable**: Sometimes, companies include stages such as Warm Lead or Hot Lead as part of their sales process. However, because these are stages that are most likely identified because of an action the prospect took with the company, such as filling out a demo form, it is considered to be an inspectable step. This means you can see this information in the contact's record inside the CRM. Your sales process needs to focus on the things that are under your team's control.

- **Buyer-centric**: The last consideration when setting up your sales process is to understand which steps must be taken by the buyer in order for the deal to move forward; for example, contract signed or POC approved.

Once you have identified a combination of rep-focused actions as well as a buyer-focused outcome, you are now ready to define your deal stages. One example of such would be the following:

- Discovery Call Booked
- Project Scope/Defining POC
- POC In Progress
- Proposal Sent

- Negotiation
- Final Contract Sent
- Closed Won
- Closed Lost

Now that you have your sales pipeline defined, the next step is to set it up in HubSpot.

Setting up your sales process in HubSpot

With your sales process clearly defined, it is time to set them up as deal stages in HubSpot. A deal stage is simply the milestones a salesperson must complete in order to move an opportunity forward. To do so, follow these steps:

1. Navigate to **Settings** on the top menu. Then, on the right-hand side menu bar, scroll down to **Data Management | Objects | Deals**. Scroll down a bit more and you will then see the fields for stage names, as demonstrated in the following screenshot:

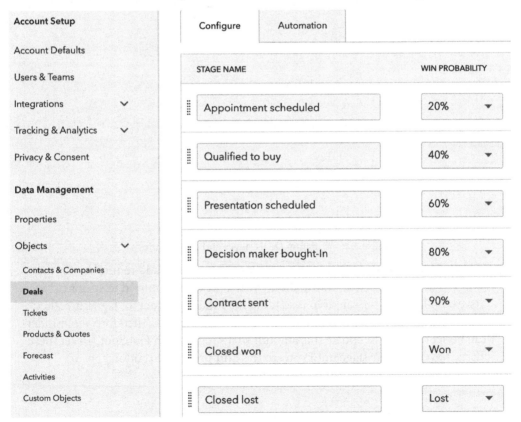

Figure 3.1 – Updating Deals stages

2. Now, replace the existing stages with your pre-defined stages. It is also important to add the probability of winning the deal to each stage. This is often a guesstimate at this stage and doesn't have to be 100% accurate. However, as your sales process becomes more precise, you can always return and update these probabilities as it will affect your forecasting reports.

3. Once completed, click **Save**:

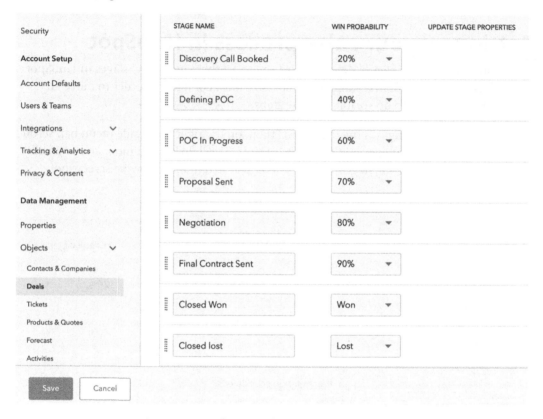

Figure 3.2 – Updating Deals stages and probabilities

4. Once you've set up your deals, the next consideration is to add reminders for the sales rep to update certain information when a prospect is moved to specific stages. For example, when the sales rep is sending the **Final Contract** for signature, they may have changed the amount following some negotiations. Therefore, a reminder can be set for them to update this amount so it's reflected in HubSpot. To set these alerts, hover over the stage until you see the **Edit properties** button appear:

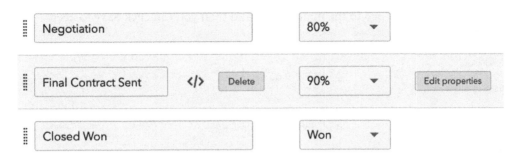

Figure 3.3 – Edit properties in deal stages

5. When you click on **Edit properties**, a box will appear from where you choose the field you want the sales reps to update by checking the checkbox on the left. In this case, it's the **Amount** field. If you have a subscription for Sales Professional in HubSpot, you can check the **REQUIRED** box, which also makes it mandatory for sales reps to fill in this information before they can move the prospect to that stage. Once done, click **Next**.

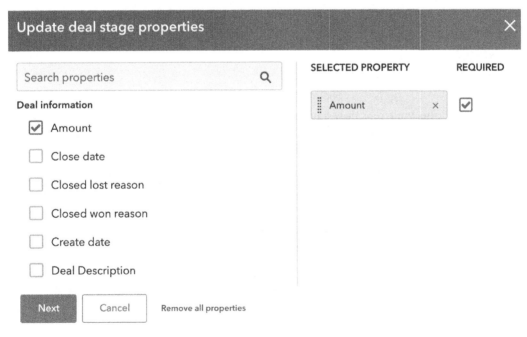

Figure 3.4 – Setting mandatory fields for your deal stages

6. You will be returned to the main screen and then you can click **Save** to keep this setting.

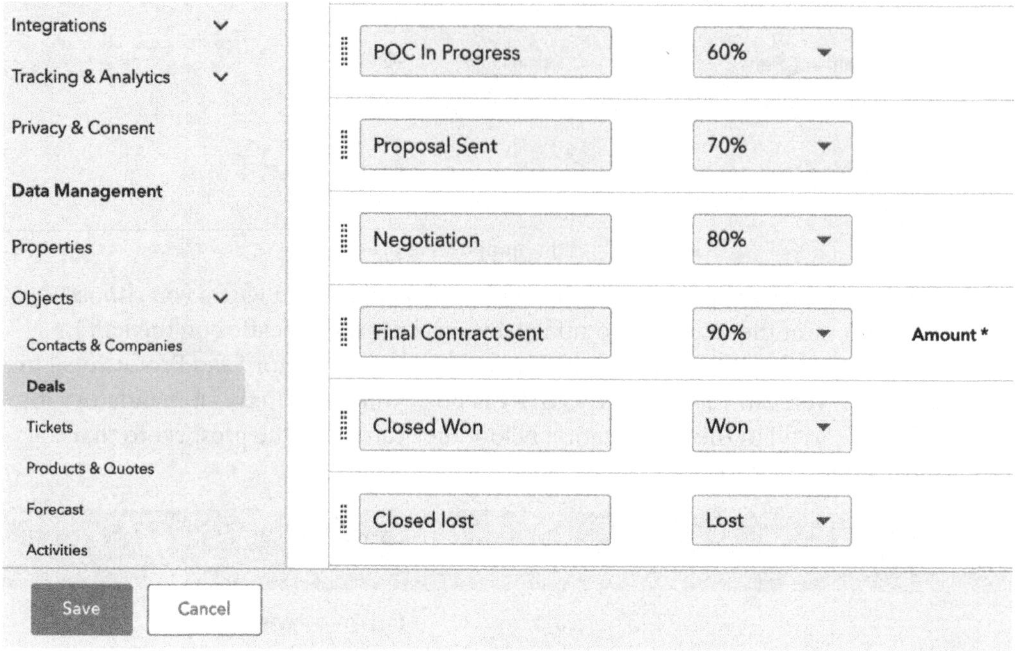

Figure 3.5 – Saving your settings

Once done, your reps now have certain fields they must fill out before moving a prospect to a specific deal stage. One more stage that should have a mandatory setting is that of **Closed lost**. Not all prospects will inevitably turn into customers, but often, management and sales reps believe that they lose customers because of price. Intentionally tracking the reasons why customers did not choose your business helps you to better understand the real reason behind their decisions.

Follow these steps to set up the processes correctly:

1. First, set up the reasons why you may lose a prospect so that it's easy for the reps to choose an option instead of creating their own version. To do this, navigate to **Settings | Data Management | Properties**. Change the filter from **Contact properties** to **Deal properties**.

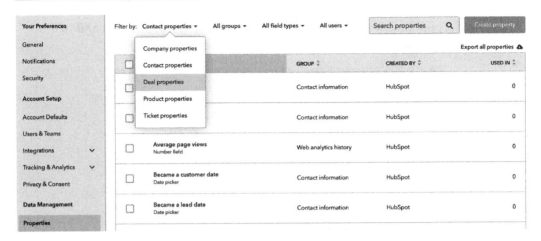

Figure 3.6 – Going to Deal properties

2. Type in reason in the Search properties bar. Click on **Closed lost reason**, as you can observe in the following screenshot:

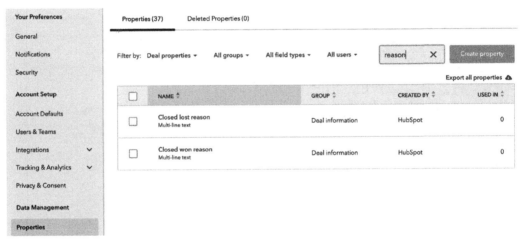

Figure 3.7 – Finding the Closed lost reason property

3. Once the pop-up box appears, click on **Field type** and then choose **Dropdown Select**, as shown in the following screenshot:

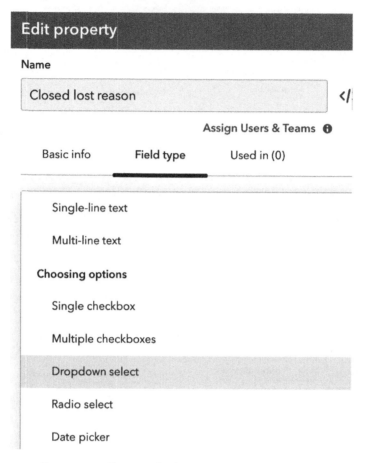

Figure 3.8 – Changing the field type to Dropdown select

4. Type in the options you generally think are the reasons why a deal is lost. Once you have included your options, click **Save**.

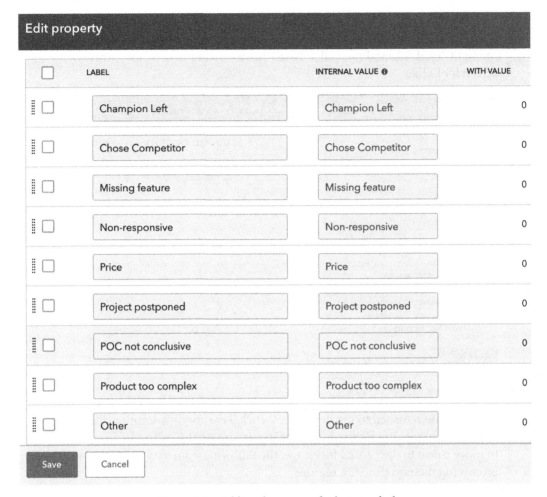

Figure 3.9 – Adding the reasons for losing a deal

5. Return to the sidebar menu and go to **Data Management | Objects | Deals**. Hover over the **Closed lost** stage and then click on **Edit properties**.

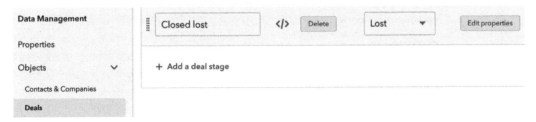

Figure 3.10 – Adding the Closed lost reasons to the Closed lost deal stage

6. Tick the checkbox on the left-hand side for **Closed lost reason**. Then, once again, if you have a HubSpot Sales Professional license, check the **REQUIRED** box on the right-hand side and then click **Next**. The following screenshot shows what the screen looks like:

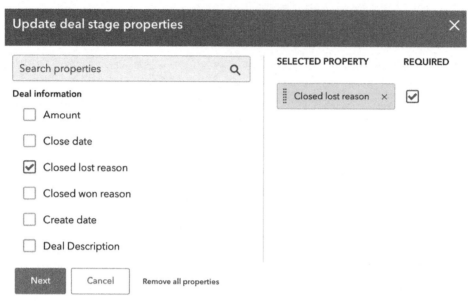

Figure 3.11 – Making the Closed lost reason feature mandatory

7. Once you are returned to the deal stages, click **Save** and this setting will now be implemented moving forward. With this particular setup, whenever a sales rep tries to move a deal to the Closed lost stage, the following notification box will pop up, prompting them to choose a reason:

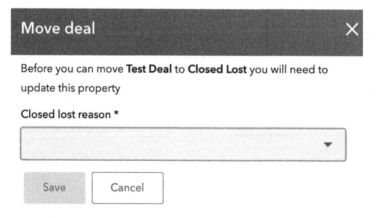

Figure 3.12 – Notification pop-up box for choosing the Closed lost reason

This concludes the main features to take into consideration when setting up your sales pipeline. But let's now look at some best practices that should be taken into account for maintaining and managing your pipeline.

Best practices for managing your sales pipeline in HubSpot

Ask any sales rep what's the least favorite part of their job and 9 out of 10 times, they will say doing administrative work. Sales reps would prefer spending time on those activities that directly contribute to their bonus plan, so unless you wish to include an incentive for keeping the CRM up to date, the alternative would be to make the process as painless as possible. So how can you achieve that? Let's examine some best practices in this section.

When to set up multiple pipelines

If you have HubSpot Sales Professional, then you have the option to set up more than one pipeline. However, before setting up another pipeline, do ask yourself the following questions:

Do you sell multiple products to various segments of your audience? For example, a company such as HubSpot sells its Marketing Hub mainly to the marketing departments of companies, while the Sales and Service Hub are sold to the sales and customer service teams, respectively, within that same company.

Do you sell across verticals? For example, selling to e-commerce companies compared to medical institutions can demand a different approach in the expected sales stages.

Does your sales cycle vary significantly from one territory to another or from one type of customer to another? For example, the sales cycle of an SMB compared to an enterprise or governmental organization can be drastically different.

Do you have distinct funnels (for example, new customers versus upsell)?

If your answer is *yes* to any of these questions, then it might be worthwhile opening a second pipeline. One popular use case that is often seen for B2B companies opening a second pipeline is when they wish to track the POC stage compared to the actual order stages. This can be especially useful when the POC stages are longer, like more than 3 months, and there is a need to follow the various steps involved in this type of sale.

To implement a second pipeline, simply follow these steps:

1. Navigate to **Settings | Data Management | Deals**. Click on **Options** on the right-hand side and then choose **Create new pipeline**.

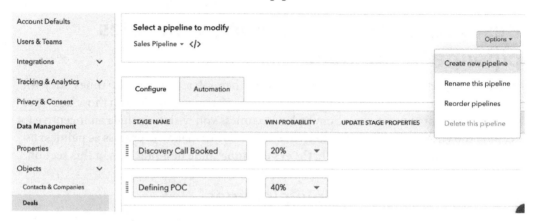

Figure 3.13 – Creating a second pipeline

2. Name your pipeline when the pop-up box appears.

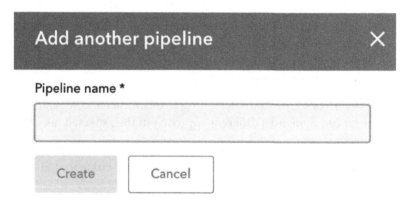

Figure 3.14 – Naming your pipeline

3. Update the deal stages as you did in the previous steps in *Figure 3.2*.

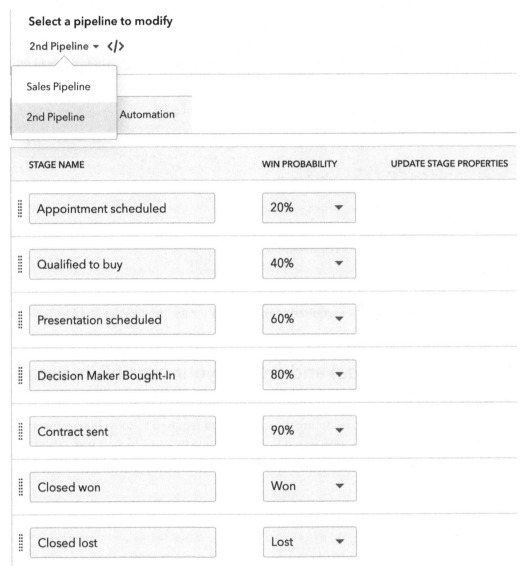

Figure 3.15 – Customizing the stages in the second pipeline

4. Now your second pipeline is created and ready to be used. To create deals in this pipeline, navigate to the top menu, click on **Sales | Deals**, and then choose the pipeline in which to create the new deal.

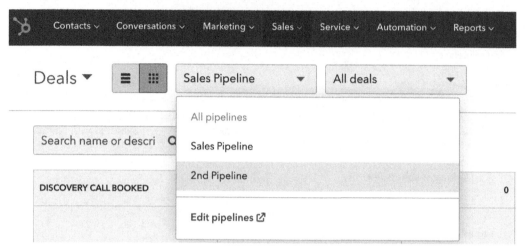

Figure 3.16 – Creating deals in your new pipeline

Now that you have the pipelines required to manage your sales process, let's look at how to create an actual deal.

How to create a deal and ensure your reps fill in all the required fields

Deals are the actual records that capture the information required to convert a prospect to a customer. There are several properties in this object and you can add your own custom fields if required.

To create a deal in either of your pipelines, follow these steps:

1. Navigate to the top menu and click on **Sales | Deals**.

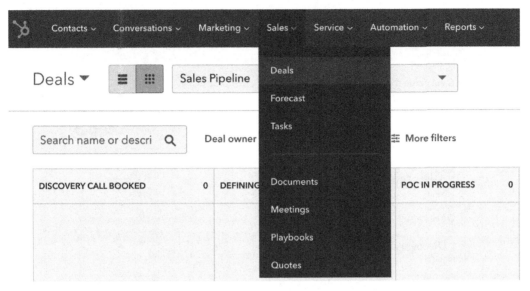

Figure 3.17 – Navigating to Deals

2. Then, click on **Create deal** in the top right-hand corner.

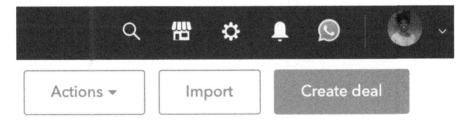

Figure 3.18 – Creating a deal

3. A pop-up box will appear. Insert all the details about the deal. Be aware that if you created two pipelines, you must be careful to choose the correct pipeline so that the deal can be created there.

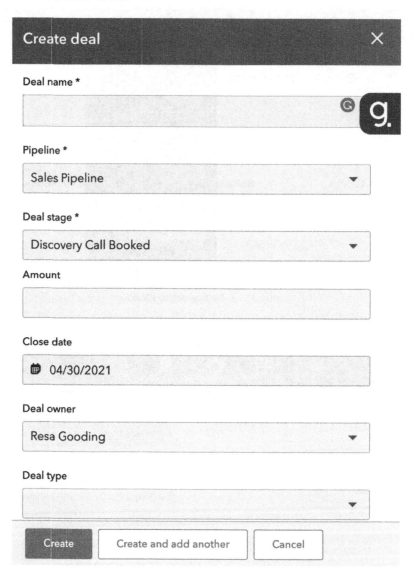

Figure 3.19 – Enter the relevant information as it relates to the respective deal

Before creating the deal, it is important to associate a company and respective contact(s) with the deal. These associations help identify which contacts are in an open process with your sales reps, meaning that when it comes to building reports and tracking the ROI on marketing campaigns, these results can be clearly seen.

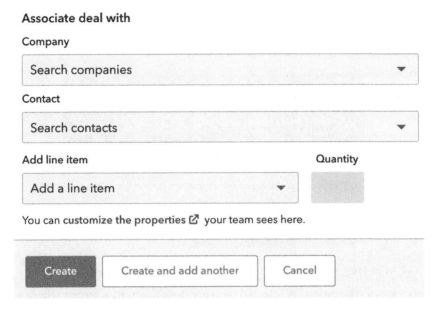

Figure 3.20 – Associate contacts and companies to the deal

Another consideration to take into account when your reps are creating deals is which fields they should see when creating a deal. To set these fields, follow these steps:

1. Navigate to **Settings | Data Management | Objects | Deals**. Then, scroll to the top and click on **Manage** for the second option, **Set the properties your team sees when creating deals**.

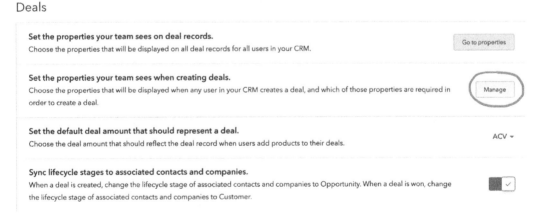

Figure 3.21 – Set the properties your team sees when creating deals

2. Once the **Manage** button is clicked, a pop-up box, as seen in the following figure, will appear asking whether you wish to start from the default properties or start from scratch. The former is recommended.

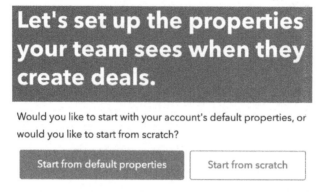

Figure 3.22 – Choosing whether to set these properties from scratch or apply the default properties

3. Once one of the options is selected, you are now taken to a screen where you can choose which properties you want the team to fill out when creating a deal (see *Figure 3.23*). Note that if you have HubSpot Sales Professional, you will also have the option to make any of the fields mandatory, meaning sales reps won't be able to create the deal without filling them in.

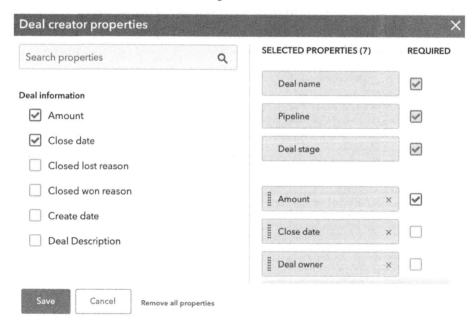

Figure 3.23 – Choosing which fields should be seen when creating a deal record

These few steps help you to save time chasing reps up to complete missing information on a deal record. Therefore, it is highly recommended to take the time to set these up. Next up is how to make it easier for the reps to see the most important information when they look at a deal record.

Customizing what field reps see on their accounts

Another important feature within the deal record is being able to customize the information that is seen when they view the record. Generally speaking, when a rep or member of the team looks at a deal record, they generally see the information they have inserted about the deal on the left-hand side under **About this deal**, as shown in the following screenshot:

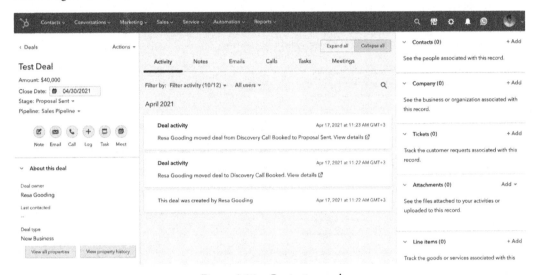

Figure 3.24 – Contact record

If you wish to add more properties that all members of the team should see, follow these steps:

1. Navigate to **Settings | Data Management | Objects | Deals**. Then, click on **Go to properties** and repeat the steps in *Figure 3.23* where you select the different properties you want your team to see.

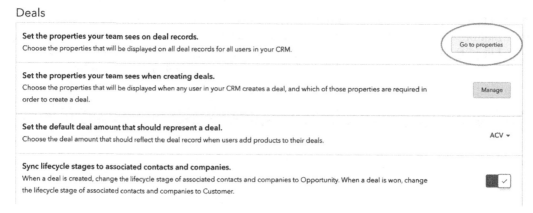

Figure 3.25 – Setting the properties your team sees on deal records

2. If a team member prefers to customize their own view, then they need to go to the contact record and click on **View all properties**.

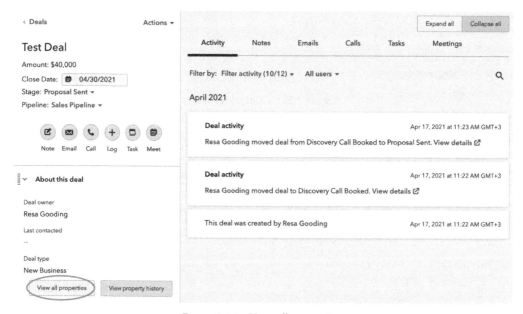

Figure 3.26 – View all properties

3. Then, once you are directed to the next page, hover over the property to be added to the view, click on **Add to your view** and return to the deal record. Note that any property added to your deal record will be shown for all deals going forward.

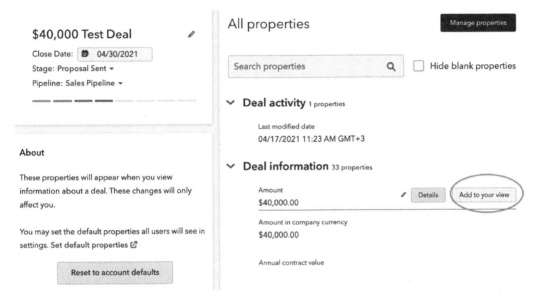

Figure 3.27 – Adding the respective property to your view

These few steps help to make it easier for your reps to navigate the system and therefore update the necessary details to provide more clarity and transparency regarding a pending deal.

There are, however, two more points that we must mention in order to ensure that everyone has the same understanding of how to interpret the information on the deal record and how to simplify the number of updates needed for a deal to move forward.

Choosing the correct deal amount on a contact record

Let's begin with the deal amount. Before we dive into this, you must first check that the default currencies are updated in your portal. You can choose to have multiple currencies if needed. To set up your currencies, complete the following steps:

1. Navigate to **Settings** on the top menu and, on the left menu bar, click on **Account Defaults**. Select the **Currency** tab on the top menu of the page and then click on **Add Currency**.

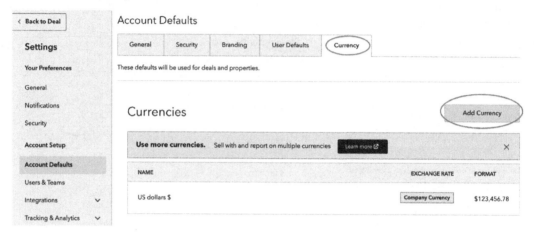

Figure 3.28 – Adding another currency

2. In the pop-up box that appears, select the other currency you wish to add.

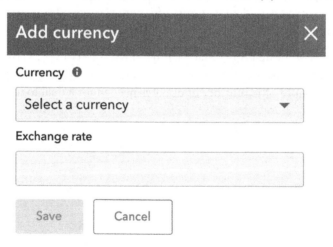

Figure 3.29 – Selecting a currency

3. Then, insert the exchange rate of this currency and click **Save**. This currency is now added to your system.

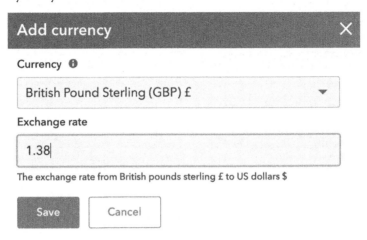

Figure 3.30 – Inserting the exchange rate for the selected currency

Now that you have the currencies added to your portal, it is time to set the default deal amount that should represent a deal. To do this effectively, you must first understand the four different types of deal amounts that HubSpot captures:

- **Annual contract value (ACV)**: ACV is the value of the deal over a 12-month period in the deal's currency, if your HubSpot account uses more than one currency.

- **Annual recurring revenue (ARR)**: ARR is the total amount of revenue earned annually for this deal. This is calculated based on the term length and values of the recurring line items associated with the deal. If there is no term length, HubSpot assumes a term of 12 months. It does not take into account the value in the Amount property. This is shown in the deal's currency if your HubSpot account uses more than one currency.

- **Monthly recurring revenue (MRR)**: MRR is the recurring monthly revenue in relation to this deal. This is calculated using the values and term length of the recurring line items associated with the deal (in other words, the total value divided by the number of months in the term's length). It does not take into account the value in the Amount property. This is shown in the deal's currency if your HubSpot account uses more than one currency.

- **Total contract value (TCV)**: TCV is the total value of the deal, based on the line items associated with the deal, including any recurring revenue and one-time charges. It does not take into account the value in the Amount property. This is in the deal's currency if your HubSpot account uses more than one currency.

If none of these fit your processes, then you have a final option called **Manual entry**.

Once you have decided which deal amount fits your business, you set it by navigating to **Settings | Data Management | Objects | Deals** and select the appropriate value under **Set the default deal amount that should represent a deal**.

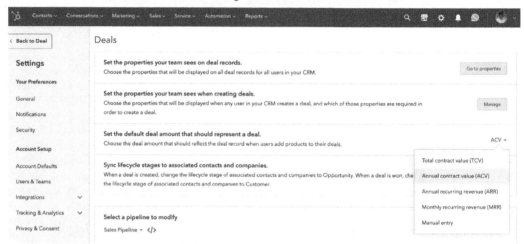

Figure 3.31 – Set the default deal amount that should represent a deal

Once you've set up your default deal amount, it's time to look at how to simplify some of these processes for the sales teams.

Using deal automation features to amplify your efficiency

We began this chapter by emphasizing the fact that our sales process can never be perfect, but we do want to minimize errors, remove friction from the sales process, and turbocharge the efficiency of your sales reps. So how do we accomplish this? Through the use of the deal automation features embedded in HubSpot software. Some of the most popular ways to use these automation features are as follows:

- Updating other properties as deals progress through the pipeline

- Creating tasks for the sales reps so leads don't fall through the cracks

- Sending internal email notifications for important updates so you don't have to spend time updating colleagues

- Sending follow-up emails once a lead reaches a certain stage in the sales process

Reporting

Adding a few of these automated processes within the pipeline allows your sales teams to remember to fill out crucial data points in the sales process or to be notified when something significant happens with a specific opportunity or deal. So do try it out.

Setting up views that allow your reps to complete their daily tasks

One of the most common questions sales reps have when starting to use any system is, "What data should I be looking at every day in this system?" The answer to this question lies in the various ways they segment the database in order to keep track of new leads or important contacts that should be followed up on. There are four views or segmentations that each sales rep should set up in HubSpot and any CRM as a matter of course:

- New Leads

- Follow-Up Needed

- VIP Leads

- Medium Priority

Let's examine in detail what each of these segments means and how they can be set up in HubSpot.

New Leads

New Leads are contacts that have just entered the database, are qualified, and no one has contacted them as yet. In *Chapter 9, Converting Your Visitors to Customers*, and Chapter 11, *Proving That Your Efforts Worked Using the Reports*, we discuss the mechanics of how to set up lead scoring and use automation to define qualified leads, but once this process is done the goal is to make sure the sales teams have easy visibility of these leads. This filter is particularly useful for inbound leads or leads generated by marketing efforts as these leads are generally the leads that fall through the cracks for follow-up by sales reps.

To set up this view, navigate to **Contacts | All Filters** and then look for the **Create date** property, as seen in *Figure 3.32*:

Figure 3.32 – Creating views using filters in Contacts

Then, consider adding some of the filters that the marketing team uses to qualify leads, such as job title or company size. In this example shown in *Figure 3.33*, we also show the option of excluding certain job titles such as "Student" so the sales team won't be distracted by unqualified leads. Also, we added the **New** lead status, so once again the reps will only see leads that have never been touched. (Lead statuses are discussed in *Chapter 11, Proving That Your Efforts Worked Using the Reports*).

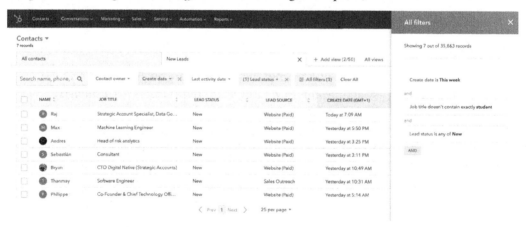

Figure 3.33 – Adding more filters to see relevant contacts

Once all the filters have been selected, you can choose to save the view by clicking **Save**, **View**, and then **Save as new**, as seen in *Figure 3.34*:

Figure 3.34 – Saving the view of chosen contacts

Once you click on **Save as new**, you are then able to choose who should see this view of contacts. Setting it to **Everyone** makes it easy for the other sales reps to choose this view as one of their options once it's created.

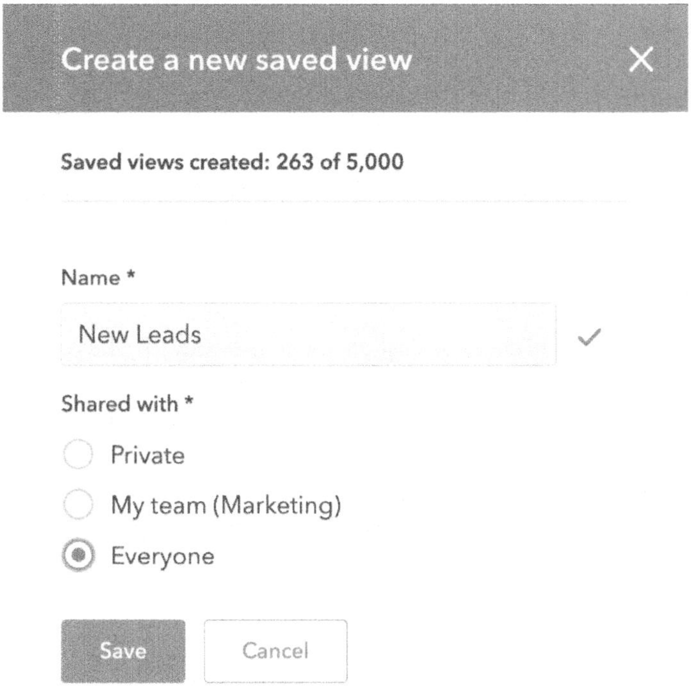

Create a new saved view   ✕

Saved views created: 263 of 5,000

Name *

New Leads   ✓

Shared with *

◯ Private

◯ My team (Marketing)

⦿ Everyone

Save   Cancel

Figure 3.35 – Saving the view for everyone to have visibility of these lists of contacts

Once this view is saved, it will appear in the top sub-menu, as shown in *Figure 3.36*, for easy access on the part of the sales reps to see the list of new contacts when starting their day:

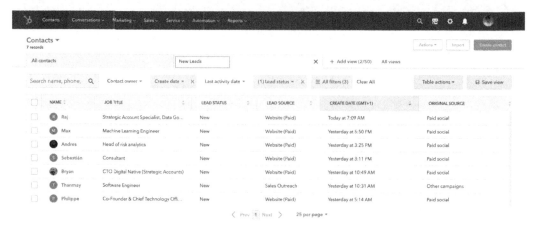

Figure 3.36 – New Leads view

This is just one view that helps give sales reps a start for the day. Let's now look at the next view.

Follow-Up Needed

This next view is supposed to show which leads have not been touched for some time. It uses a property called **Last Contacted in HubSpot**, which collects the time when a contact was last emailed by a team member personally or called. Note that this does not include marketing emails, just sales emails that are tracked when a sales rep connects their email to HubSpot.

To build this view, the same process described above is followed. The only difference in this view is the properties used to filter the relevant contacts. In this case, we used the following properties: **Last contacted** is a period that is considered too long for a sales rep not to have been in touch, for instance, last month; **Lead status** is any status you have currently incorporated into the system to represent the fact that some follow-up is needed, for instance, **Open** and **Attempting to Contact**, and **Job title** doesn't include any irrelevant titles that sales reps shouldn't deal with, such as student or teacher. See *Figure 3.37* for an illustration:

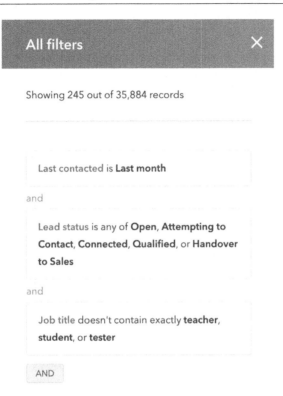

Figure 3.37 – Filters for creating a view of contacts that should be followed up

Once the filters are saved, the view can now be seen at the top, as shown in *Figure 3.38*. This ensures that whenever a sales rep logs in to the system, there will be a daily view of the relevant contacts that should be followed up with.

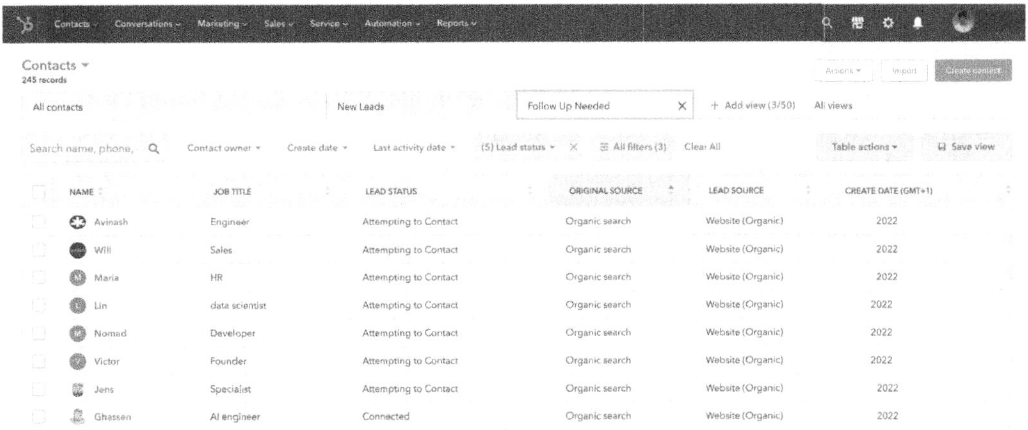

NAME	JOB TITLE	LEAD STATUS	ORIGINAL SOURCE	LEAD SOURCE	CREATE DATE (GMT+1)
Avinash	Engineer	Attempting to Contact	Organic search	Website (Organic)	2022
Will	Sales	Attempting to Contact	Organic search	Website (Organic)	2022
Maria	HR	Attempting to Contact	Organic search	Website (Organic)	2022
Lin	data scientist	Attempting to Contact	Organic search	Website (Organic)	2022
Nomad	Developer	Attempting to Contact	Organic search	Website (Organic)	2022
Victor	Founder	Attempting to Contact	Organic search	Website (Organic)	2022
Jens	Specialist	Attempting to Contact	Organic search	Website (Organic)	2022
Ghassen	AI engineer	Connected	Organic search	Website (Organic)	2022

Figure 3.38 – View of contacts that the sales rep should follow up with

VIP Leads

This view should be used to fast-track contacts so that they get the sales reps' immediate attention, for example, contacts that filled out a demo form or contact us form. *Figure 3.39* shows an example of what the filters can be for this view:

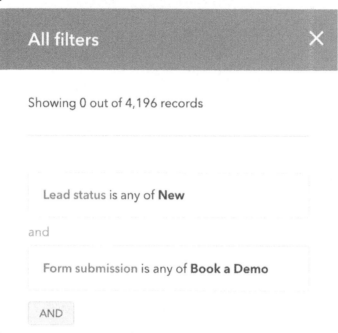

Figure 3.39 – Filter for creating a view of VIP leads

The next important view is that of Medium Priority.

Medium Priority

These contacts are leads that could potentially be of interest to sales but haven't yet shown an interest in speaking to sales. To set up this filter, lead scoring, if implemented, can be used as a possible criterion. *Figure 3.40* shows an illustration of how to set up these filters. Another easier criterion to use in lieu of lead scoring is probably adding the website pages you deem to be of high intent to purchase pages such as a pricing page or an about us page.

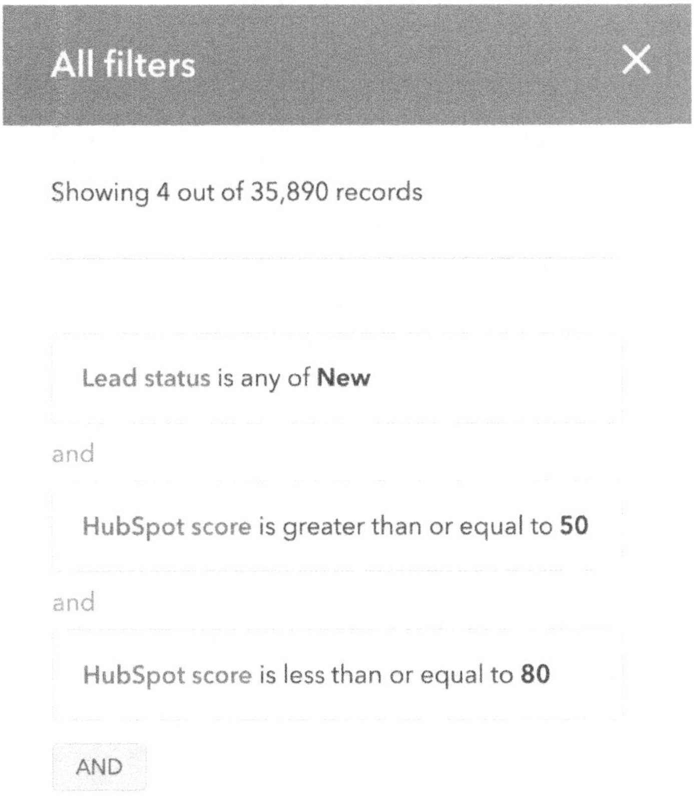

All filters   X

Showing 4 out of 35,890 records

Lead status is any of **New**

and

HubSpot score is greater than or equal to **50**

and

HubSpot score is less than or equal to **80**

AND

Figure 3.40 – Filters for setting up views for contacts that are not such a high priority

These are just a few views that can be quickly implemented in your setup of HubSpot for your sales teams. It helps to give them some focus and action items when using the portal. There are a few points to note, however, regarding the tips discussed in this section as you may be wondering why you wouldn't use lists instead to do this:

- First, lists tend to get lost in the mayhem as there could be hundreds of lists created eventually. Hence, the point of doing this exercise to ensure that the sales reps know exactly which contacts to focus on once they open their computers at the start of the day would be lost if yet more lists were used for this exercise.

- Also, at the time of writing, when creating filters for views in contacts, there is no "OR" option, only "AND". For lists, this is possible. So, if you wish to add multiple filters you will need to create separate views.

Summary

By completing the steps in this chapter, you now have a clearly defined sales process set up in HubSpot and your sales teams can now begin following through with respective opportunities until they are closed-won. Note that although many companies have operated thus far without such a process, having one brings a level of clarity to the team and management on exactly where prospects stand and allows them to see which opportunities currently exist in their pipeline, the stages they are at, and when it is forecast that they will be closed.

In the next chapter, we will learn how to manage HubSpot CRM and Sales Hub for sales teams and managers. We will also learn how to use the HubSpot tools to create meetings, tasks, and functions only designed for sales.

Questions

Let's now see whether the concepts in this chapter have resonated with you:

1. What are two conditions you should consider when setting up the sales pipeline?
2. When should you open a second pipeline?
3. What are two actions you should consider automating in your pipeline?

Further reading

- How to document your sales process: `http://www.marketingmo.com/strategic-planning/how-to-document-your-sales-process/`

- How to design your sales process in HubSpot: `https://blog.hubspot.com/customers/how-to-design-your-sales-process-in-hubspot-crm`

- HubSpot Academy Lesson – Set Up Your HubSpot CRM for Growth: `https://academy.hubspot.com/courses/set-up-your-hubspot-crm-for-growth?library=true&_ga=2.36803296.1117529161.1633694052-1936490580.1584861075`

4
Empowering Your Sales Team through HubSpot

HubSpot is more commonly known for its marketing automation capabilities than its sales capabilities. However, in recent times, their sales tools have become more robust, often putting them ahead of the competition as it helps remove the friction that can exist between a prospect and salesperson. Today, more companies are using the platform to also power their sales activities as, first, it is mostly free to access, and second, it provides a few key advantages, as follows:

- It allows both marketing and sales teams to see the entire journey of the customer from the first interaction with your business to the moment they became a customer.

- It creates the perfect setup for sales and marketing teams to work closely together since they each have full visibility into each other's activities.

- It reduces the company's investment in technology as they now only need to invest resources in paying for and managing one platform instead of two different platforms.

This chapter will focus on helping your sales teams achieve three main goals using HubSpot sales tools:

- **Identifying new leads in less time**: We will review tools such as the prospects tool, email templates and sequences, and shared inbox profiles.

- **Connecting with a prospect at exactly the right time**: Tools such as email tracking, email scheduling, and notifications and calls will help you know when the best time is to reach out to a prospect.

- **Landing more meetings and close more deals**: Tools such as meetings, documents, and quotes will help you secure more meetings and turn those prospects into customers faster.

By the end of this chapter, you will be able to increase the efficiency of your sales teams by reducing the amount of administrative work required, as well as improving their deal-close rate. If you wish to understand how to create pipelines and use the deals specifically in HubSpot, please read the previous chapter.

Technical requirements

To ensure you get the most out of this chapter, be sure to have Admin access to your HubSpot account. Most of the elements discussed here are included in the free version of HubSpot, so even having a free version of the account can be very useful.

Identifying new leads in less time

In *Chapter 2, Generating Quick Wins with Hubspot in the First 30 Days*, we mentioned Google Analytics as a surefire way to understand which pages of your website attract the most visitors. However, one limitation of Google Analytics is that it cannot tell you *who* exactly came to your website. This is one of the major advantages of having a platform such as HubSpot. In the following sections, we will show you how the prospects tool or notifications can help you identify unique visitors.

Using the prospects tool

HubSpot has a proprietary tool called the prospects tool, which uses the HubSpot tracking code to detect the **Internet Protocol (IP)** addresses of visitors to your website. Note these visitors may not yet exist in your database, meaning they have not yet given you their contact details but will still appear in the prospects tool.

The tool is free to all users of HubSpot and works because, as most companies have unique IP addresses, once they visit your website using their company's internet network, the prospects tool populates your HubSpot portal with publicly available information about that company.

To access the prospects tool, navigate to **Contacts | Target Accounts** and activate this feature by clicking on **Get started**:

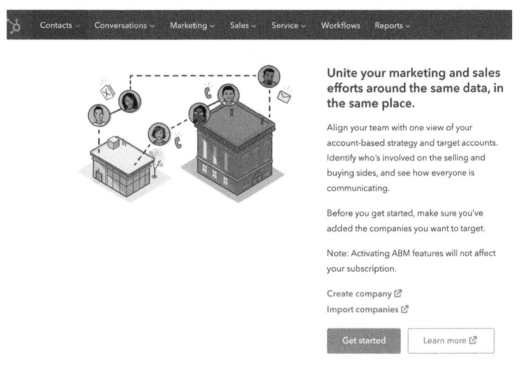

Figure 4.1 – Navigation bar to the prospects tool

Once the **Target Accounts** feature is activated, you will arrive at the following page, where you will find the **Prospects** tool in the bottom left menu:

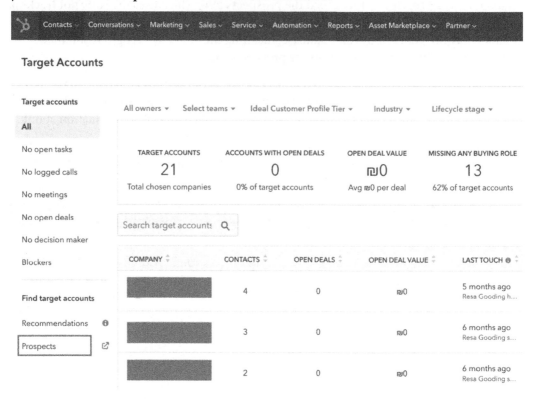

Figure 4.2 – Navigation bar to the prospects tool

Clicking on the **Prospects** tab takes you to a page where you will see a lot of information about companies. Note, if you do not see any information appear you will need to double-check that your website is connected to HubSpot. Refer to *Chapter 1, Overview of HubSpot – What You MUST Know*, where we discussed the technical setup, for guidelines on how to do this.

Remember, this information is collected via IP addresses, so because of GDPR and personal privacy regulations, HubSpot cannot at this stage tell you who visited your site, as most times, these contacts have not yet opted in. So, it will only tell you which company was on your site, how many people from that company came to your site, how many pages they visited, and when they were last seen.

NAME ⇕			NUMBER OF VISITORS ⇕	NUMBER OF PAGE VIEWS ⇕
🐾 rostkredo.com.ua	Preview	+	2	3
Net One Systems Co., Ltd.	Preview	+	1	2
🐀 Econet Editora	Preview	+	2	2
xgate.co.kr	Preview	+	37	109

Figure 4.3 – Prospects tool

You can also add more columns to see which sources or channels bought these contacts, for instance, social media or direct traffic, as well as which countries they came from based on the IP location.

Note, for smaller companies or individuals visiting your site from the comfort of their home, the IP address will appear as their generic internet service provider, such as Verizon or Orange.

But, how exactly can your sales teams use this information?

One way is, first, by understanding whether certain target companies are visiting your site, the sales team can then research the relevant persona on LinkedIn and connect with them. For instance, if you are a cybersecurity company, then most likely the person from the company visiting your site is a CIO or systems security engineer, and you can then connect with such persons from the company on LinkedIn.

Another angle for which both your marketing and sales teams can use this tool is to build an **account-based marketing (ABM)** campaign targeting the companies that visit your website. You can start this campaign by setting up retargeting ads for these companies in HubSpot and then building an email sequence for this list of companies containing sales emails coming from the respective sales team members. And, once the prospects are converted, they will be added to the database for further follow-up by the sales teams. This brings us to our next tool – email sequences.

Prospecting better with email templates and sequences

Email templates are emails that can be set up to send repetitive content directly from your personal inbox. On the other hand, sequences are a combination of templates set up to be sent automatically at predefined intervals.

In *Chapter 9*, *Converting Your Visitors to Customers*, we will discuss marketing emails and workflows that exist in the Marketing Hub of HubSpot and are basically the equivalent of email templates and sequences. The main difference is that the former is sent directly from the inbox of the sales team members, while the latter is sent from HubSpot as a marketing email. Although both are automated emails being sent to the contacts at defined intervals, the advantage of using sequences is that it is a more personalized approach, as the emails will look exactly as if they are coming from your regular inbox. Unlike marketing emails, there is no design or unsubscribe link (if you choose not to add it).

Templates

Templates are also a free tool in HubSpot and found in the top menu by navigating to **Conversations | Templates**:

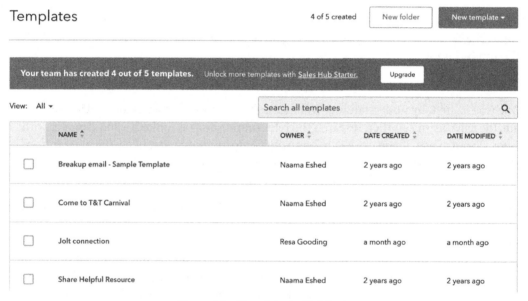

Figure 4.4 – Templates in HubSpot

From this page, you can click on the orange **New Template** button and choose either the **From scratch** or **From template library** option and begin creating your desired email content. As always, HubSpot shares with you a wealth of resources to help you get started; it's highly recommended to check out their library of email templates to get some ideas on how to position your email to a prospect.

Sticking to our cybersecurity example and setting up an email sequence that your sales teams can use as a follow up from leads identified from the prospects tool and enlisted to your ABM campaign, here's a sample of an email template with which you can begin:

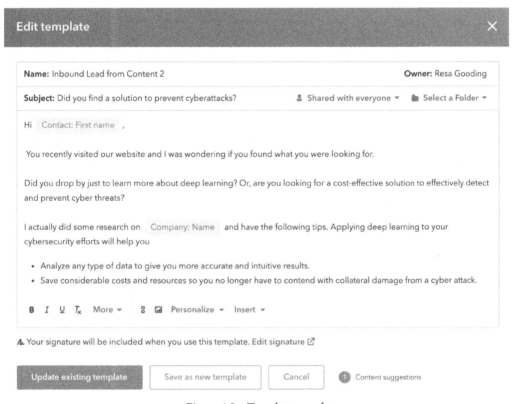

Figure 4.5 – Template sample

Note a few things about the template:

- The content found in the **Subject** line will be populated in the email subject, so be sure to choose something that will encourage people to open the email.

- There are personalization tokens inserted in the email for the contact's first name and company name.

Once you've set up at least three of these types of templates, the next step is to set up the email sequence.

Automating your outreach with email sequences

Email sequences are a paid feature of HubSpot as part of the Sales Professional package. If you have access to this feature, you will find it under **Automation | Sequences**.

As mentioned previously, it is essentially a workflow that allows your sales teams to send automated emails to prospects directly from their inbox. It is a great tool to use when trying to follow up with a prospect to book a meeting or after sending a contract or any other sales-related activities that usually demand more than one email before getting the contact to respond. One of the most popular uses for setting up a sequence is when there is a need for your sales team to follow up with someone who booked a demonstration or trial of your product. Here's an example:

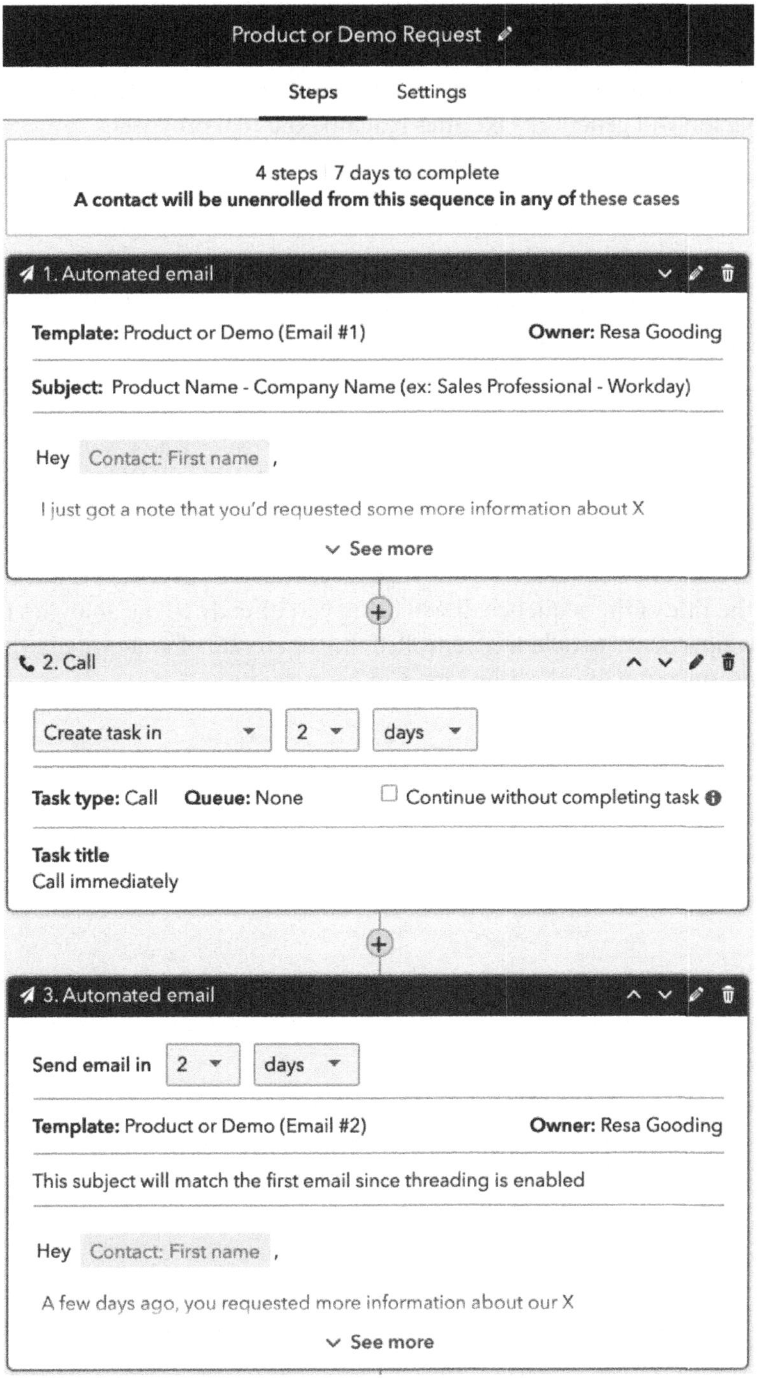

Product or Demo Request ✏

Steps   Settings

4 steps   7 days to complete
A contact will be unenrolled from this sequence in any of these cases

✈ 1. Automated email   ⌄ ✎ 🗑

Template: Product or Demo (Email #1)   **Owner:** Resa Gooding

Subject: Product Name - Company Name (ex: Sales Professional - Workday)

Hey   Contact: First name ,

I just got a note that you'd requested some more information about X

⌄ See more

⊕

📞 2. Call   ⌃ ⌄ ✎ 🗑

| Create task in | ▾ | 2 ▾ | days ▾ |

Task type: Call   **Queue:** None   ☐ Continue without completing task ⓘ

Task title
Call immediately

⊕

✈ 3. Automated email   ⌃ ⌄ ✎ 🗑

Send email in 2 ▾   days ▾

Template: Product or Demo (Email #2)   **Owner:** Resa Gooding

This subject will match the first email since threading is enabled

Hey   Contact: First name ,

A few days ago, you requested more information about our X

⌄ See more

Figure 4.6 – Sequences tool

Here are a few points to note about HubSpot sequences:

- It can be a combination of emails, tasks, reminders, or any other action that a salesperson will generally take after reaching out to a prospect.

- You can enroll a single contact or multiple contacts at a time by putting them all in a list.

- You can decide on the intervals for when the next action should take place.

- Once a sequence is sent, you can see the statistics on its performance, specifically, open rate, click rate, and reply rate.

- You can view the performance of each of your emails, so you know which type of message resonated best.

- Last but not least, contacts will only be able to exit the sequence if they reply to your email or book a meeting.

Once you have enrolled contacts in your sequence, you can check its performance by clicking on the title of the sequence. It will bring you directly to the analytics page where you can view how many people were enrolled, the open rate of your emails, the click rate, reply rate, meeting rate, unsubscribe rate, and bounce rate:

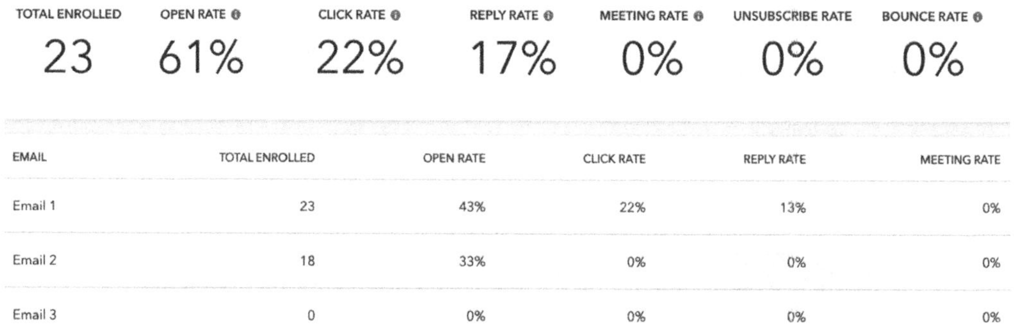

TOTAL ENROLLED	OPEN RATE	CLICK RATE	REPLY RATE	MEETING RATE	UNSUBSCRIBE RATE	BOUNCE RATE
23	61%	22%	17%	0%	0%	0%

EMAIL	TOTAL ENROLLED	OPEN RATE	CLICK RATE	REPLY RATE	MEETING RATE
Email 1	23	43%	22%	13%	0%
Email 2	18	33%	0%	0%	0%
Email 3	0	0%	0%	0%	0%

Figure 4.7 – Analytics of a sequence

As shown, you can also view the performance of each individual email so you can determine which type of email gets the best reaction and replicate these patterns.

Centralizing all communication with prospects using a shared inbox

Another popular channel through which leads often come is your company's generic inboxes, such as `support@companyname.com` or `info@companyname.com`.

These inboxes usually exist in the email domain that manages all your company's email inboxes, so understanding who has visibility to the emails coming in from these inboxes can be difficult. With HubSpot's shared inbox feature, you can now have any emails sent to these inboxes filtered into HubSpot, so that your sales teams can have visibility into the content that is being sent to each of them, and source any new leads that come in via this channel.

To connect a shared inbox to HubSpot, simply navigate to **Settings | Tools | Inboxes**. From there, choose **Create a channel** as seen in *Figure 4.8* and follow the instructions, which prompt you to choose your email provider and allow connection to the inbox. You must have access to the inbox itself as you will be required to sign in.

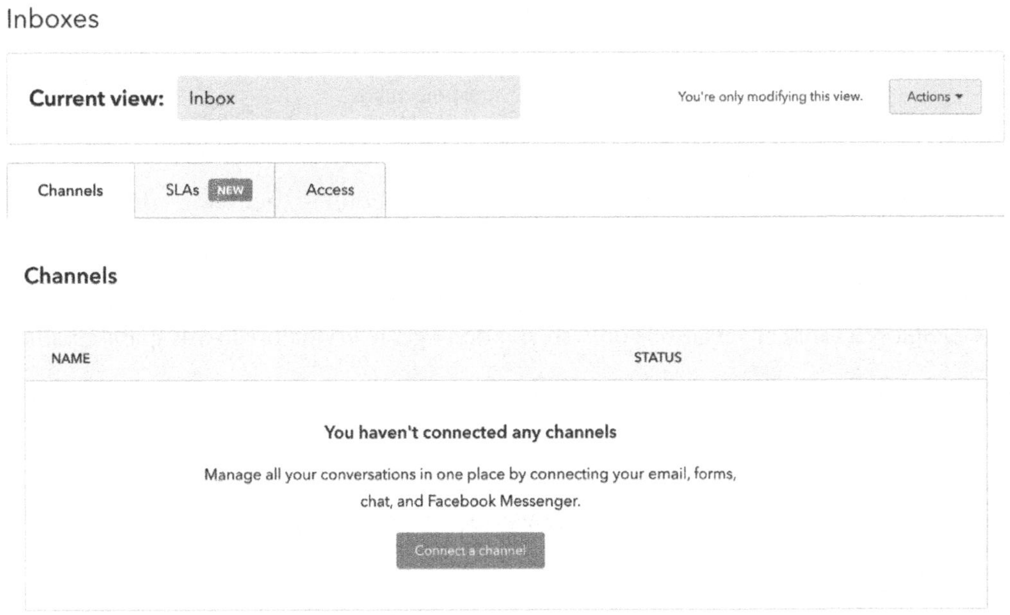

Inboxes

Current view:	Inbox	You're only modifying this view.	Actions ▾

Channels   SLAs NEW   Access

Channels

NAME	STATUS

You haven't connected any channels

Manage all your conversations in one place by connecting your email, forms, chat, and Facebook Messenger.

Connect a channel

Figure 4.8 – Connecting a shared inbox

Once your shared inbox is connected successfully, you can view the information in this inbox by navigating to your top menu and choosing **Conversations | Inbox**. Here, you will find all messages that either come through your support inbox or your chat:

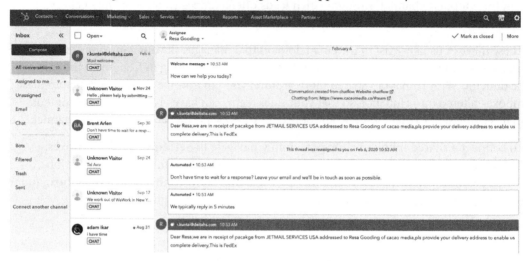

Figure 4.9 – Conversations inbox

Connecting your shared inbox allows your sales team to perform the following tasks:

- Identify which leads need urgent attention and respond to them immediately.

- Assign or include another member of the team in the conversation so they can also be in contact with the lead if deemed necessary.

- Filter relevant conversations only so you don't get overwhelmed with spam emails.

This gives your sales teams the ability to prioritize which leads need their urgent attention; the next step is to help them know when is the best time to reach out to that prospect.

Connecting with a prospect at exactly the right time

Timing is everything, right? But, as a salesperson, you often operate in the dark wondering when it is really the best time to call or connect with a prospect. How do you avoid, or at the very least minimize, that dreaded voicemail or out-of-office email response?

Fortunately, HubSpot has a host of useful tools (all free, by the way) that allow you to maximize your outreach and optimize the response rates you get. Some of these tools are email tracking, email scheduling, calling, and meeting calendars, all of which will be covered in the following sections.

Email tracking

One of the most useful tools in a salesperson's arsenal is knowing not just if someone *receives* your email but also knowing if they *opened* the email and *when*. Connecting your personal inbox to HubSpot allows this feature to be activated, so that each time someone opens your email, a notification will pop up in the email sent.

But first, let's make sure you have your personal inbox connected correctly to HubSpot. To connect your inbox to HubSpot, navigate to **Settings | General | Email**. Pay attention to selecting the **Connect an inbox** option under **Personal Inbox** and not **Shared Inbox**. Once you've selected this option, simply follow the prompts that direct you to complete the integration.

The following screenshot shows you a successfully connected inbox to HubSpot:

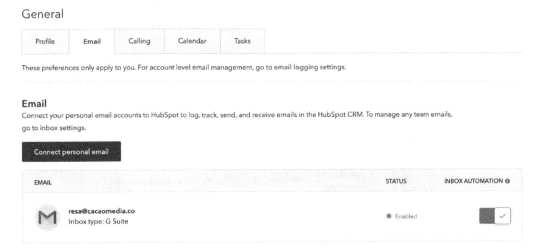

Figure 4.10 – Difference between shared inbox and personal inbox

Note, when connecting a shared inbox, everyone with access to HubSpot will have visibility to the emails sent to that inbox from within HubSpot. Therefore, this is another incentive to ensure you connect your personal inbox correctly so you can control what information you wish to be logged into the system from your personal inbox.

Email scheduling

Research shows that the best time to send an email is between 8 a.m. and 9:30 a.m. That being said, you aren't always available to write an email at this time or press the send button, even if it is ready in your drafts. So, the best alternative is to write that email whenever you can and schedule it to be sent at the time you wish the recipient to get it.

Hubspot's email scheduling tool, which is part of the integration of connecting your inbox to HubSpot, allows you to schedule the email to be sent when you choose.

Simply compose the email in your inbox, and at the very bottom where the **Send** button appears, click on the arrow, and you will see **Schedule Send**. Clicking on this option will reveal a list of dates and times to select to send the email:

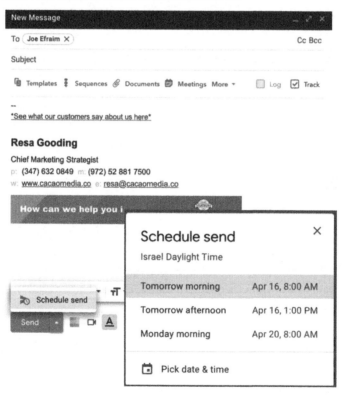

Figure 4.11 – Email scheduling feature

Remember that to activate this feature, you must also download the HubSpot extension to your inbox when integrating your emails.

Getting instant notifications when prospects land on your website

Another helpful and free feature that allows you to coordinate your interactions with prospects at exactly the right time is the notifications feature, which exists in the prospects tool described earlier. As you may recall, the prospects tool tracks visitors to your website. So, if you wish to connect with a prospect who's been hard to connect with, receiving a real-time notification when they are on your site can be a great time to pick up the phone and connect with them, as it indicates you are on their mind at this very moment.

To activate this notification, you once again navigate to **Contacts | Target Accounts**, then scroll to the bottom of the page and click on **Prospects**. Once arriving on the page, in the top right-hand corner, click on **Actions | Manage Notifications**.

A box, as shown next, will then appear inviting you to activate either personal notifications or team notifications so your entire team can receive these alerts. This allows you (or select members of your team) to get real-time notifications when companies visit your site for the first time or return after some time:

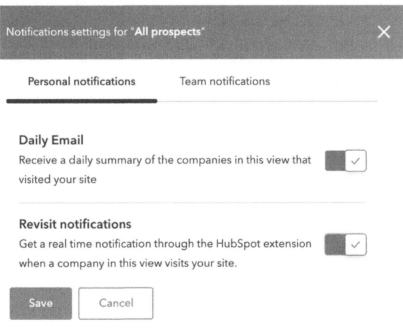

Figure 4.12 – Notifications tool

Having this feature activated makes it very convenient for your sales teams to connect with prospects at a more convenient time.

Connecting over the phone and keeping a record with the calling feature

This brings us to another great feature, calling, which helps sales teams to record a call with a contact and set up follow-up tasks immediately after the call.

To activate this feature, navigate to **Settings | Sales | Calling** and connect your phone number as prompted:

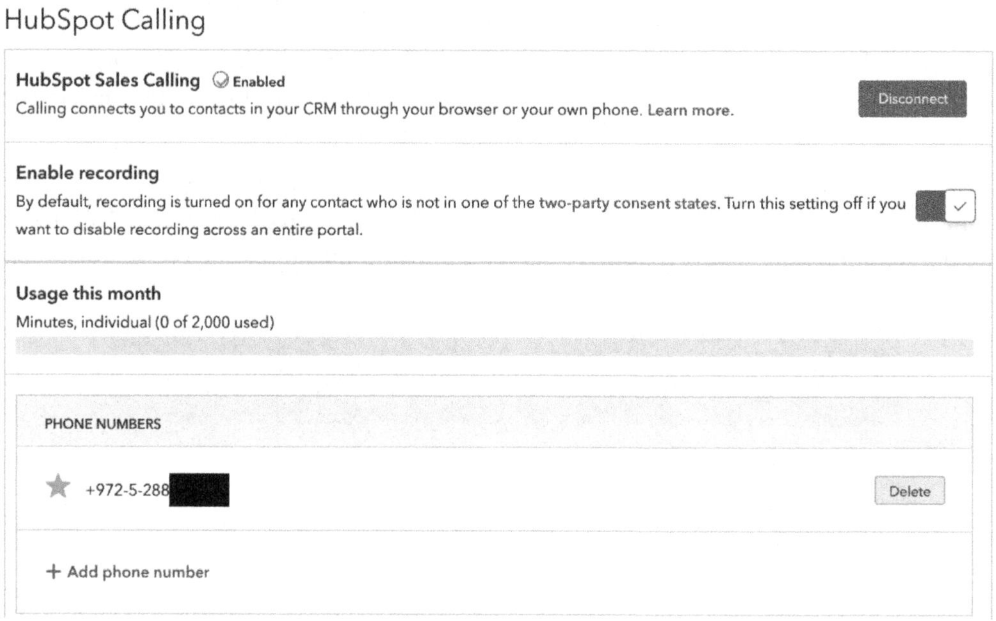

HubSpot Calling

HubSpot Sales Calling ⊘ Enabled

Calling connects you to contacts in your CRM through your browser or your own phone. Learn more.

Disconnect

Enable recording

By default, recording is turned on for any contact who is not in one of the two-party consent states. Turn this setting off if you want to disable recording across an entire portal.

✓

Usage this month

Minutes, individual (0 of 2,000 used)

PHONE NUMBERS

★ +972-5-288▮▮▮▮

Delete

+ Add phone number

Figure 4.13 – Calling tool

Here are a few useful tips to help you use this feature once the integration is set up:

- You can make a call to the contact directly from your phone or from HubSpot.

- The contact must have a phone number associated with their record for the call to be recorded. You can add this information manually to the contact if needed.

- If a contact opts out of all marketing communication, then you won't be able to call the contact from HubSpot or record the call under their record.

The calling tool is effective to reach potential customers and log this activity with them. But, one phone call is never enough to convert someone into an actual customer. According to statistics, it can take up to 14 interactions with a lead before they convert to the next stage. HubSpot tools such as the meeting calendar, documents, and quotes can be quite handy for helping move a prospect along your sales process. Let's take a closer look at how they work.

Landing more meetings and closing more deals

HubSpot Sales Hub is commonly used to track the progress of deals and the pipeline in which your sales team is actively engaged. To make this process more efficient, HubSpot has added a suite of tools such as the meetings tool to help sales teams book more meetings, the documents tool to help sales teams keep track of how prospects are engaged with the documents sent to them, and the quotes tool to get the prospect to confirm their interest in purchasing and the sales teams to close more deals.

Save time booking meetings

The first of such tools is the meetings tool. This tool is a free feature of HubSpot that connects your calendar with HubSpot, so you can provide a calendar view of your availability and time for the prospects to easily book a meeting with you. The advantage of using HubSpot's meeting tool instead of another platform is that it will automatically take contacts out of any email that they may currently be enrolled in when they book a meeting.

To set up the meetings tool, first, connect your calendar to HubSpot by navigating to **Settings | Sales | Meetings**. Once you get to this page, you will arrive at the view shown in the following screenshot. Choose to connect your calendar depending on the email platform you use and follow the instructions as seen:

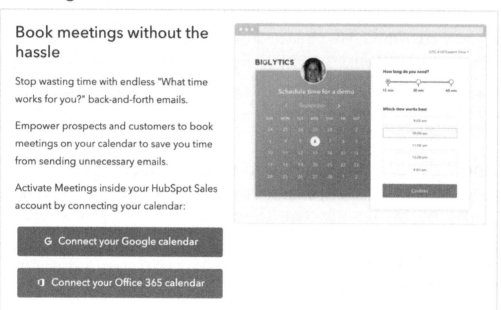

Figure 4.14 – Connecting your calendar to HubSpot

Once your calendar is connected, it's time to set up your meeting link so users have a view of your availability. To set up your meeting calendar, follow these steps after connecting your calendar to HubSpot. If you missed the popup to set up your meeting link, go to your top menu and navigate to **Sales | Meetings** and you will be able to set it up accordingly:

1. Click on **Details** in the left bar and in **Meeting headline**, enter the headline you would like users to see on your meeting calendar, for instance, Meet with Resa Gooding:

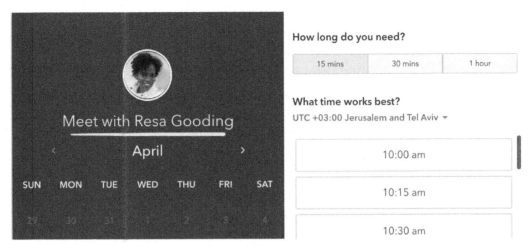

Figure 4.15 – The headline feature in the meetings tool

2. Then, enter the name of the meeting in **Meeting name**, for instance, `Demo with [Your Company Name]`. This is what the link will be called when inserting it into an email.

3. Choose the ending of your URL, for instance, a demonstration or free consultation. This URL cannot be changed once you create it, so choose wisely.

4. Enter the duration of time that people can book a meeting with you, for instance, 30 mins, 1 hour, and so on:

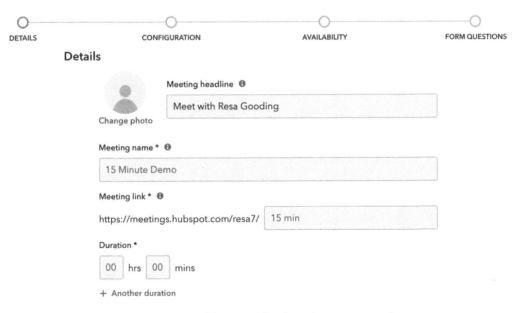

Figure 4.16 – Adding your details to the meetings tool

Once these steps are completed, click on **Configuration** on the left side menu.

In the **Configuration** menu, you will set the details the user will see in the calendar invite once they book the meeting with you:

1. Enter the **Location** details. Note, if you typically have meetings online and you use a video conferencing tool such as Zoom, you can connect it to HubSpot, so it will automatically send a Zoom link to anyone who books a meeting with you.

2. Fill in the **Invite subject** textbox, which can have a personal token or company token in it, so it can read `Meeting with [Your Name] + [Company Name / Contact Name]`.

3. Enter the **Invite description** details, which will provide a short description of what people can expect from the meeting.

4. Set the **Booking page language** option to your prospect's language, or if you work internationally, it is recommended to leave the settings as **Default to visitor's browser settings** so it can adjust automatically.

5. Set **Date and time** to your preference, or if you work internationally, it is recommended to leave the settings as **Default to visitor's browser settings** so it can adjust automatically.

6. For **Email notifications**, ensure the toggle button is on so users will automatically get a confirmation email once they book a meeting with you. In addition, it is recommended to set the email reminders for 1 day before and 1 hour before, so no one 'forgets' they booked a meeting with you 3 weeks ago.

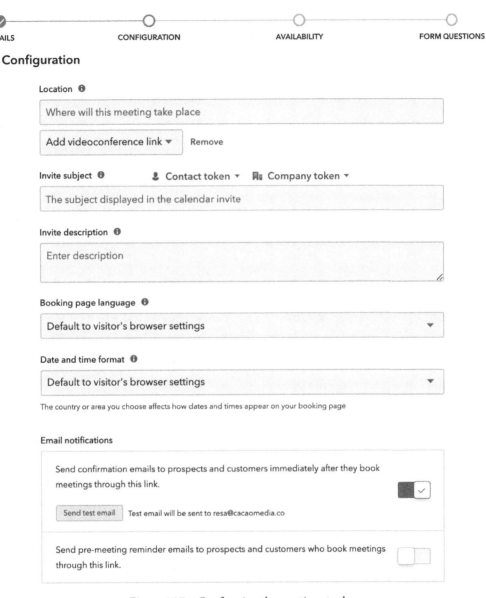

Figure 4.17 – Configuring the meetings tool

7. Once your details and configurations are set, the next step is to decide when you actually want to take meetings. Navigating to **Availability** on the left sidebar allows you to choose the days and range of times you wish to be available for meetings:

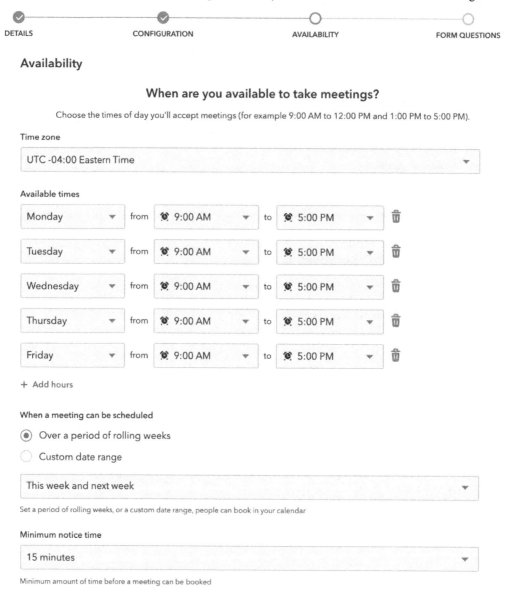

Figure 4.18 – Choosing your availability in the meetings tool

8. First, select the time zone you typically operate in. This will adjust automatically for international visitors to your calendar link.

9. Then, select the days and times you wish to be available. Note, if you want to show your availability between select hours of a day, for instance, Fridays 09:00-11:00 and then again 17:00-21:00, you will need to select the day twice, as shown:

Figure 4.19 – Selecting multiple time ranges on the same day

You can then choose how you wish your calendar to be seen, either constantly over a period of time or just for a select period because you are going to a trade show or conference between specific dates and are inviting prospects to book a meeting with you.

And finally, you choose the following:

- **Minimum notice time**: The minimum time a meeting can be booked for. Recommended notice time is 24 hours.

- **Buffer time**: The time between meetings, so you aren't booked for one meeting after the other.

- **Start time increment**: The frequency of your meeting start times, for instance, every 15 minutes, 30 minutes, or 1 hour.

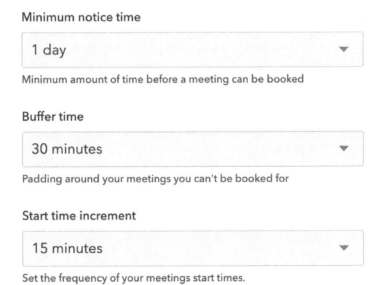

Figure 4.20 – Setting minimum time, buffer time, and start time increment on the meetings tool

10. In order for a prospect to book a meeting with you, they must answer the minimum questions of **First Name**, **Last Name**, and **Email**. However, if you have upgraded to Sales Professional, you can then also add a custom question, which can be used as a further qualifier before someone books a meeting with you:

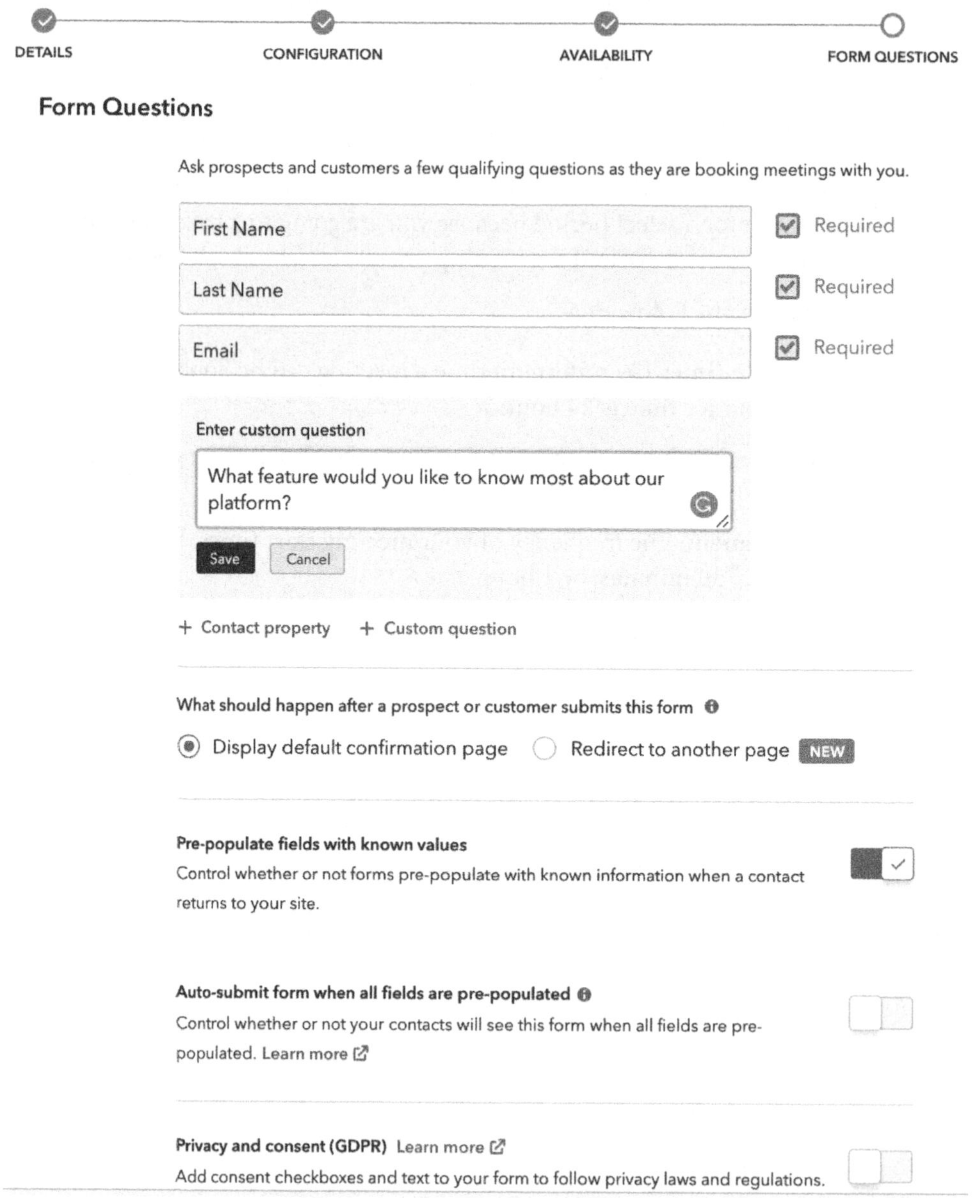

Figure 4.21 – Adding questions to your meeting link

11. Once you have completed these steps, click on **Save** and your meeting link is ready, as shown here:

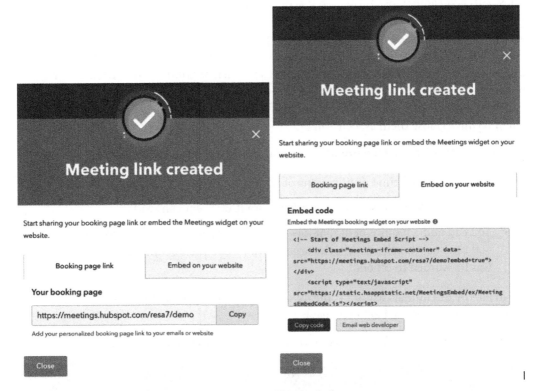

Figure 4.22 – Meeting link

You now have two options to use this meeting link:

- **In an email**: You can use it within the body by hyperlinking text when sending an email to a prospect to book a meeting with you or in your signature so people can easily book time with you.

- **On a website page**: You can use the embed code to include the link on a website page so visitors can easily book time with you.

Sending documents and knowing if they were read

HubSpot has two places where you can store files you wish to use in your marketing or sales outreach campaigns. Those two places are **Files and Templates** and **Documents**. Files and Templates will be discussed in later chapters, but in a nutshell, it is used to store all collateral that is used in marketing campaigns, for instance, images, assets such as case studies, ebooks, and so on. The documents feature in HubSpot is used for sales outreach campaigns, especially when sending sensitive data such as contracts, or specifications based on a client's requirements. The good thing is that they are both free features of HubSpot and can give the sales teams much-needed insights as to where a prospect stands when trying to close them as a customer.

The advantages of using **Documents** instead of **Files and Templates** are as follows:

- You can get real-time notifications of who opened it and how much of it they read.

- You can limit access so only those to whom it was sent can read it.

- You can add a requirement that new eyeballs need to enter their email addresses so you can see who else within the organization read the document and if the email was forwarded to others.

All in all, the documents feature is meant to give the sales teams more insights into how their sales collaterals are being received.

To access **Documents**, navigate to the top menu and **Sales | Documents**:

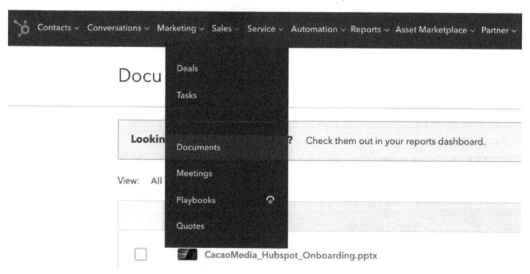

Figure 4.23 – Navigation bar to the documents feature

Once you are there, you can upload any document you wish to share with a prospect. So, next time you send them an email, you can insert a link to the document that is hosted here and see the analytics of how people interacted with it:

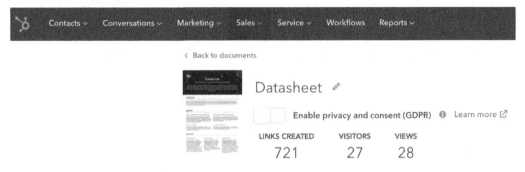

Figure 4.24 – Analytics from documents

By turning on the GDPR consent button, people are prompted to enter their email addresses before accessing the document. This is quite a handy feature to increase qualified leads as when your sales teams are doing cold outreach to contacts who are not yet in your database, they would be automatically added should they choose to access the document.

Using the quotes tool to get signed deals

The quotes tool in HubSpot is an integral part of helping sales teams achieve their KPIs as it makes it easy for them to create, send, and track how prospects view their quote. The quotes tool is a paid feature of HubSpot Sales Professional and can be found by navigating to the top menu and clicking on **Sales | Quotes**:

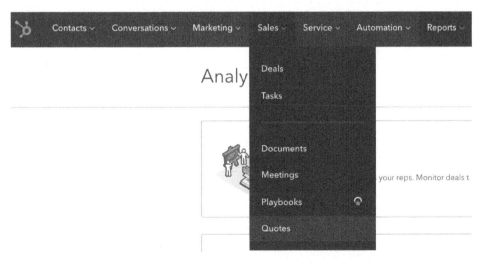

Figure 4.25 – Navigation bar to the quotes tool

Once in the **Quotes** section, follow these steps to create a quote:

1. Associate an existing deal with the quote. This means you have to create a deal first, which is discussed in *Chapter 3, Using HubSpot for Managing Sales Processes Effectively.*

Figure 4.26 – Quote details

Choose the following:

- **Quote template**: HubSpot gives you three options of design to decide upon.

- **Quote name**: The name you wish to have on the quote as it reflects the service or product from which you are quoting.

- **Expiration date**: How long this offer is valid.

- **Comments to buyer**: Any additional information you wish the buyer to know.

- **Purchase terms**: Any information regarding the purchase terms can be added here:

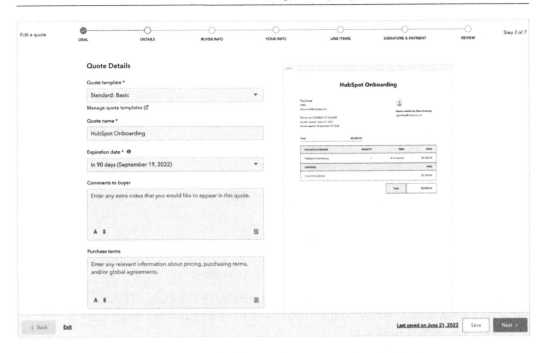

Figure 4.27 – Quote details – template, name, and expiration date

Add the buyer's information and company name, which is typically the person who will be responsible for ensuring the quote is signed off internally in their company:

Figure 4.28 – Buyer's information

Add your information as the sales representative sending the quote:

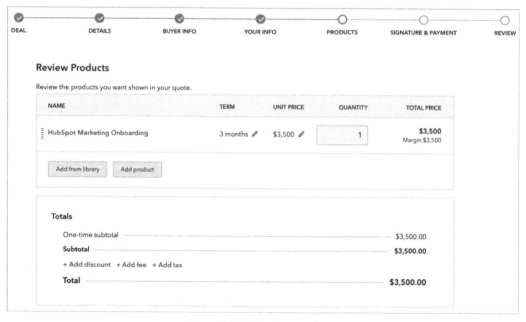

Figure 4.29 – Seller's information

2. You can add the products that should be included in the quote. These should be previously added to the product library or can be added at the quote stage by clicking on **Add product**:

NAME	TERM	UNIT PRICE	QUANTITY	TOTAL PRICE
HubSpot Marketing Onboarding	3 months 🖊	$3,500 🖊	1	**$3,500** Margin $3,500

Review Products

Review the products you want shown in your quote.

Add from library   Add product

Totals

One-time subtotal $3,500.00

Subtotal **$3,500.00**

+ Add discount   + Add fee   + Add tax

Total **$3,500.00**

Figure 4.30 – Review products

3. Add the signature and payment options. Currently, HubSpot only supports Stripe if you wish to add a payment option. In the near future, there will be further options. However, to currently add Stripe, you must first visit the HubSpot App Marketplace, download the Stripe app, and follow the instructions to connect the app to HubSpot.

4. If you simply need to receive a signature on the quote to confirm the purchase, you have the option to allow the recipient to sign by e-signature or to physically print and sign the document. If you select e-signature, you will see the following:

Figure 4.31 – Signature and Payment with space for signature

5.   Review the quote and confirm all the information is correct:

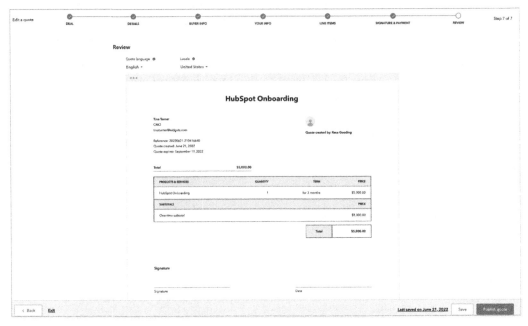

Figure 4.32 – Final review of the quote

6.   Click on **Save**, and the link that is created with the quote can be inserted in an email when sending the quote:

A web page for your quote has been created

Copy the web page link below to share with prospects or choose to write an email with the quote included. You can access any of your active quotes from the deal's Products page.

Figure 4.33 – Link for the quote

It is understandable that most businesses might require a more sophisticated quoting tool as there might be many nuances to be added before a quote is accepted. However, on many occasions, these businesses have used HubSpot's quote tools as a pro forma invoice so the prospect can at least sign an intent to purchase, and then a more official quote can be sent from your finance team.

All in all, the sales tools provided in this chapter can be quite useful to your sales teams as they help them to reduce the amount of administrative work needed as well as close any gaps where deals might be falling through the cracks. Most of the features are free, as we identified, and are quite sufficient to bring real value to their everyday tasks. So, do try them.

Summary

Overall, we discussed the sales tools in this chapter, such as email scheduling, calling, templates, sequences, the meetings tool, documents, and prospects, among others. However, the upgraded version of HubSpot Sales Professional further empowers your team to reach potential customers with a more personalized and human approach without leaving anything to chance.

The bottom line is that there is no better time than now to improve the way your sales teams sell.

In the next chapter, we will take you back to marketing, as we explore how to ensure leads find your products and services online so your sales team can actually use these tools.

Questions

For most businesses, it is imperative to help their sales teams focus more on selling instead of dealing with administrative tasks. So, let's make sure you understand the value of implementing some of these free tools right away:

1. Which sales tool helps a sales team member to send personalized yet automated responses – sequences or workflows?

2. Does HubSpot have a meeting calendar tool that allows prospects to see your availability and book a mutually convenient time?

3. What is the benefit of using the documents tool to send a contract instead of just sending it as a regular email attachment?

Further reading

To learn more about HubSpot's sales tools and some creative ways businesses are empowering their sales teams, do check out the following resources:

- HubSpot sales blog: `https://blog.hubspot.com/sales`
- HubSpot case studies: `https://www.hubspot.com/case-studies-directory?product=crm`

Part 2: Scaling Your Business with HubSpot

Once your portal is set up correctly, the next step is to use the various tools within HubSpot to optimize and scale your marketing efforts. From reaching your target audience to converting those contacts to qualified opportunities and customers, HubSpot has a suite of tools and features that assist marketers in building revenue-generating campaigns and tracking their results. Read each of these chapters to understand how to use these various tools and learn how to check every once in a while that your portal is set up correctly.

This part contains the following chapters:

- *Chapter 5, Increasing Online Visibility Using HubSpot's SEO Tool*
- *Chapter 6, Getting Known through Social Media on HubSpot*
- *Chapter 7, Expanding Your Reach with Paid Ads Managed in HubSpot*
- *Chapter 8, Conducting a Portal Audit*
- *Chapter 9, Converting Your Visitors to Customers*
- *Chapter 10, Revive Your Database with the HubSpot's Email Marketing Tools*
- *Chapter 11, Proving That Your Efforts Worked Using These Reports*

5

Increasing Online Visibility Using HubSpot's SEO Tool

The mastery of **search engine optimization (SEO)** is an art. Most people and companies understand the importance of implementing an SEO strategy, but it is often overlooked or not prioritized when building and executing a content strategy. Marketers often start producing blogs, redesigning their websites, and creating other pieces of content, such as e-books, white papers, and webinars, without giving any serious thought to SEO.

HubSpot, as the pioneer of inbound marketing, recognized the importance of including an SEO tool as part of their platform, so marketers can have it at the forefront of their marketing strategy. Using HubSpot's SEO tool as an integral part of your content marketing when creating landing pages, blogs, or content for website pages ensures that you see better results in a shorter space of time.

In this chapter, we will focus on the following topics and explain the value each of these steps will bring to you, so you can decide whether it is important for you to do them or not during your setup. Although we spent some time giving as complete an overview as possible of SEO without making it the entire focus of the chapter, feel free to skip over any sections you may already be familiar with and proceed to those areas you may have overlooked in the initial setup so you can go back to fix them.

Here's what you can expect to understand from this chapter:

- The importance of SEO and how it can be used to increase your organic traffic
- An overview of the HubSpot SEO tool and how it works
- Gaining insights from the analytics in the SEO report to further increase your website traffic
- Learning which other tools are important to integrate with the HubSpot SEO tool for a holistic picture of your content's performance

Technical requirements

To get the most out of this chapter, you will need the following:

- HubSpot Marketing Professional
- Super admin access to your HubSpot portal
- An account with Google Search Console

Knowing the importance of SEO and how it increases your organic traffic

In order to understand how to use SEO to increase organic traffic and the importance of it, let's start by understanding the different terms and the reason why they are so important to your organization.

SEO 101 – understanding the basics

To understand SEO, let's first set the *stage*. Think about yourself and how you find information today. With anything you are looking for, from recipes to deciding on your next vacation, or even trying to find out more about something as serious as an illness, you turn to a search engine such as Google, Bing, or Yahoo. Some of us who are old enough will recall Ask Jeeves. These are all platforms where we can ask a question and they will, in seconds, return a list of results based on our queries.

Google today is the most popular search engine, accounting for more than 92% of the market share when it comes to search engines. It is so widespread that it is now a verb. We all say, "*Just google it*" in response to any query we get that we don't have a ready answer to.

Therefore, to understand how Google works is to understand how SEO works as SEO is the backbone of Google's algorithm.

In its simplest terms, SEO is the process of increasing the number of visitors from search engines to your website. Traffic from search engines is categorized as *organic traffic* as it means that people came to your online content without paying. However, as you may have realized in your many personal searches, there are millions, if not billions, of results today on almost every single topic for which you can search. Generally, people don't venture further than the second or third page of these results when looking for an answer. So, this is in effect SEO—the process of increasing the rank of your online content so you hopefully appear on the first page. This is done mainly through the use of keywords, meta tags, competitor analysis, backlinks, and content creation.

With billions of searches done every day on Google, it is every business's dream to appear on the first page of Google to get those visitors landing on their content. However, to achieve this, you must understand a few basic terms that will allow this to happen. Let's start with understanding the difference between on-page SEO and off-page SEO, as well as some other key terms:

- **On-page SEO**: This form of SEO is probably the quickest win as it relies solely on your effort. The goal is to optimize your page content for search engines using various tools, such as meta tags and alt descriptions.

- **Off-page SEO**: This is the method of achieving outbound links from other websites that will redirect users to your website. In the beginning, many sites, in an attempt to increase their number of backlinks, attempted "keyword stuffing," which was simply linking content wherever possible. However, since then, Google has updated their algorithms to ensure that users can depend on the information received and that sites are trustworthy. So, any backlinks used must be contextual and the site that is giving the backlink should be reputable and not considered spammy.

- **Page rank**: Another caveat Google created in an effort for sites to build trust and authority is page rank. This checks both the quality and quantity of links of websites from different sources and uses these factors to determine how important a page is. The page rank scale is 0-10 with 10 being of the highest authority. The best way to improve page rank is by getting many quality external links that point to the website page organically. In order to create these links, you first need to understand what keywords are.

- **Keywords**: Keywords are the foundation of SEO. Their main purpose is to help search engines such as Google and Bing to track and index your website pages. Recall how you use a search engine today and what your expectations are—you expect to receive the right content at the right time for any given search. This, however, as we explained previously, led to many sites engaging in keyword stuffing, also known as black-hat SEO. Therefore, search engines have become more sophisticated and now also rank pages based on relevance and credible information, which ties in with the next two most important tactics in SEO.

- **Link building**: In its simplest terms, link building is your attempt to get other websites to hyperlink a few keywords in their content to a piece of content you own. It is often considered one of the most difficult parts of SEO mainly because it relies on your ability to either create content that is so good that other sites organically want to refer to you or you are able to build relationships with reputable websites and convince them to link to your content. Effective link building can have a direct impact on increasing your website traffic, which will eventually impact your revenue. Some of the most popular ways to generate these referral links are through reaching out to other blogs, posting on forums, and even ensuring your own references to your business anywhere on the web contain a link back to your business.

- **Anchor text**: Anchor text is text that is hyperlinked to another page on a website. It is usually highlighted by another color from the rest of the text on the page or underlined. The main purpose of anchor text is to link a relevant keyword to its corresponding page.

Adding tags

Tags are crucial to on-page SEO as search engines don't just show text content as part of their results. They also show images, videos, books, and so on. So, how do you ensure all of your content is sufficiently recognized by the algorithms?

- **Alt text/tag**: By now, it is a common practice to include images in your content, whether it is website pages, blogs, or landing pages. To get readers interested, it's important to choose an image that will back up your message and get you a good ranking in the search results. But don't forget to include alt text when uploading the image. "*Why*," you ask? Alt text is a written description of an image; this is what appears instead of the picture on a website if the image fails to load. Alt text also helps different screen-reading tools to understand what the image is about, in order to aid visually impaired readers. This also allows search engines to better crawl the page and rank your website better.

Featured image

Enabled featured image

Choose or upload an image to be used when sharing your post on social media or on your listing page.   ON ✓

Image alt text

The fundamentals of building an Effective SEO Content Strategy in HubSpot

Figure 5.1 – Alt text for images

- **H1**: Also known as a heading, H1 is the first header tag visible on a page. It is used for the title of a page or post. It is typically the largest text on the page and presents the main idea. For blogs, this is often the name of the blog post. It can be similar to the title but not the same to maximize SEO efforts. There have been lots of trends in SEO that have come and gone, but H1s have never lost their significance. Keep in mind that a good H1 tag should be around 20-70 characters.

- **Title tag**: The HTML element on a web page represents the most relevant keyword and information about the page. A title tag appears to users at the top of their browser and in search engine results. The title tag is one of the most important factors when ranking a web page for a particular keyword.

You can see the title tags marked in yellow in the following screenshot:

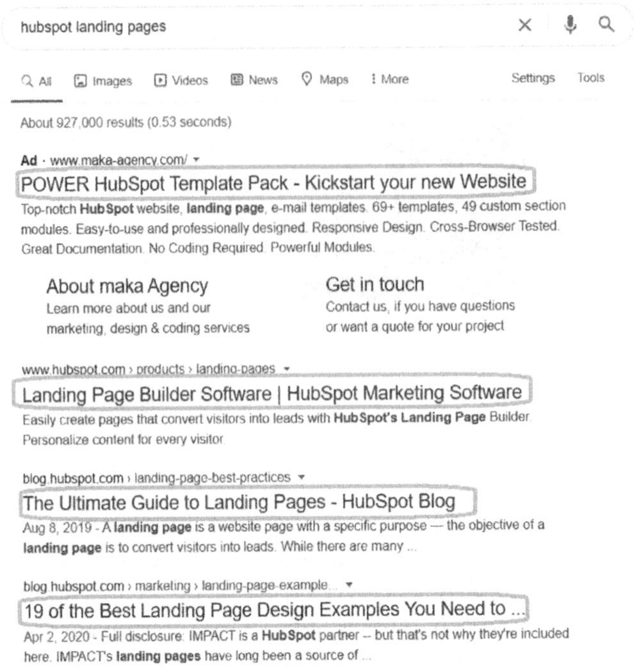

Figure 5.2 – Title tags in Google search engine

- **Meta description**: The meta description is a short description between 50 and 160 characters long about the page content. When searching on search engines, you'll see the meta description under the title tag, so by optimizing the meta description to describe the page better and connect to the key term you searched, you'll get a better ranking for the page. Therefore, this step is crucial. Keep the text within the recommended length; otherwise, the search engine will cut the text. Meta descriptions can also impact a page's **click-through rate** (**CTR**) on Google, this having a positive impact on a page's ranking ability.

Here, you can see the HubSpot meta description section on a landing page:

Meta description * ⓘ

Tomer Harel, CEO, Key Scouts, an SEO focused HubSpot agency covered the fundamentals of building an effective SEO Content Strategy in this workshop

● Great! You're within the limit. 8 characters remaining

Figure 5.3 – Meta description text placed in the setting of your blog or website pages

Let's see how the meta description looks on a search engine:

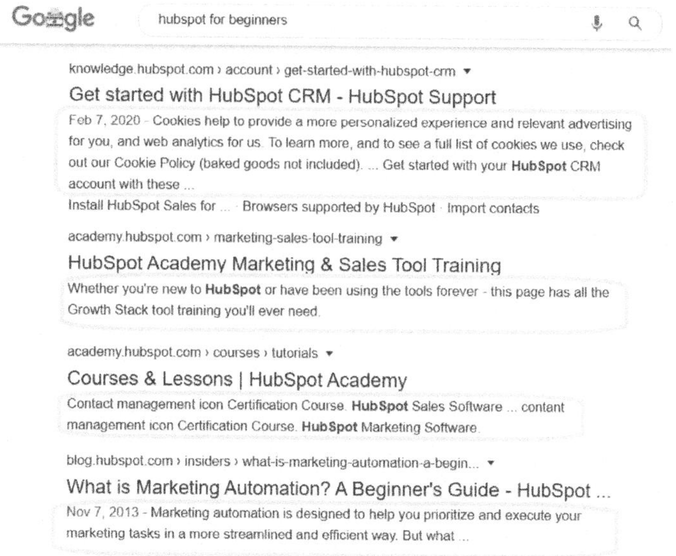

Figure 5.4 – Meta descriptions in Google search engine

Here's an example of a fully optimized SEO page in the following figure:

Figure 5.5 – Fully optimized SEO page

On this page, we see that all elements, such as the title, crawling and index, meta descriptions, images, and headers, are optimized for SEO. This was done within HubSpot, which allows your page to have the proper ranking it needs on search engines.

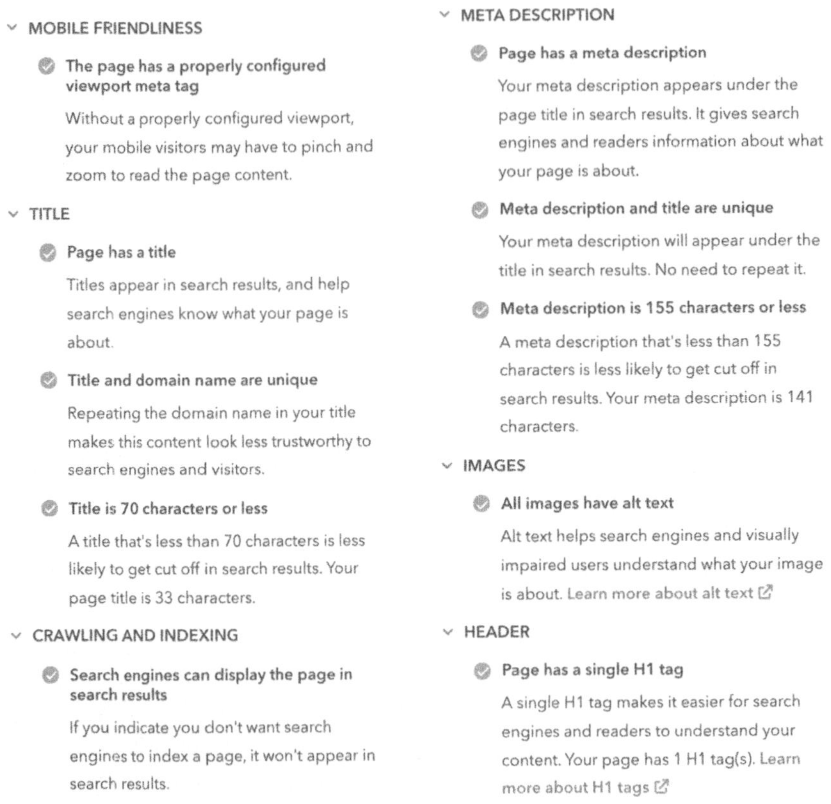

∨ MOBILE FRIENDLINESS

✅ **The page has a properly configured viewport meta tag**

Without a properly configured viewport, your mobile visitors may have to pinch and zoom to read the page content.

∨ TITLE

✅ **Page has a title**

Titles appear in search results, and help search engines know what your page is about.

✅ **Title and domain name are unique**

Repeating the domain name in your title makes this content look less trustworthy to search engines and visitors.

✅ **Title is 70 characters or less**

A title that's less than 70 characters is less likely to get cut off in search results. Your page title is 33 characters.

∨ CRAWLING AND INDEXING

✅ **Search engines can display the page in search results**

If you indicate you don't want search engines to index a page, it won't appear in search results.

∨ META DESCRIPTION

✅ **Page has a meta description**

Your meta description appears under the page title in search results. It gives search engines and readers information about what your page is about.

✅ **Meta description and title are unique**

Your meta description will appear under the title in search results. No need to repeat it.

✅ **Meta description is 155 characters or less**

A meta description that's less than 155 characters is less likely to get cut off in search results. Your meta description is 141 characters.

∨ IMAGES

✅ **All images have alt text**

Alt text helps search engines and visually impaired users understand what your image is about. Learn more about alt text ⧉

∨ HEADER

✅ **Page has a single H1 tag**

A single H1 tag makes it easier for search engines and readers to understand your content. Your page has 1 H1 tag(s). Learn more about H1 tags ⧉

Figure 5.6 – Elements of a fully optimized SEO page

Now that you understand the basics of SEO, it is time to delve into how HubSpot helps you organize all these efforts.

An overview of HubSpot's SEO tool

As part of your HubSpot account, you will find some SEO tools and solutions that can be used to optimize your content for search engines. Start by scanning the entire domain and its associated subdomains, whether it's hosted on HubSpot or another CMS. To begin, go to **Marketing | Planning and Strategy | SEO**.

On this page, add a new URL by clicking on the right-hand side orange button and filling in the URL you would like to scan.

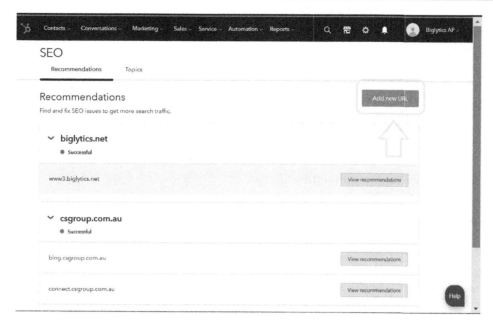

Figure 5.7 – Add your website to HubSpot's SEO tool

Now HubSpot will run and scan your domain and subdomains. This scan will present an improvement recommendation. Next to the domain name, you'll find a **View recommendations** button.

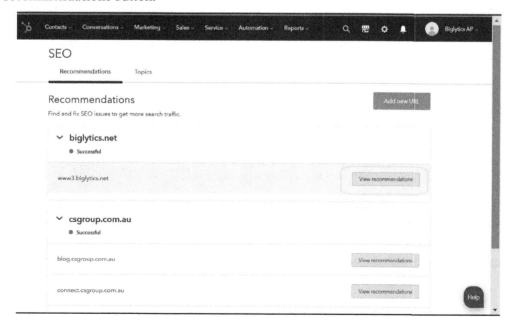

Figure 5.8 – Accessing the SEO recommendations from HubSpot

When clicked, this button will show you the results. It will lead to a page segmented into four parts:

- **RECOMMENDATIONS**: The title of the recommendations
- **PAGES AFFECTED**: How many pages it will affect
- **IMPACT**: Scale from low to high of how important the impact is
- **REASON**: Why this change is necessary

The following screenshot shows these parts:

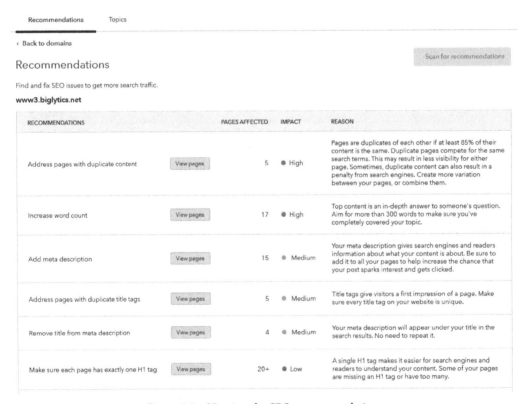

Figure 5.9 – Viewing the SEO recommendations

In order to fix a HubSpot-hosted page or blog post, click on the **View pages** button and then on the **Fix in editor** button. If your pages are hosted outside of HubSpot, click on the page URL to see which page needs to be updated and make the changes in your CMS.

SEO

Recommendations   Topics

‹ Back to SEO recommendations

Increase word count

Top content is an in-depth answer to someone's question. Aim for more than 300 words to make sure you've completely covered your topic.

blog.cacaomedia.co

PAGE NAME		WORD COUNT	VIEWS ❶
Content Israel 2020 https://blog.cacaomedia.co/blog/content-israel-2020 ☑	Fix in editor ☑	56	2
Optimize Selling Time Through Organizational Alignment https://blog.cacaomedia.co/blog/optimize-selling-time-through-organizational-alignment ☑	Fix in editor ☑	67	2
Marketing Activities Your Company Can Do During Slow Periods https://blog.cacaomedia.co/blog/marketing-activities-your-company-can-do-during-slow-periods ☑	Fix in editor ☑	99	1
How to Scale your Online Events Using Marketing Automation https://blog.cacaomedia.co/blog/how-to-scale-your-online-events-using-marketing-automation ☑	Fix in editor ☑	101	1

Figure 5.10 – Fixing the SEO recommendations

Next to the **Recommendations** page, you will also find the **Topics** page.

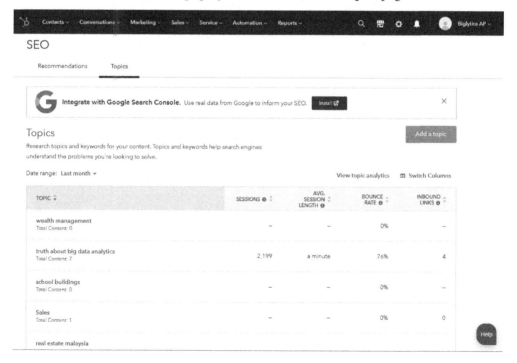

Figure 5.11 – Defining your topics in HubSpot

On this page, you can plan and create your content strategy. This tool will help to define relevant topics to write about based on all the existing content on your domain.

First, you need to define a core topic that is broad but relevant to your product term and has a significant amount of search volume, as well as containing between two and four words.

To add a new core topic, click on the **Add a topic** button on the right side of the page, as shown:

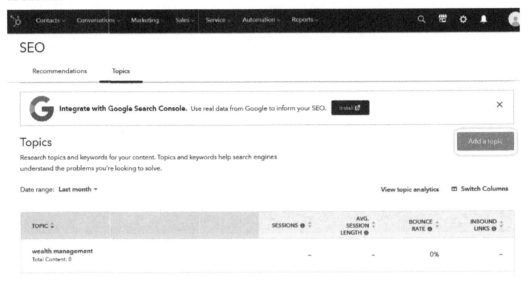

Figure 5.12 – How to add a topic to your HubSpot SEO tool

By clicking on this button, a new page will open, and you'll need to define the country and the topic. Write the new topic into the text box and click on **Add**.

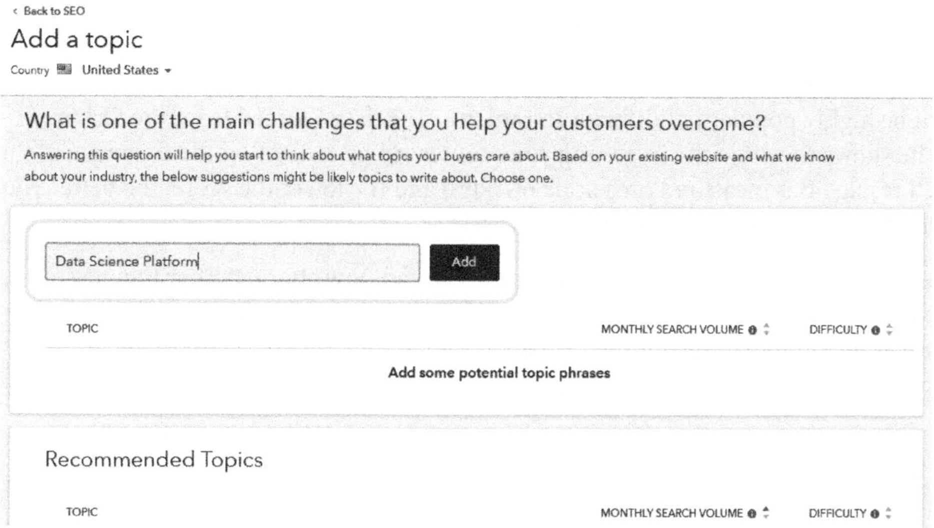

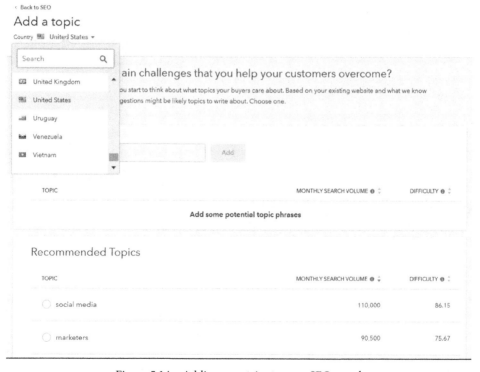

Figure 5.13 – Adding the topic to the HubSpot SEO tool

On this page as well, you can find topic recommendations based on the country you choose at the top of the page.

Figure 5.14 – Adding countries to your SEO search

Next to the recommended topics, you'll see the monthly search volume (this number is based on the average monthly searches for a keyword in search engines). Longer or more niche terms might have no results or low monthly search volume, and broader terms might be highly popular but difficult to rank for. The data sourced from the SEMrush website shows the difficulty in getting your content to be ranked on the first page of the search results. It is measured on a scale of 1-100 and the lower the score, the better your chances of ranking for this topic/keyword.

Once you've analyzed the recommendations, you can now choose either the new topic that you've created or one of the recommended topics. Clicking on the **Create Topic** button at the bottom of the page adds your core topic to the pillar page (discussed shortly).

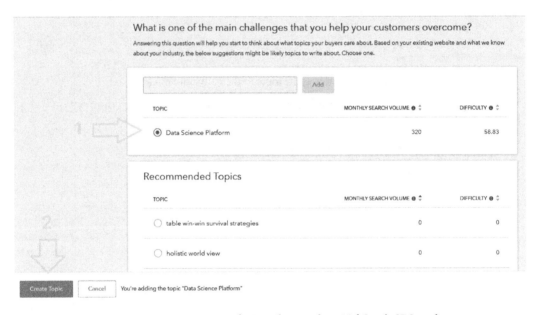

Figure 5.15 – Saving your subtopics/keywords to HubSpot's SEO tool

Now, a cluster page map will appear, and in the center of the page, you'll find your core topic with the option to attach content related to your subtopics.

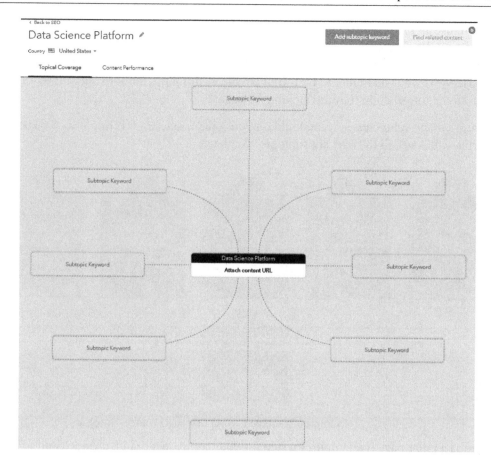

Figure 5.16 – Pillar page in HubSpot

This is the place to add your pillar content, which will define this cluster map. You have two ways to add subtopic content: by adding an external URL, such as a website page hosted outside of HubSpot, or by selecting an existing HubSpot page, whether it's a blog post or landing page created on HubSpot.

Pillar pages

So, what exactly is a pillar page? In short, a pillar page covers a main topic in depth and the cluster content gives further insight into one aspect or angle of that topic.

Pillar pages are generally longer than average website pages because of all the information that they include. They are usually around 2,000 words or more and are closely tied to the subtopics that will eventually be linked to the page. The information on this page will cover as many possible angles on the topic but at a high level. The subtopic pages will give the opportunity to explain in depth each angle covered in the pillar page.

You can use all kinds of tactics to make your audience spend more time on this page, such as adding a short video that explains the topic or including diagrams or micrographics. In addition, to make the navigation on this page easier, you can add a submenu (not to be confused with your main menu) that will help the visitor jump to more relevant sections and find the information they are looking for faster.

There are many submenus you can build on your pillar page, but it is important to choose one that will cover all the relevant subtopics you have.

Figure 5.17 – Example of a submenu of a pillar page. Source: HubSpot

Creating a pillar page is an important step for your company's brand, product, and marketing. This could be the chance to showcase your thought leadership and deep knowledge of a specific topic. Don't think only about keywords when creating the pillar page; think about the topic that you would like to own and be thought of as the go-to resource for as it relates to your company's brand, product, or services.

Once the topic is defined, now is the time to start thinking about related keywords, which will eventually turn into your subtopics.

Subtopics

Once you've created your pillar page and attached it to the cluster, as shown in the following diagram, it is time to define subtopics or keywords. The best approach when doing this is to try to think from your customer's point of view about what the search term they will likely use to find information on your related topic will be. You can even type a few options in Google to see what they suggest as related searches at the bottom of the page:

Figure 5.18 – Defining your subtopics in HubSpot

To add a subtopic keyword, click on the **Add subtopic keyword** button in the top-right corner of the page. Enter your subtopic keywords into the text box and click on **Research Subtopic Keywords**.

Figure 5.19 – Researching your subtopic keyword

The tool will generate a list of related keywords with their monthly search volume. It is recommended to choose a subtopic with at least 300 monthly searchers, but it really depends on your industry and niche, so don't be afraid to choose keywords with smaller search volumes if they are particularly relevant to your market. Finally, choose the most relevant subtopic keyword and click on **Save**.

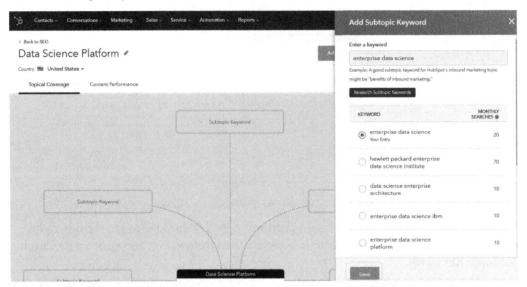

Figure 5.20 – Understanding the relevance of your subtopic/keywords

Now that your new subtopic has been added to the cluster page, the next step is to attach the related content to your subtopic. This content can be a blog post, a website page, or a landing page.

You then repeat this process each time you have related subtopic content or use it in your plan to create new content. The goal is to have at least eight subtopic pieces connected to your pillar page but keep in mind that the quality of the subtopic keywords and content is better than the quantity.

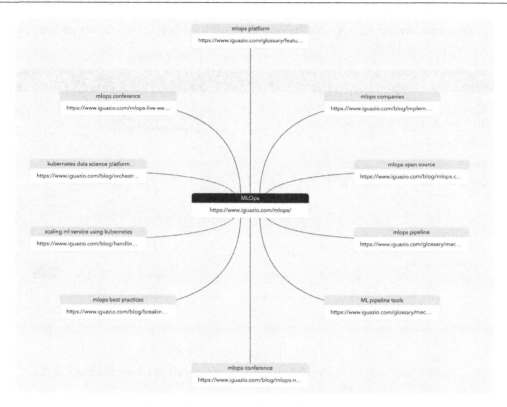

Figure 5.21 – A topic cluster built in HubSpot

Once the topic cluster is built with the pillar page and subtopic keywords, you should then see a diagram like that shown in *Figure 5.21* allowing you to ensure all your content pages are properly linked to your pillar page. This provides your pillar page with more authority and helps you to rank higher on search engines.

Gaining insights from the analytics in the SEO report to further increase your website traffic

After you've created a pillar page and an informative cluster, it is time to analyze and see your content performance.

By navigating to **Marketing | Website | SEO | Topics**, select the topic you would like to analyze. Then click on the **Content Performance** tab at the top of the page.

This page is segmented into two sections:

- **Pillar Page:** This shows the performance of the pillar page as it relates to time per page and bounce rate.

- **Subtopic content**: This shows the measures of the subtopic pages, such as time per page view and bounce rate.

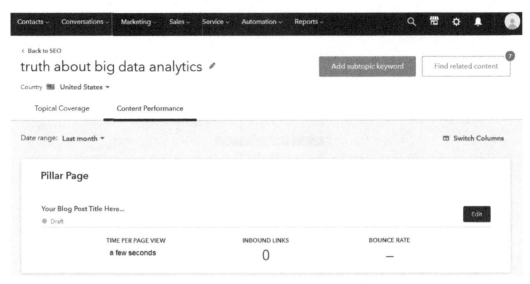

Figure 5.22 – Analyzing the pillar page's overall performance

Subtopic content looks at the subtopic keywords, time per page views, inbound links, bounce rate, and link to the pillar page.

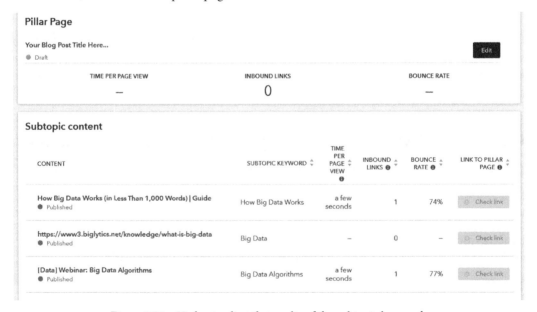

Figure 5.23 – Understanding the results of the subtopic keywords

If the content is properly linked to the pillar page, you will see **Linked** in that column.

Figure 5.24 – Checking whether the subtopics are linked to the pillar page

To get a deeper analysis of your cluster performance, go to the topics list from **Marketing | Planning and Strategy | SEO | Topics** and click on **View topic analytics** on the right-hand side of the page.

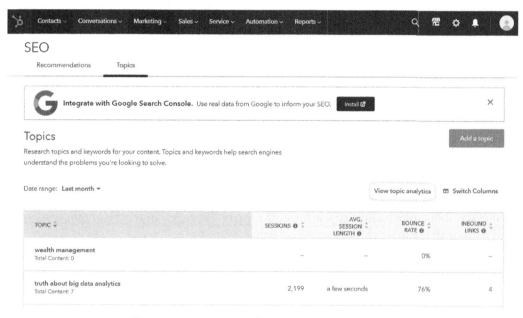

Figure 5.25 – Accessing the top analytics in HubSpot

The page that now opens shows a graph of different information that you can change according to the options in the dropdown.

Figure 5.26 – Graph showing the analytics of the subtopics

You can segment the information on this report according to a date range and the frequency of the information appearing at the top of the page. Under the graph, you can find a list of all the topic clusters based on name.

The table will present the following:

- **SESSIONS**: The number of sessions that started from search to content in this topic for the selected date range

- **SESSION TO CONTACT RATE**: The number of new contacts divided by the number of sessions for the selected date range

- **NEW CONTACTS**: The number of new contacts that have been added in this period

- **CONTACT TO CUSTOMER RATE**: The number of customers divided by contacts for the selected date range

- **CUSTOMERS**: The number of new contacts added during this date range who became customers

- **BOUNCE RATE**: The number of sessions with exactly one analytics event, divided by the total number of sessions

- **SESSION LENGTH**: The average time between the start and end of a session
- **New visitor session**: The number of sessions from visitors that have not been on your website before
- **New session %**: The percentage of total sessions from new visitors
- **Page views \ sessions**: An average of the number of unique page views per session

These are shown in the following screenshot:

All topic clusters >

Edit columns

TOPIC CLUSTER	SESSIONS	SESSION TO CONTACT RATE	NEW CONTACTS	CONTACT TO CUSTOMER RATE	CUSTOMERS	BOUNCE RATE	SESSION LENGTH
truth about big data analytics	2,269	0.44%	10	0%	0	77.13%	1 second
inbound marketing	1,519	0.07%	1	0%	0	75.58%	1 second
big data analytics	241	0%	0	0%	0	74.27%	1 second
Total	**4,029**	**0.27%**	**11**	**0%**	**0**	**76.37%**	**1 second**

Figure 5.27 – Topic cluster analytics

On every report, you can see up to seven columns. If you wish to edit which columns are seen in your view, click on **Edit columns** in the top-right corner above the table.

All topic clusters >

Edit columns

TOPIC CLUSTER	SESSIONS	SESSION TO CONTACT RATE	NEW CONTACTS	CONTACT TO CUSTOMER RATE	CUSTOMERS	BOUNCE RATE	SESSION LENGTH
truth about big data analytics	2,269	0.44%	10	0%	0	77.13%	1 second
inbound marketing	1,519	0.07%	1	0%	0	75.58%	1 second
big data analytics	241	0%	0	0%	0	74.27%	1 second
Total	**4,029**	**0.27%**	**11**	**0%**	**0**	**76.37%**	**1 second**

Figure 5.28 – Adding more information to your reports

Then choose the seven columns you would like to see and click on **Save**.

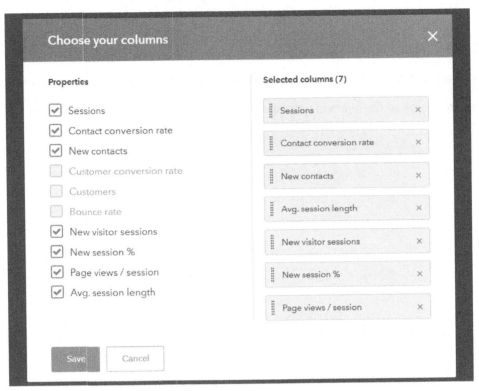

Figure 5.29 – Selecting the columns you wish to add to your report

It's important to fix the SEO section but it's even more important to analyze it to see whether your changes are giving you the results you wanted. If not, don't give up; search again for relevant keywords and make the changes accordingly.

Getting a holistic view of your content's performance

Another cool feature you can use is to connect your Google Search Console in order to use real data to inform your SEO.

By clicking on the **Install** button, you'll be led to **HubSpot App Marketplace**, where you will need to search for this app.

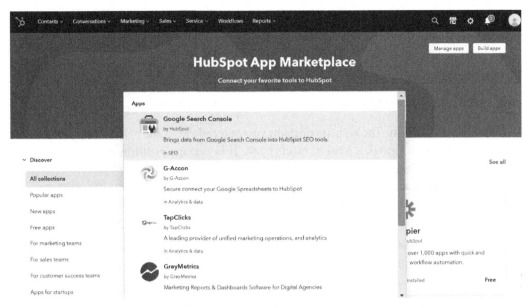

Figure 5.30 – Searching for the Google Search Console app in HubSpot

Choose the **Google Search Console** app and in the top right-hand corner, choose **Connect app**.

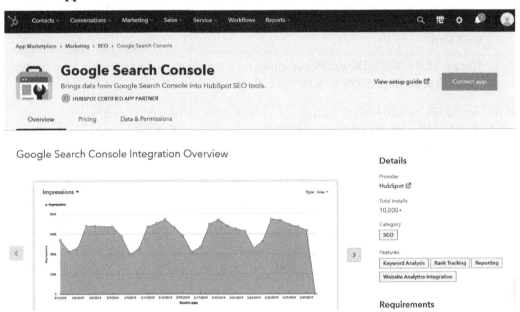

Figure 5.31 – Adding Google Search Console to HubSpot

You'll now need to connect your account by entering your Google credentials, then click on **Allow to grant HubSpot permission** to connect your Google account.

What will this integration give you?

Your SEO tool and optimization tab will have the following five metrics:

- **Average position**: The website domain you entered gets a numeric value based on its position on Google's search results page. This average position number gives you a better understanding of how your website is performing in search results related to your topic. Keep in mind that this position can be different from the one you see if you actually entered the keyword or phrase in your Google search engine. It is based on history, location, and other factors. This is why this value is an average.

- **Total impressions**: This is counted each time your content appears in search results for your topic phrase.

- **Average CTR**: This is the average number of times someone clicked on your web page on the Google search results page. If an individual clicks on the same link multiple times, it will only be counted once.

- **Top search queries**: These are the search terms where your web page appears in Google search results. You can see top search queries in the **Optimization** panel on the page or blog post editor and in the subtopic content details panel in your SEO tool.

- **Clicks**: This is the total number of clicks on a search engine page result for a specific query that sends a visitor to your page.

If you would like to add Google Search Console metrics to your SEO dashboard, navigate to **Marketing | Planning and Strategy | SEO**, then click on **Topics** to view your **Topics** dashboard. In the top-right corner of the page, click on **Switch Columns**.

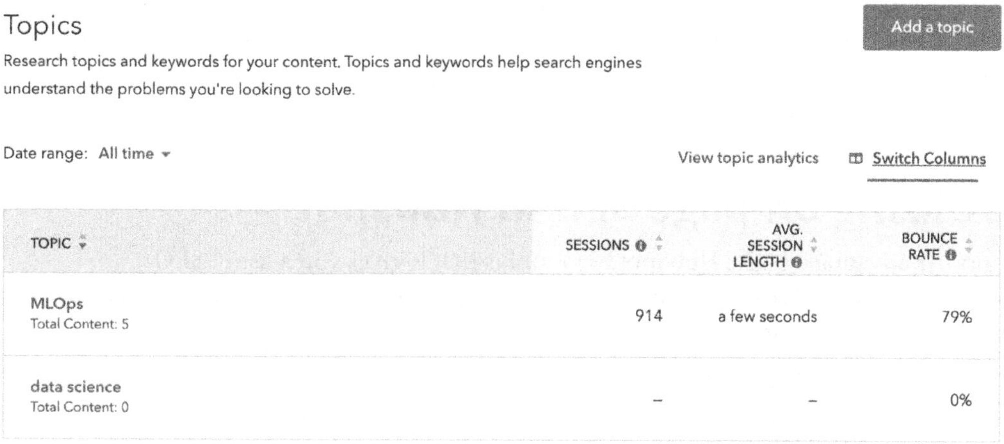

Topics
Add a topic
Research topics and keywords for your content. Topics and keywords help search engines understand the problems you're looking to solve.
Date range: All time
View topic analytics
Switch Columns
TOPIC
SESSIONS
AVG. SESSION LENGTH
BOUNCE RATE
MLOps
Total Content: 5
914
a few seconds
79%
data science
Total Content: 0
-
-
0%

Figure 5.32 – Analyzing further the SEO analytics using Google Search Console

When the popup opens, select the checkbox for the Google Search Console metrics you want to view on your dashboard (total impressions, average CTR, clicks) and then click on **Save**.

Choose which columns you see
Choose which columns are displayed by default. Choose 5 columns.
COLUMN OPTIONS
Sessions
Avg. session length
Bounce Rate
Monthly Search Volume
Requires Google Search Console Integration:
Avg. position
Total impressions
Avg. click through rate
SELECTED COLUMNS
Sessions
Avg. session length
Bounce Rate
Avg. position
Total impressions
Save
Cancel

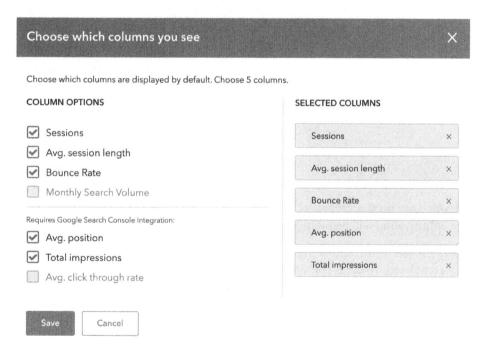

Figure 5.33 – Adding Google Search Console analytics to your reports

We have already mentioned how important it is to analyze your work. Also, when you're working with different platforms and integration, it's important to check whether the numbers are right in both systems (the integration is working correctly) and if not, fix it so you don't have gaps.

Utilizing on-page SEO in HubSpot

Another advantage of the HubSpot SEO tool is that it gives you a list of SEO recommendations for optimizing every landing page, blog, or website page hosted on HubSpot. Let's look at optimizing landing pages, for instance.

Under **Marketing | Website | Landing pages**, you will find a list of all the landing pages you have already created or will create. After creating a landing page, in the editor mode, you'll find an **Optimize** tab at the top of the page.

Figure 5.34 – Accessing the on-page SEO tool within HubSpot

This tab will open on the left side of the screen and a list of all SEO aspects with regard to on-page optimization will be highlighted.

Some of them will be marked with a green checkmark that shows this recommendation has been completed, whereas some will be marked with a gray checkmark, which means that these recommendations should be completed.

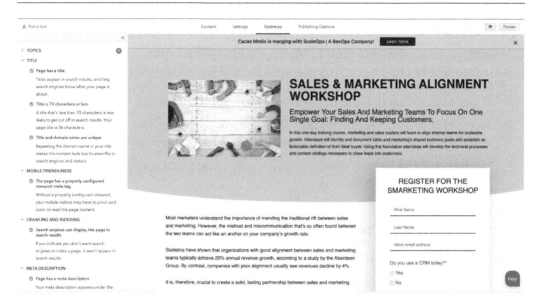

Figure 5.35 – Analyzing the recommendations of the SEO tool

Next to the title of the section with the recommendation to implement, you'll see a red circle with a number that presents how many recommendations you still have left. The goal is to go through each of these recommendations and implement them to the best of your ability.

Summary

SEO is both a science and an art. To be successful, it requires consistency and creativity in order to make an impact. In this chapter, we covered the basics you need to get your SEO process started within HubSpot. With this as a starting point, you can now focus your resources and efforts. Start with creating a list of keywords, understand and analyze the possible traffic you can gain with specific keywords, pay attention to the difficulty of ranking, and optimize your content based on the relevance of your brand and its products or services.

Once you've connected your HubSpot to your website domain, define the main topic and related subtopics. You can now use this to inform your content strategy and continue building upon this to produce relevant and search engine-friendly content.

In the next chapter, we'll explore the social media tools and functionalities of HubSpot and show you how to generate amazing campaigns and reports all in one tool.

Questions

To ensure you understand the value of the steps you've just completed, let's practice some common troubleshooting tactics you can implement if faced with any of these issues:

1. If you want to search for a new topic in a specific country, what should you do?

2. If one of your team members asks why you need to use the HubSpot SEO tool when you already use Google Search Console, what would be your response?

3. If you would like to plan content creation where you could search for topics and keywords that you can focus on?

Further reading

- Search Engine Journal: `https://www.searchenginejournal.com/`

- *SEO Starter Guide* from Google: `https://developers.google.com/search/docs/beginner/seo-starter-guide`

- *19 SEO Tips Straight From the Mouths of HubSpot's SEO Team*: `https://blog.hubspot.com/marketing/seo-tips`

- *The Beginner's Guide to SEO* (MOZ): `https://moz.com/beginners-guide-to-seo`

- *What Is SEO? (Learn How to Do It in 5 Minutes)* by Neil Patel: `https://neilpatel.com/what-is-seo/`

6
Getting Known Through Social Media on HubSpot

As part of your daily routine, I'm sure you are finding yourself scrolling through Instagram, Facebook, and LinkedIn more often than you would like. Have you stopped to consider how much time you spend on these platforms each day? Are there companies or even personalities whose content you look forward to consuming? Is there a special type of content you prefer over others, such as images, text, or videos?

This is exactly why it's a wide phenomenon among marketers to have their businesses present on social media. Although more widely adopted by B2C companies than B2B companies, social media has become an integral part of almost every type of business' marketing strategy.

But how do you start planning and implementing a social media marketing strategy that will work for your specific business? In this chapter, we will focus on how B2B companies can use social media and show how, together with HubSpot, they can scale their businesses quickly when the right strategy is implemented.

In this chapter, we will cover the following topics:

- Deciding which platform is right for your business
- Understanding the importance of your company's presence on social media
- Understanding HubSpot's social media tool
- Connecting social media platforms to HubSpot
- Creating and implementing a social media strategy

Technical requirements

For this chapter, you will need the following:

- Admin access to your HubSpot portal
- Admin access to each of your business's social media platforms (LinkedIn, Facebook, Instagram, and Twitter)

Deciding which platform is right for your business

When planning a social media strategy, you will need to consider the different approaches for each social network, think about which platform your audience is mostly present on, and in what format they usually prefer to consume content. Before we dive into deciding which platform is right for your business, let's understand how each network works:

Platform	No. of Active Users	Relevant Industries	Best For
Facebook	2.6 billion	B2C and B2B	Brand awareness, lead gen, advertising
LinkedIn	600 million	B2B	B2B relationships, business development, employment marketing
Instagram	1 billion	B2C	Natural-looking media, behind-the-scenes, user-generated content, advertising, and employees' social lives

Twitter	335 million	B2C and B2B	Public relations, customer service
YouTube	2 billion	B2C and B2B	Brand awareness, entertainment, and king of all things videos (tutorials, products, music, and so on)
Pinterest	335 million	B2C	Visual advertising, inspiration
Snapchat	300 million	B2C	Brand awareness; advertising

To understand the impact and reach of each platform mentioned in the preceding table, take a look at the following diagram, which illustrates the number of active users each platform held in 2021:

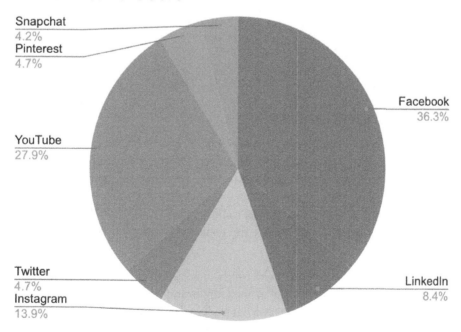

Figure 6.1 – Percentage of active users per social media channel

Now that we have a clear understanding of the potential reach and impact each social network has, let's explain why social media marketing is important and exactly how it could be beneficial to your business.

Understanding the importance of your company's presence on social media

Oftentimes, when a company is doubting whether they should be active on social media or not, it is because they are trying to do too much too soon. Social media, as you have probably come to recognize by your personal use, can be very time-consuming. Therefore, as a company, even if you are considering hiring a dedicated resource or outsourcing your services, there still will never be enough hours in the day for any one person to keep up. So, once you've decided which platform(s) is right for your business, the next step is to decide on your goal. Typically, social media can help you achieve four goals:

- Increase brand awareness.

- Generate leads or increase conversions.

- Nurture engagement with followers or customers.

- Spy on the competition.

Let's take a deeper look at each of these incentives to be on social media.

Increasing brand awareness

As mentioned previously, the number of users each platform boasts should be enough reason to create a social presence. Exposure to even 1% of their audience could be a game-changer for your business. The ability to share content related to hot industry topics or promote your products and services, as well as boost your company's perception via the different channels, has the potential to build brand awareness. This, according to the latest Hootsuite research, is one of the top goals for companies to have their presence on social media.

Social media has been proven to be the primary channel that companies turn to when they are looking to build brand loyalty or measure brand sentiment. Instead of using focus groups, they can often accurately detect what people think at any point in time by likes, shares, and comments.

Generating leads and increasing conversions

Lead generation is a key goal for investing in your company's social media presence. Promoting your content on social media is a great way to increase conversions and sales. This is because you are promoting to people who generally have an active interest to engage with you since they are following your account.

Here are five examples of how B2B or B2C companies can use social media to generate more leads:

- **Promoting gated content**: This is one of the most common ways to generate leads. Here, you can create a post that includes a link to a landing page, where the visitor is eventually prompted to exchange their email address for a piece of high-value content. It is important to note that for these posts to be effective, the content must capture the interest of your followers. This doesn't just relate to the text but how your posts tell the story visually as well.

- **Special offers or contests**: Running a special offer or a contest is a great way to promote your brand on social media. It allows you to present your company creatively and ask your audience to engage with your brand to win. Although more commonly used by B2C companies, B2B companies can also benefit from this tactic if done cleverly as contests can generally attract irrelevant people. However, the upside is that you can get more people to follow you and engage with you as they can potentially share the contest with their networks, helping you to reach more people. And then, through lead nurturing, you can filter out any irrelevant leads.

- **Hosting live videos**: Publishing on a live stream is an effective way to engage in real time with your followers and customers. As a B2B company, you can use this tactic to make announcements about products, provide updates or details about exciting news at your company, answer your audience's questions, get feedback, or simply host a guest speaker and discuss a specific topic. Live streaming allows you to position your brand as a thought leader in your industry. You can find the channel that brings the most value to your brand and run a live stream on it. From Facebook Live to LinkedIn live or Tweet chat, you have various options to engage with your clients in the place they are mostly present.

- **Setting up a shop or Showcase page for your products**: Social media platforms give you another place to sell your products or services. You can enable Facebook's Shop section, Instagram's shopping feature, or a Showcase page on your LinkedIn company profile. This feature will allow your followers to click on a picture you've shared of a product. By clicking on the bag icon, they'll get more information about the product, such as its price, material, and size availability. With this feature, your visitors can easily checkout through the platform and buy the product directly from you. Although this feature is more commonly utilized by B2C companies, B2B companies can also use it as an opportunity to generate leads for demos and free trials.

- **Paid social ads**: All the tactics described previously are based on organic traffic. However, the algorithm on each social media platform is improving all the time, making paid ads more important than ever. If you wish to reach your audience more effectively today on social media, you will need to invest in paid ads.

    Paid ads don't just randomly flood users with irrelevant promotional content. They allow for personalization. They can track your target audience's habits, including the sites they visit and the google searches they make, thus giving them more targeted and relevant content that they would be interested in viewing, which means they will be more likely to click on it.

    Each social platform has unique demographic criteria that allow you to create targeted ads, including job title, industry, gender, age, interest, and more. By knowing the differences between the platforms, you can leverage the right ads and targeting options to ensure you're publishing to the right audience. Ensuring you get the most bang for your buck requires having some expertise in different areas, such as A/B testing, ongoing analysis, and budget adjustments. This will be discussed in a later chapter.

Nurturing engagement with followers and customers

Constantly engaging with your social media followers and customers allows you to build trust and a longer relationship between them, you, and your business. You can achieve this by creating relevant posts, responding to their comments and questions, and providing them with any knowledge resources and help they may need.

You can also start a viral conversation by asking your followers questions about your products and their pain points, or create surveys to increase their trust and show them how their input and information are valuable to you.

Checking your competitors' actions

Social media is a great platform to keep track of your competitors – it is where you can understand their social media tactics, the products they're promoting, their keywords and target audience, the campaigns they're running, or their level of engagement with followers.

Simply put, social media allows you to get a closer look at your competitors, to understand what's working or not working for them. This is a place for you to learn and adjust accordingly to build a better strategy for your company. It is not just a place for engaging and posting content just for the sake of staying seemingly active – it is a place for you to be creative, unique, and outstanding with your brand.

Understanding HubSpot's social media tool

By now, you should be convinced that it is worth setting up your company on social media if you are not already there. But I am sure you are realizing that there is so much you can do and with your plate already full, you may be wondering how you will ever manage to do any more.

Today, many social media tools can help you organize and schedule your posts, monitor engagement, and analyze it. The HubSpot social media tool is no exception. It is a consolidation of everything you need to do on social media platforms in one place, with the bonus of being able to track which contacts in your database are actively engaged with you on social media. This information is invaluable as it allows you to deliver a very personalized experience and reach potential leads and customers where they feel most comfortable.

So, how do you get started with HubSpot's social media tool? You must go through the following steps:

1. Connect social media platforms and set up your preferences (note that HubSpot only connects to LinkedIn, Facebook, Instagram, and Twitter as it's a platform mostly for businesses).

2. Create posts (including adding images, videos, and links).

3. Check engagement (such as likes, shares, and comments).

4. Analyze the results.

So, let's jump right in!

Connecting social media platforms to HubSpot

Apart from connecting your business social media accounts to HubSpot, it is also advisable to connect select personal profiles from your company, such as sales teams, biz dev, product managers, and more. It is a great opportunity to set them up as thought leaders. You will need access to their accounts to connect them. To connect a social media account to HubSpot, follow these steps:

1. Navigate to **Settings | Marketing | Social**.

2. Click on **Connect Account** at the top right-hand corner, as shown here:

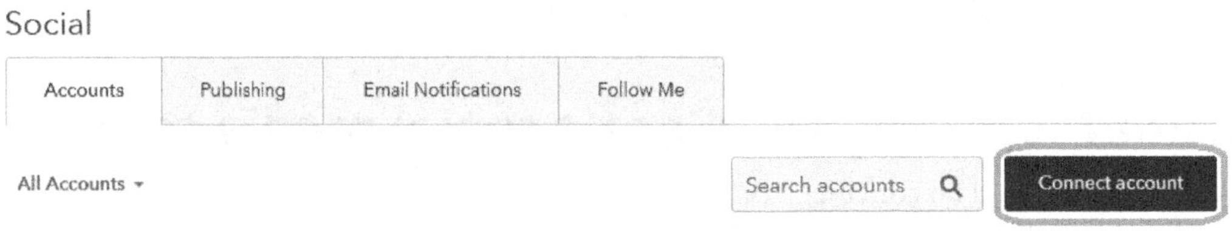

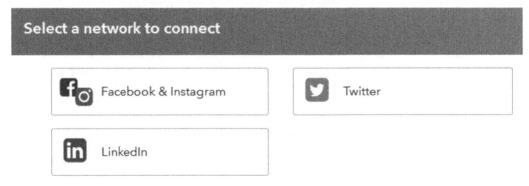

Figure 6.2 – Connecting your social media accounts to HubSpot

Now, choose the platforms where you have accounts. You can choose from **Facebook & Instagram**, **Twitter**, and **LinkedIn**:

Figure 6.3 – Choosing your platforms

Once you've chosen a social media platform, a new page will open to authorize the app and connect to your user. For example, the following screenshot shows the page that will appear if you choose to connect your Twitter profile to HubSpot:

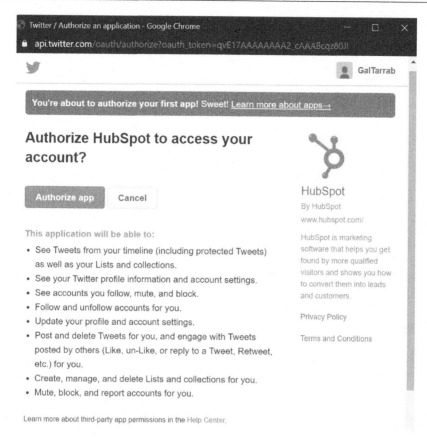

Figure 6.4 – Authorizing HubSpot to connect to your social media apps

You can repeat these steps for each platform you wish to connect to.

Once your social media platforms are connected, click on **Settings | Marketing | Social**. Then, from the top sub-menu, click on **Publishing**. A calendar with various days and times will appear that allows you to select your preferred times for publishing posts. The calendar looks like this:

Social

Accounts	Publishing	Email Notifications	Follow Me

Schedule

SUNDAY	MONDAY	TUESDAY	WEDNESDAY	THURSDAY	FRIDAY	SATURDAY
11:00 AM	11:00 AM	11:00 AM	11:00 AM	11:00 AM	11:00 AM	11:00 AM
2:00 PM	2:00 PM	2:00 PM	2:00 PM	2:00 PM	2:00 PM	2:00 PM
4:45 PM	4:45 PM	4:45 PM	4:45 PM	4:45 PM	4:45 PM	4:45 PM

Figure 6.5 – Choosing your designated times for publishing posts

To delete time or add more time slots, hover over the desired day and click on the trash icon or the **Add time** button:

Figure 6.6 – Adding or deleting additional times

On this page, you can also define the ways you want the posts to be published. Here, you can choose to **publish like a human**, which makes your publishing schedule appear natural and spontaneous. Your posts will publish at various times within 10 minutes of the time you choose:

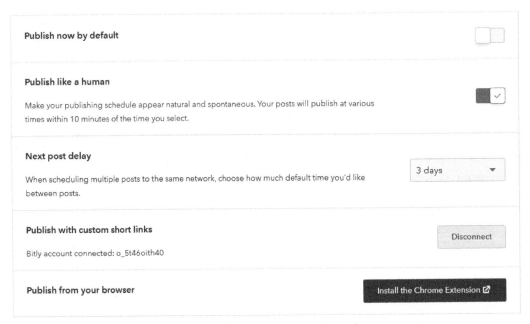

Figure 6.7 – Publish like a human, connect your Bitly account, or decide on the time gap between posts

Here, you can also define the time gap between multiple posts that are scheduled to be posted on the same network.

If you use Bitly, which is a platform that helps you shorten your links so that you stay within the word count limit (this is especially useful for Twitter), you can connect your Bitly account here as well.

One last thing to help you publish posts easier is to install the HubSpot Chrome extension, which allows you to share a post you are reading instantly to the HubSpot social media tool for posting. To do so, just click on the **Install the Chrome Extension** button. The Chrome web store will open, as follows:

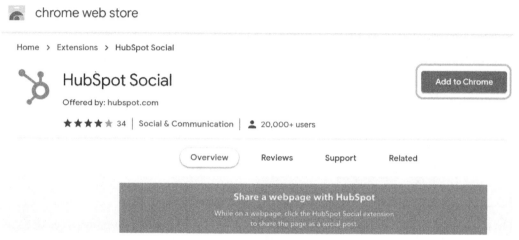

Figure 6.8 – Installing the Chrome extension to post web articles directly to HubSpot

Then, click on the **Add to Chrome** button to install this option.

You can decide how and when you would like to receive notifications for your social media activity. On the **Email notifications** tab, you can choose when you would like to receive notifications about all new social interactions, conversions, and Twitter followers. You can choose either **Daily**, **Twice daily**, or **Weekly notifications**.

You can also choose if you want to receive a monthly summary of your social activity and the effect it's had on your business:

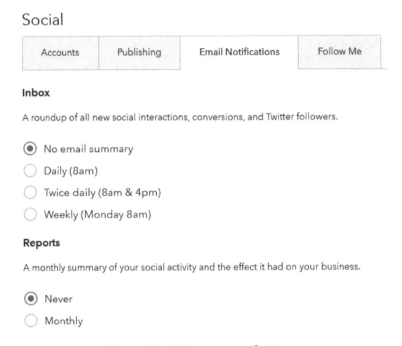

Figure 6.9 – Setting your notifications

On the last tab, called **Follow Me**, you can add all the social media company pages that you own:

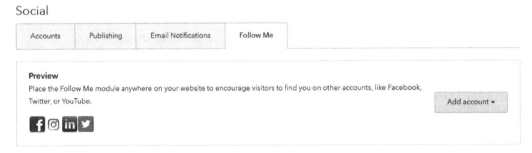

Figure 6.10 – Setting up your Follow Me buttons

Then, you can **Place the Follow Me** module anywhere on your website to encourage visitors to find you on other accounts, such as Twitter, LinkedIn, or YouTube.

Creating social posts

Once you've completed all the technical setup, it is time to create your first social media post. To do so, navigate to the top menu and click on **Marketing | Social**. The following screenshot shows how you can access the Social tool in HubSpot:

Figure 6.11 – Accessing the Social tool in HubSpot

On this page, you can publish, monitor, and report about your social media activity.

To create a new social post, click on the **Create social post** button at the top right, as shown in the following screenshot:

Figure 6.12 – Creating your social posts

Choose the social platform you would like to post on (LinkedIn, Twitter, Facebook, or Instagram), write your new post, choose the account and time you want this post to publish, and attach an image, video, file, or even an emoji if it's relevant.

You can choose to schedule another post on the same platform or a different social platform by choosing the **Schedule another** option and the respective platform:

Figure 6.13 – Scheduling another post

Once you've finished writing the post, you can choose to **Schedule post** or **Save as draft**.

On the **Publishing** page, you'll see all the published posts segmented by publish date, the number of clicks, and the number of interactions. From the top menu, you can choose to filter the posts by network, date, campaign, and user. The menu on the left also allows you to view posts that have been scheduled or posts that are in draft form. The draft feature is particularly useful if you wish to add another layer of approval before a post goes out, especially when someone else is responsible for creating the posts:

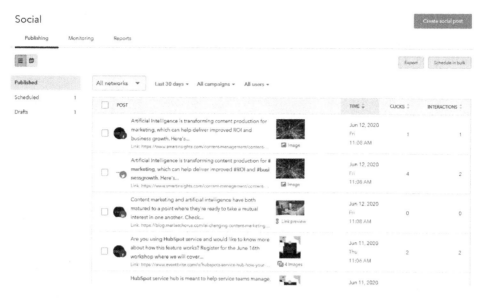

Figure 6.14 – Viewing your list of scheduled, published, or posts in draft form

Recently, HubSpot integrated a new Facebook feature that allows newbies on social media to reach larger audiences by targeting specific countries or languages. To use this feature, your Facebook page must have less than 5,000 likes, and your page admin must enable the **Audience selection** and **Post visibility** options regarding your Facebook page settings. Once you've set up everything on the Facebook side, go to HubSpot, create a new post, and click on **Public audience**. A pop-up box will appear, prompting you to choose the countries and languages you would like to target:

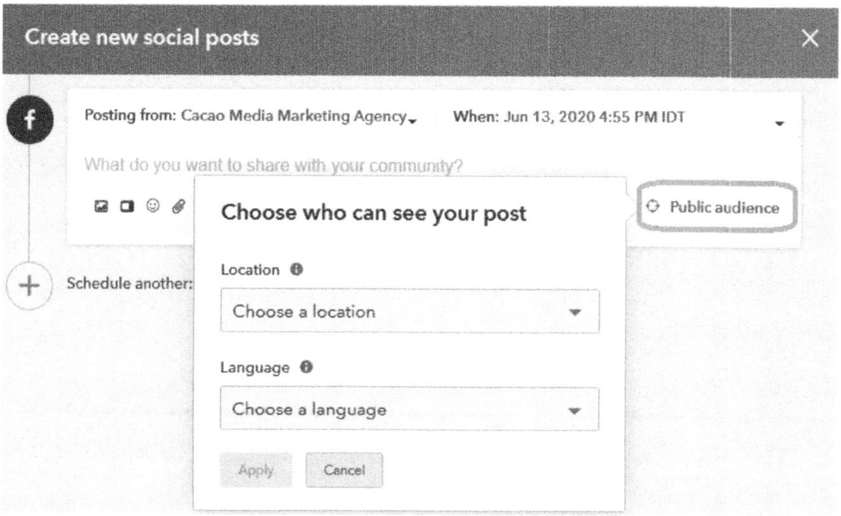

Figure 6.15 – Creating a public audience

Additionally, you can choose multiple actions for each post. By hovering over the image of a post, an **Action** button will appear that will give you the options to clone the post, delete the post, view the post on the respective social media platform, or create an ad based on this post:

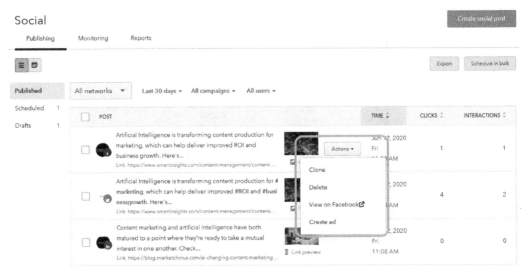

Figure 6.16 – Accessing more actions for your posts

To get a full view of your social media calendar, you can view the publishing page. There are two ways to see the publishing page: as a list or as a calendar. You can change your choice by clicking on the calendar icon on the left:

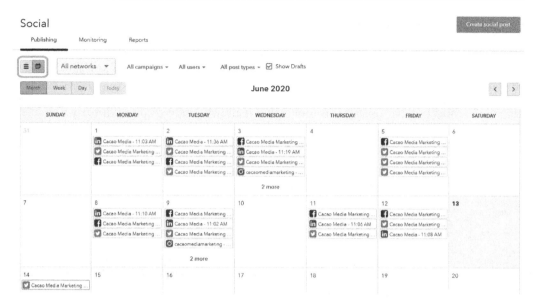

Figure 6.17 – Viewing the calendar tool

You can change the focus of the calendar to daily, weekly, or monthly presentations by clicking on any of the respective highlighted buttons:

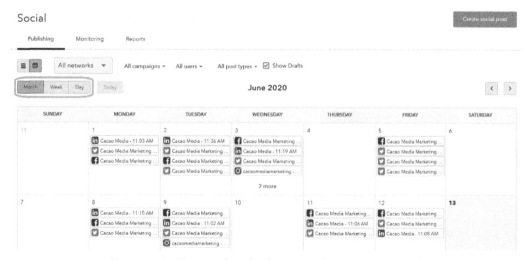

Figure 6.18 – Viewing the calendar tool within a specific period

The calendar view can be very useful as it allows you to see and plan your social media posts. At a glance, you can see if you have too many or too few posts scheduled over a specific period.

Checking engagement

On the **Monitoring** tab, you can view your business's social interactions with other people, such as Twitter retweets, new followers, Facebook and LinkedIn likes, shares and comments, and much more.

One of the most popular uses of this tool is that it allows you to respond directly to comments without logging into the respective social media platforms. By clicking on **Conversations** from the left-hand menu, you can sort all activity to show only those posts that have comments:

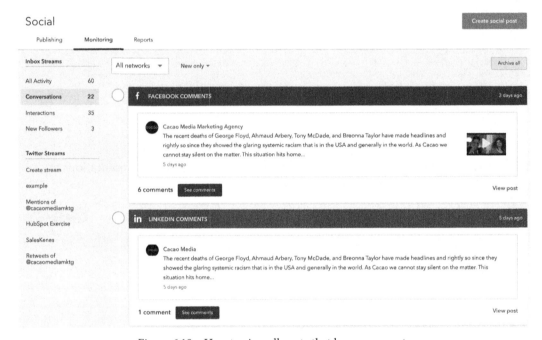

Figure 6.19 – How to view all posts that have comments

If you wish to respond to the comment, you can easily click on **See comments**. A window will open so that you can respond to the comments and post them directly on the respective channels:

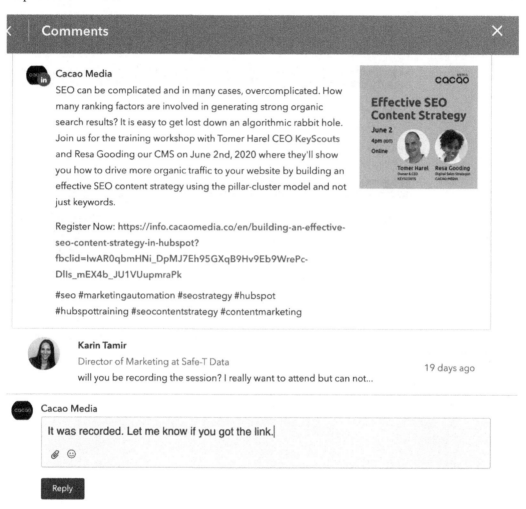

Figure 6.20 – Responding to comments on social media posts

If you wish to keep up to date with only the most recent updates, you can choose to approve each update by clicking the circle next to the post, as shown in the following screenshot:

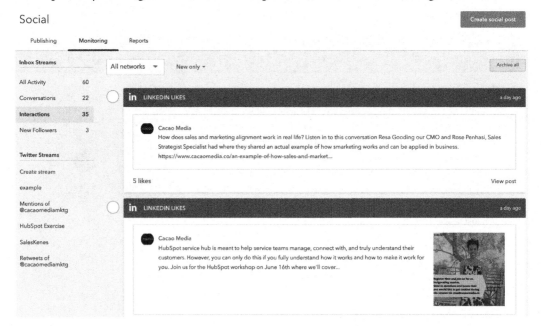

Figure 6.21 – Keeping up to date with the most recent interactions

You also have the option to view just those posts that have received **Likes** or **Shares** by clicking on **Interactions**.

You can also say welcome to your new followers by clicking on **New Followers**:

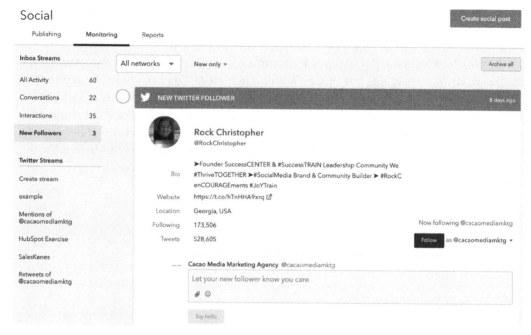

Figure 6.22 – Viewing all new followers from Twitter

The **Conversations** tab in the social media tool can be quite useful as it reduces the time that's needed to log in to each social media platform to check and respond to comments.

Analyzing the results

On the **Reports** tab, you have different social reports where you can see the analysis of your social media activity in one dashboard. From interactions to clicks, published posts, sessions, new contacts, and top posts, you can gain insights into which channels are performing best, which types of posts are resulting in more engagement, how your social media activity is impacting your business, and much more. You can choose to see all the channels at once in a combined report or focus on only one channel at a time within a specific period or as it relates to a specific campaign. The following screenshot shows the statistics of your social media effort. For instance, the **Audience** report shows how much your audience grew in each channel during a specific period, while the **Published Posts** report shows how many posts you published within that specific period:

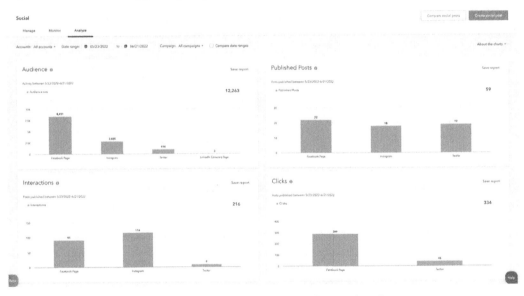

Figure 6.23 – View of all the reports for social media

These reports show if certain inferences can be made, such as whether more posts contribute to an increase in your audience and engagement, such as likes, shares, and more.

Apart from tracking your growth on social media, some of the more meaningful reports you can track are as follows:

- **Visit-to-lead conversion**: One of the main goals of social media is to drive traffic to your website. However, to close more sales, you need to track how many of those visitors convert into actual leads and flow through your funnel. Knowing exactly how much social media helps in the lead generation process will help you meet your monthly/quarterly lead goal. It will give you the historical full picture to set an educated goal based on how much social media brings in, and what that rate of growth looks like month over month for the leads to progress from lead to **marketing qualified leads (MQLs)** to **sales qualified leads (SQLs)**, opportunities, and customers:

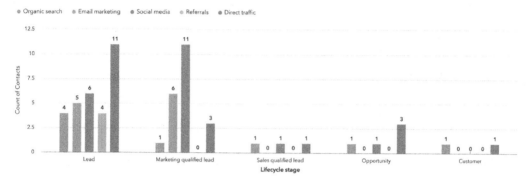

Figure 6.24 – Visit-to-lead conversion report based on life cycle stages

Additionally, to improve your visit-to-lead conversion, you can analyze various posts that have been published on different days to see which days had higher conversions:

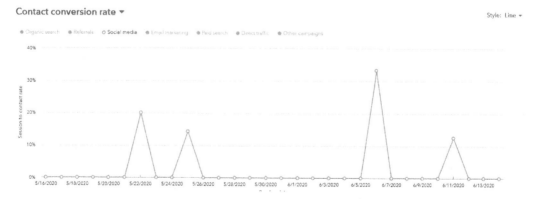

Figure 6.25 – The performance of social media posts on different days

- **Measure social media platforms together and separately**: Every social media platform has its strengths. Therefore, you need to look at the performance of your social media activity – not only as one source compared to other sources but also to deep dive into the different sources to see which one brings the most value to your business. Most importantly, you can look at the relevant traffic to help you meet specific sales and marketing goals:

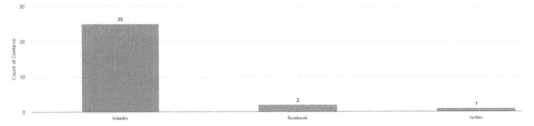

Figure 6.26 – Viewing a combined report of all social media platforms' performance

- **Lead source-to-deal conversion**: Now that you have an understanding of how many contacts you get from each social media platform, it is useful to track which source brings in the most customers. This insight shows you which channel is most lucrative in bringing you the qualified leads that turn into customers. It also highlights opportunities to improve the process for channels that are performing poorly. The following screenshot shows an example of conversions from different lead sources:

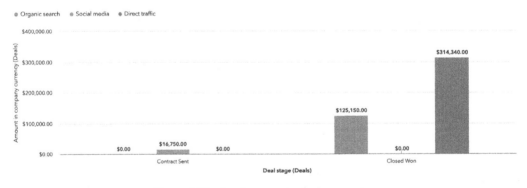

Figure 6.27 – Lead-source-to-deal conversion

Reporting on your social media activity is crucial to your success as a marketing manager as most leaders undervalue the importance of these platforms. To achieve their confidence, it is important to include reports that they care about, which are mostly reports that affect the bottom line. So, when presenting to management, leave out the number of followers and likes you have on your posts, and instead focus on how many opportunities are being created for the sales team from social media.

Summary

Today's customers demand that you make the effort to reach them where they are. As much as you may doubt the usefulness of social media to your business, its importance should never be underestimated. After all, every business transaction is with a person, not a business, and your target audience is on one of those social media platforms, whether it's for personal or business reasons.

In this chapter, we covered how you can effectively use social media for your business. We focused specifically on how the HubSpot social media tool can help you be more effective and efficient in managing and implementing your social media strategy. Remember to start by connecting your social accounts to HubSpot, creating posts, monitoring engagement, and analyzing all the information to improve the ROI of your social media efforts.

In the next chapter, we will expand your reach with paid ads and show you how to generate results-focused campaigns, all using the HubSpot platform.

Questions

To ensure you understood the value of the steps you've just completed, let's practice some common troubleshooting tactics you can implement if faced with any of these issues:

1. Which social media platforms are most relevant for B2B businesses?

2. When connecting your social media account, should you only connect your company profiles or some members of your team as well?

3. Which types of reports help you track whether your social media efforts are resulting in opportunities for your sales team?

Further reading

To learn more about the topics that were covered in this chapter, take a look at the following resources:

- Social Media Examiner: `https://www.socialmediaexaminer.com/`

- *9 Types of Social Media and How Each Can Benefit Your Business*: `https://blog.hootsuite.com/types-of-social-media/`

- HubSpot Academy – Social Media Courses: `https://www.hubspot.com/resources/courses/social-media`

7

Expanding Your Reach with Paid Ads Managed on HubSpot

As we discussed in the previous chapter, your target audience is spending time on social media. Therefore, every company needs to ensure it has a presence on social media in one form or another. However, if you've noticed lately that your posts are not getting a lot of traction and engagement rates are low, it is because social platforms prefer you to pay to play. So, advertising on social media has become an essential part of every marketer's strategy.

It is important to note that social media advertising is not a replacement for SEO or organic social media posting. On the contrary, social media advertising needs to be a complementary action to an organic strategy.

When thinking about which social media channel to use for advertising, it is best to start with the channel where you already perform relatively well organically or where you know for sure your target audience is hanging out.

In this chapter, you will learn about the following:

- How the HubSpot ads tool works

- How to connect LinkedIn Ads to HubSpot

- How to connect Facebook ads to HubSpot

- How to connect Google Ads to HubSpot

- How to create retargeting ads for contacts within HubSpot

- How to create audiences from your database within HubSpot that can be targeted in the ad platforms

- Tips for optimizing the ROI from your ad campaigns

- How to analyze ad reports in HubSpot

By the end of this chapter, you will be able to successfully set up a paid campaign and use it to generate and convert relevant leads.

Technical requirements

To get the most out of this chapter, you will need the following:

- HubSpot Marketing Professional

- Super admin access to your HubSpot portal

- Admin access to each of your business's social media ad platforms (LinkedIn, Facebook, and Google AdWords)

Getting to know how the HubSpot ads tool works

Managing your social ads can be difficult when using different platforms and analytics tools to get insights or manage your media budget for various campaigns. Having the ability to manage all your campaigns in one platform can give you better insights as you are able to compare the performance of different ads across different platforms, as well as cross-checking different ads within different campaigns and platforms.

With HubSpot's Ads tool, you are able to achieve this cross-comparison of your ads' performance across LinkedIn, Google, and Facebook ads in order to achieve the insights to understand how to optimize your campaigns for better results. The integration of your ads with HubSpot's Ads tool allows you to do the following:

- Get a complete picture of your ads' performance.

- Sync contacts from your lead generation ads.

- See which contacts engaged with your ads.

- Create target audiences based on lists of contacts and website visitors with a simple installation of your ad accounts' tracking pixels.

To use HubSpot's Ads tool, you first need to connect your Linkedin, Facebook, and Google accounts. For every platform, the requirements are slightly different. In the following sections, we explain exactly how this is done.

Connecting your LinkedIn Ads account to HubSpot

The HubSpot user who connects the LinkedIn Ads account must have Publish access to the HubSpot ads tool and be an account manager in that LinkedIn Ads account.

Once the appropriate access is acquired, follow these steps to connect LinkedIn to HubSpot:

1. Navigate, from the top menu, to **Settings | Marketing | Ads | Connect account**, as shown in the following screenshot:

Figure 7.1 – Connecting an Ads account to HubSpot

2. Then, choose the desired platform from the popup. In this case, select **LinkedIn**.

Figure 7.2 – Ads platforms to connect in HubSpot

3. After selecting **LinkedIn**, a popup will appear prompting you to sign into your personal LinkedIn account. It does not take information from your personal account but simply uses it as a conduit to get to your company's Ads account.

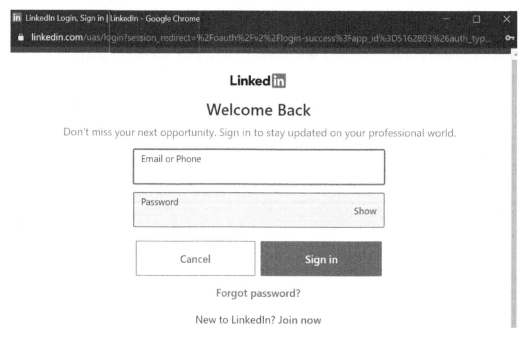

Figure 7.3 – LinkedIn connection

4. Once you have signed in, you will then be asked to select the LinkedIn Ads account to connect to HubSpot. If you want to track contacts that interact with your ads, leave autotracking on, as seen in *Figure 7.4*. This will apply HubSpot tracking to your LinkedIn ads. Click **Connect**.

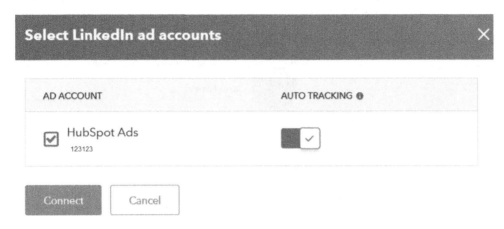

Figure 7.4 – HubSpot Ads autotracking switch on

Once these steps are completed, your LinkedIn Ads account is connected and you will be ready to launch and track your existing and future ads on LinkedIn. Next, let's see how we connect Facebook ads to HubSpot.

Connecting your Facebook Ads account to HubSpot

The HubSpot user who connects the Facebook ads account must have Publish access to the HubSpot ads tool and be an admin of the ad account in Facebook's Business Manager account.

In order to connect Facebook to HubSpot, follow the instructions shown in the previous section, the same as connecting a LinkedIn Ads account. When prompted to select an ad account, you will choose **Facebook** instead of **LinkedIn** at *Step 2* and proceed.

Alternatively, you can also connect your company page and ad account from Facebook so the lead ad forms used in Facebook ads will appear as one of the form options in HubSpot, allowing you to easily sync the leads that complete the form. To complete this integration between HubSpot and Facebook lead ad forms, follow these steps:

1. Navigate to your Facebook page.

2. From the side menu, click on **All Tools**.

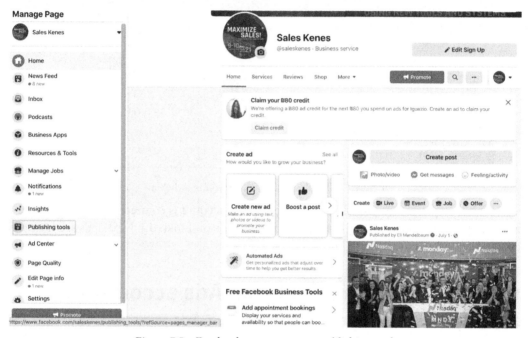

Figure 7.5 – Facebook company page publishing tool

3.   On the left-hand side menu, navigate to **Instant Forms**.

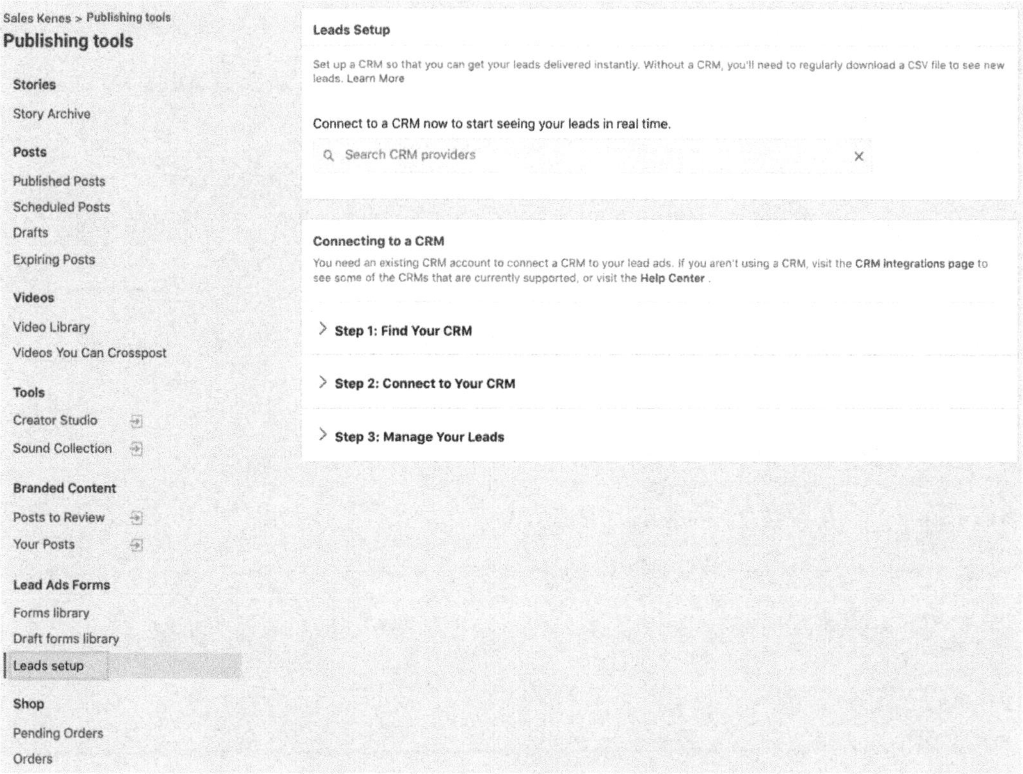

Figure 7.6 – Lead setup page on Facebook

4. Click the **Search CRM providers** field and search for **HubSpot**. Then, select the corresponding entry in the dropdown when it appears.

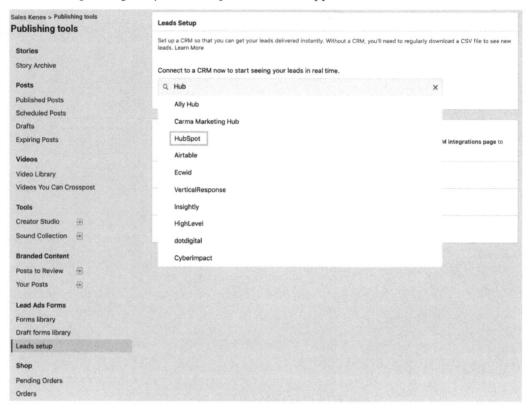

Figure 7.7 – Searching for HubSpot

5. Next to **HubSpot**, click **Connect from Website**. You will then be redirected to log in to your HubSpot portal.

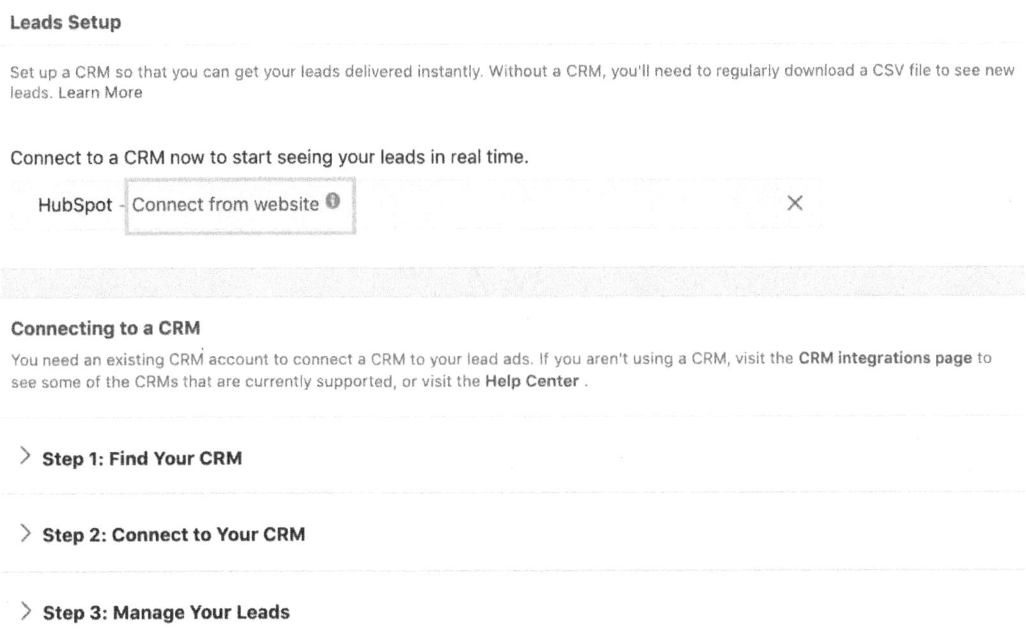

Leads Setup

Set up a CRM so that you can get your leads delivered instantly. Without a CRM, you'll need to regularly download a CSV file to see new leads. Learn More

Connect to a CRM now to start seeing your leads in real time.

HubSpot - Connect from website ❶   ✕

Connecting to a CRM

You need an existing CRM account to connect a CRM to your lead ads. If you aren't using a CRM, visit the **CRM integrations page** to see some of the CRMs that are currently supported, or visit the **Help Center** .

> **Step 1: Find Your CRM**

> **Step 2: Connect to Your CRM**

> **Step 3: Manage Your Leads**

Figure 7.8 – Connecting HubSpot to the website

6.   Sign in to your HubSpot account and select the ad account you want to connect to HubSpot.

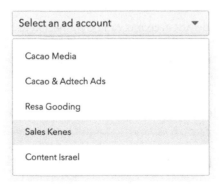

Figure 7.9 – Selecting the relevant Facebook ad account to connect to HubSpot

7. Then, click **Connect ad account**. A message will then appear confirming that leads from your Facebook ad account will sync to HubSpot, and HubSpot will also apply tracking to the ads in your Facebook ad account.

Success! Leads from this page will now be synced to your
HubSpot CRM.

All lead generation ad leads from the past 90 days will also sync over to HubSpot. When new people
convert on your lead generation ads, their contact data will be automatically synced to your HubSpot
CRM.

Go to HubSpot Ads dashboard

New to HubSpot? Click here to get started!

Figure 7.10 – Facebook lead setup connection on HubSpot

Now that our Facebook ads and lead forms are connected, our next step is to connect Google Ads to HubSpot.

Connecting your Google Ads account to HubSpot

The HubSpot user who connects the Google Ads account must have Publish access to the HubSpot ads tool and admin access to the Google Ads account.

> **Tip**
> Only individual Google Ads accounts can be connected to HubSpot. Google Ad Manager accounts cannot be connected to HubSpot. So, any Google Ads account that is managed in a manager account should be connected to HubSpot individually.

In order to connect a Google Ads account to HubSpot, the following steps must be completed:

1. Navigate, from the top HubSpot menu, to **Settings | Marketing | Ads | Connect account**.

2. In the popup, select **Google Ads**.

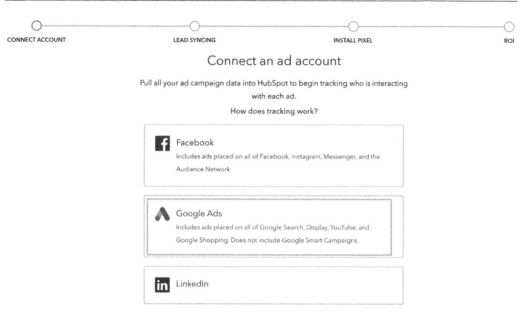

Figure 7.11 – Connecting a Google Ads account to HubSpot

3. In the dialog box that opens, log in to your Google account using the email address associated with your Google Ads account.

4. Then, click **Allow**.

5. Select the Google account you wish to connect to HubSpot and click **Connect**.

Select Google ad accounts

Your selected Google Ad account(s) will be added to HubSpot's Google Manager account. You will receive an email from Google confirming this. By connecting your Google Ads account to HubSpot, you agree that Google may share information about your use of Google Ads with HubSpot, including the amount you spend on Google Ads. Google may use this information to further its business relationship with HubSpot, including to calculate or pay commissions or bonuses owed to HubSpot. Learn more

AD ACCOUNT	AD ACCOUNT ID	AUTO TRACKING ❶
☑ Google Ads account		✓
☐		

Connect   Cancel   Create ad account

Figure 7.12 – Selecting the relevant Google Ads account

Once the connection is successful, you'll be redirected to the Ads dashboard in HubSpot, where existing ad information will be synced to the HubSpot Ads section. This allows HubSpot to track advertising performance across users' ad accounts.

Installing the pixel tracking code

After connecting the paid ad accounts (Facebook, Linkedin, and Google) to HubSpot, you can install a pixel from an external ad network, such as the Facebook pixel, Google conversion tracking tag, and LinkedIn Insight Tag, on all your HubSpot-hosted pages or external pages where your tracking code is installed.

The pixel tracking code will help you create a website visitors' audience directly in the HubSpot ads tool instead of the social media networks. You can just use HubSpot's tracking code and it will still work and attribute contacts to your ads, but the social media pixel will give you more information in a smoother way.

In order to install the pixel tracking code, follow these steps:

1. Navigate to **Settings | Marketing | Ads**.
2. On the top menu, click on **Pixels**.

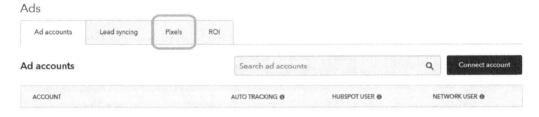

Figure 7.13 – Google pixel tracking code

3. Click on **Add pixel**.
4. Choose the pixel you would like to install from the drop-down menu that opens.
5. Click **Add pixel**.

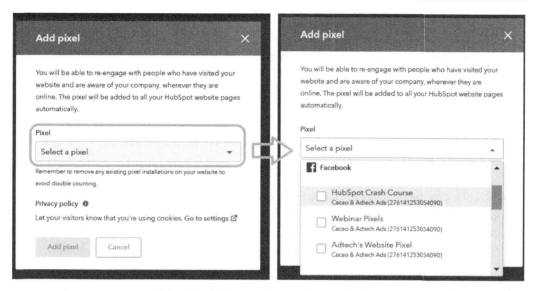

Figure 7.14 – Selecting pixel code from HubSpot

The Facebook pixel will automatically be added to HubSpot pages such as landing pages, blog pages, and web pages or to external pages that contain your HubSpot tracking code.

Building an ad audience

Now that the technical part of connecting the ad accounts is completed, it is time to create your ad audience.

Your ad audience will affect the entire ad. You decide how wide or narrow to make this audience in your Facebook, Google, and LinkedIn ads. HubSpot gives you three ways to create your audience based on your website visitors, HubSpot contacts, and existing audiences.

Before you start creating the ad audience, it's important to understand the different requirements each platform has.

The criteria for **Google Ads** audiences are as follows:

- For Google Search Network, the audience should be at least 1,000 visitors within the last 30 days.

- For Google Display Network, the audience should be at least 100 visitors within the last 30 days.

- For Facebook ads, the audience needs to contain at least 20 users.

- For LinkedIn Ads, the audience needs to contain at least 300 users.

The advantage of creating an audience in HubSpot instead of the ads platform is that first, you get to use your own data if you already have contacts in HubSpot, and additionally, you can create audiences over time that match certain criteria you wish to focus on and target just these contacts in your ads.

Creating a website visitor's audience in your HubSpot account

Sometimes, you would like to set up a retargeting campaign for contacts who visit your website. This will allow them to see your ads as they browse through their social media platforms, allowing you to gain additional opportunities to convert them to a lead or move them through the funnel to become an opportunity. The following steps show you how to create such an audience:

1. Navigate to **Marketing | Ads | Create audience**.

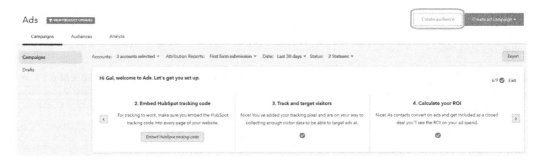

Figure 7.15 – Creating an audience for ads on HubSpot

2. In the pop-up page that opens, select **Website visitors**.

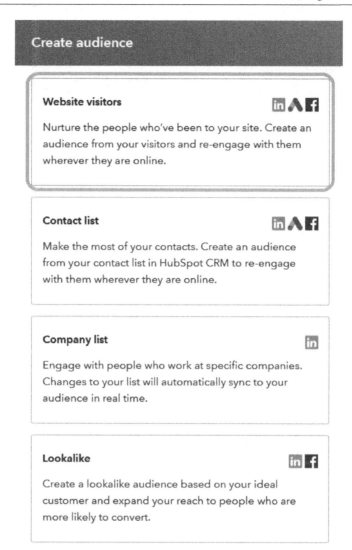

Figure 7.16 – Creating an ad audience by website visitors

3. Under **Source pixel**, click **Select a pixel**. A drop-down menu will appear.

4. Select your Facebook, Google Ads, and/or LinkedIn Ads pixel.

5. To add a new pixel, click **Add a pixel**.

6. Segment the audience based on the pages they are visiting based on ad time estimation of the visits.

7.   Give the audience a name and click **Create audience**.

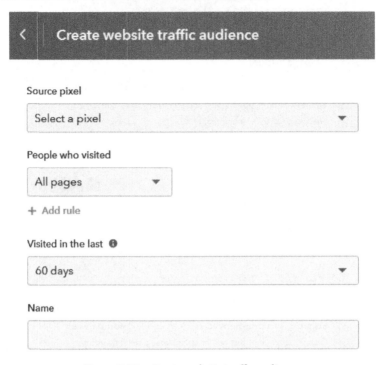

Figure 7.17 – Create website traffic audience

HubSpot makes it easy for its customers by creating an audience to include visitors to all website pages. However, if you have a Marketing Hub Starter, Professional, or Enterprise account, you can choose specific website pages that you want to include the audience from.

You can also create a contact list audience, not based on the pages they visited but based on the contacts themselves. Let's have a quick rundown of how that is done.

Creating an audience list

In order to create an audience list that contains specific contacts from your database, the following steps are necessary:

1.   Click on **Marketing | Ads | Create audience | Contacts list**.

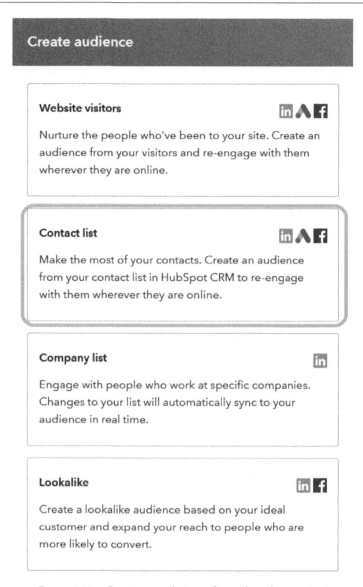

Figure 7.18 – Creating a website audience based on contact

2. Check the **This contact list was not purchased, rented, appended, or provided by a third party** checkbox.

3. Choose the ad account you'd like to use this audience for.

4.   Give this list a name and click on **Create audience**.

Figure 7.19 – Creating a contacts list

Once this contact list is created, it then appears in the relevant social media platform that was chosen and these contacts can then be targeted in future campaigns.

Now, let's look at how to create these ads for these campaigns.

Creating ads

After you've connected the ad accounts and created audiences, it's time to create the ads:

1. Click on **Marketing | Ads** on the top menu in your HubSpot account.

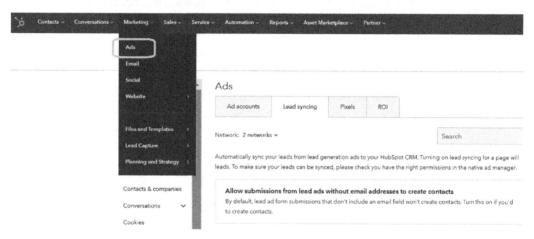

Figure 7.20 – Ads option in HubSpot

2. Click on **Create ad campaign** in the top-right corner of the page and choose the social media platform you want.

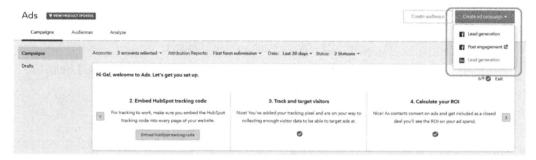

Figure 7.21 – Create ad campaign

3. After selecting the platform to advertise on, insert all the needed information.

4. In the **Ad** tab of the LinkedIn campaign page, fill in the ad account with the required information, such as an image or video, body text, a headline, and a **call to action** (**CTA**) from the drop-down options, as well as a Linkedin lead gen form.

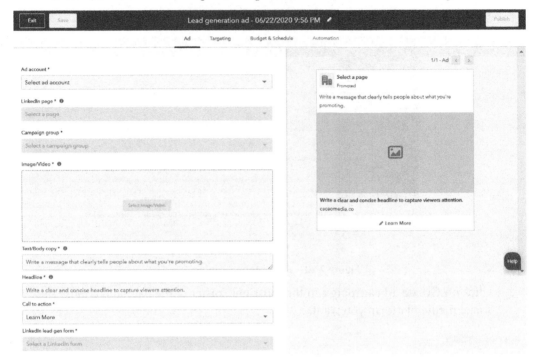

Figure 7.22 – Ad creation page in HubSpot

5. On the **Targeting** tab, fill in the **Remarketing and lookalike audiences**, **Location**, and **Interests/Behaviors/Demographic** lists.

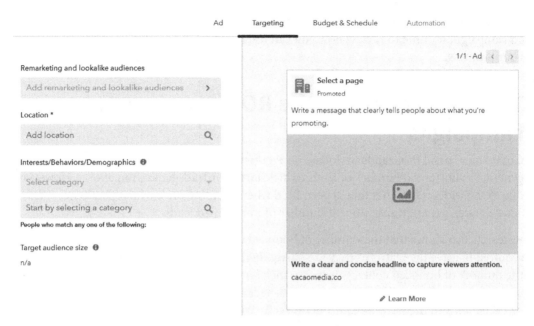

Figure 7.23 – Targeting section in ad creation

6. On the **Budget & Schedule** tab, fill in the budget and the dates the ads will run.

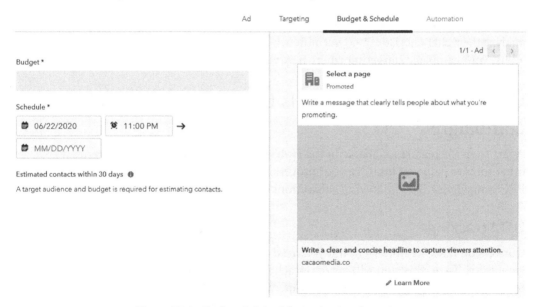

Figure 7.24 – Budget & Schedule section in ad creation

7. After you've inserted all the information, it's time to publish the ad.

Now that you have connected the ad accounts to HubSpot and created your first ad campaign, it's time to review how you can use the HubSpot paid ads tool for your business.

Tips for optimizing the ROI from your ad campaigns

Companies spend thousands of dollars on **Pay-per-Click** (**PPC**) campaigns in order to generate a substantial number of leads to kickstart their lead-generation efforts. However, due to the wide-casting net that is permitted when deciding on the target audience, these ads can often generate a significant number of unqualified leads.

Research also shows that the number of bounced contacts increases when a user is required to leave the platform they are currently in to get to your offer. One tip to reduce the number of bounced contacts is to use social media internal forms and not redirect the user to a landing page. This allows your prospect to first fill out the form within LinkedIn or Facebook and then access your offer directly within the platform, improving your conversions and **Click-Through Rate** (**CTR**).

Another advantage of generating leads directly on Facebook or LinkedIn through their lead-generation forms is that you will also generate more leads at a lower cost per lead. In addition, once these contacts are directly synced to HubSpot, you are able to better analyze their characteristics to determine whether they are indeed qualified and then adjust your campaign, targeting where necessary to better align with your buyer persona.

Using other HubSpot tools to optimize your ad campaigns

Apart from the features available in the HubSpot ads tool, HubSpot provides many other tools to help you improve your process for generating quality leads from your PPC campaigns. In the following subsections, we cover a few of them.

UTM tracking

Conversion rates are important but you need to also make sure you are converting the right leads. To do this, you will need to track more elements in the campaign. The data from URL tracking allows you to determine which campaign and platform a lead came from, the keyword they searched for, the device they were on, and so on.

One of the best ways to accomplish this is by using UTM links. The UTM is built with special parameters. These parameters append to the end of your landing page URLs. They look something like this: `www.yourpagelink.com/?utm_source=linkedin&utm_medium=ad&utm_cmapign=name`.

There are six parameters that you can add to your URL:

`utm_source`	Ad platform where you're running your ads, for example Google.
`utm_medium`	Type of channel, in our case, it will be CPC (short for cost per click).
`utm_term`	Keyword defined in your ad campaign. Set it to {`keyword`} to automatically pass the keyword that the user searched for.
`utm_campaign`	Name of your PPC campaign.
`utm_device`	Type of device, such as computer, tablet or mobile. Set it to {`device`} to automatically pass the device that the user is on.
`utm_matchtype`	Keyword match type, such as broad, phrase, or exact. Set it to {`matchtype`} to automatically pass how your keyword will be matched.

Figure 7.25 – URL parameters

The three main parameters are the source, medium, and campaign.

Targeting relevant keywords

Keywords are not only essential for SEO and the generation of organic traffic to your website, but they're also the essence of every paid search campaign (mostly relevant for Google advertising).

The first step in keyword creation is to identify the most focused and relevant keywords. Then, you need to segment your campaigns and search for keyword ideas within each segment. There are a lot of excellent keyword research tools that you can use to find the best ones, such as Google Keyword Planner, Google Trends, Keyword Tool.io, or Ubersuggest.

In order to reach the quality contacts that are at the bottom of the funnel, you have to start thinking like your customers. When planning the campaign, you can see the list size, and with this, you can also decide how narrowed and focused you would like to make this campaign. The more assets you connect to the campaign, such as keywords, ads, and landing pages, the better your leads will be.

Additionally, in your text, you can use long-tail keywords, which consist of four or more words. You can search these keywords directly in Google, or try and use different tools. In Google, you can find the related keywords by searching for a relevant keyword, scrolling to the bottom of the search page, and looking at **Related search**.

Removing irrelevant keywords

Create a report for all the used keywords to determine whether you are getting any irrelevant clicks and leads from your ads. If you find any, remove these keywords by adding them to your negative keywords list. This will tell the search engine not to show your ads for any of these keywords.

With this action, you'll create a list of keywords that have produced opportunities (and customers) for your company. For these keywords, you can search for new, related long-tail keywords to increase exposure, increase the bids so your ads' rank at the top of search results, and use these ones on a new campaign that is more targeted and relevant for these customers.

Generating a pre-qualify ad copy

With your ad copy, you should pre-qualify visitors so that the traffic you get will be a lot more relevant and targeted to your company and not focused solely on increasing the CTR. You can do this by adding the following elements to your ad copy:

- **Target persona**: Create segmentation in your ad copy for pre-qualifying your ad traffic and even personalizing your ads. You can do this with text such as *Report guide for CTO* or *All the analysis that a CMO of start-ups will need.*

- **Business size**: Reflect your intention and target business size in your ad copy. For example, if you want to target small businesses, you can add "start-ups" to your ads and create copy such as "start-ups" plan for analyzing real-time information."

- **Industry**: Focus all your effort on the specific industries that are relevant to you instead of advertising to all the industries there are.

- **Pricing**: It's not very common to see ads with a price on them, but this is a good way to weed out contacts who may not have the budget for your solution. You can do this by adding text such as "Starting at $999/month."

- **Determine which offers drive the most results**: Create A/B tests for every ad campaign. Different people prefer different ads. A/B tests will enable you to see which ad and which campaign gets the most traction and gives you better results. Make sure you're not analyzing just the CTR, but you also check which offers are producing the most conversions and eventually opportunities.

It's a good place for you to test all types of campaigns from free trials and scheduling a demo to a webinar invitation and content download. But most importantly, when creating the A/B test, remember to change and test only one single object at a time to isolate the effect of that element on performance. Some elements you should test on include the following:

- **Headline**: Test different versions of your main point or offer.

- **Call to action** (**CTA**): You can try different copy, colors, sizes, and placements.

- **Images**: Test different images or videos for your header or background.

Determining ROI

Calculating ROI shows how much money you are getting from the ads. This will show you whether you should invest more money in paid ad campaigns or rethink and change your strategic plan. The HubSpot paid ads tool helps you to analyze the ROI.

IMPRESSIONS		CLICKS		CONTACTS ❶		CUSTOMERS ❶		AMOUNT SPENT ❶	ROI ❶
24M	0.3%	77K	3.1%	2,391	0.7%	17		$124,844.53	1,695%
		$1.62 each		$52.21 each		$7,343.80 each			

Figure 7.26 – ROI chart from paid ads

In the preceding chart, you can clearly see that a media budget spent of $124,844 resulted in an ROI of 1,695% since the revenue generated from 17 customers that originated from paid ads sources greatly exceeded the budget spent.

Running buyer persona targeting

On Facebook, there is a feature to build an audience based on a look-alike list of people. This allows you to specifically find more people that fit the criteria of the existing contacts in your database. The goal is to expand your reach to find more people based on the characteristics you have already identified as relevant to your target audience. Since you're connecting your HubSpot to your Facebook ad account, you can build these look-a-like audiences inside HubSpot to expand your ads' reach even more.

To do this, you first create lists of leads or of people who fit your buyer persona in HubSpot. This is a quick and easy way to get started with look-a-like audiences. You can use the Facebook Ads Manager for more look-a-like features.

By using the look-a-like list, you'll broaden your paid reach while also staying hyper-focused on tight targeting and your buyer personas.

Creating retargeting ads for contacts within HubSpot

Retargeting refers to advertising to people based on their previous internet actions. Retargeting ads are therefore generally promoted to contacts who already visited your website or are even part of your database.

Advertising to people who already have an interest in you and your product or service usually gives better results and is a better investment of your money. The HubSpot paid ads tool can also be used to create retargeting ads for contacts in the middle and bottom of the funnel. The contacts generated from these campaigns often tend to be of higher quality with a low cost attached to them, but the overall number of conversions will be lower compared to other ad campaigns.

To ensure your retargeting ad campaigns are effective, it is important to install a tracking code on your website. You can create retargeting campaigns based on audience segmentation if you have a sufficient volume of traffic to your website. Unlike remarketing, which focuses on sales or marketing emails sent to re-engage customers, retargeting focuses on pulling in new audiences or customers through ads on social media, email, or other platforms.

There are many great tools for retargeting, such as Perfect Audience, AdRoll, ReTargeter, and Bizo. You can also use Facebook for retargeting, which allows you to launch ads to a large pool of mirror audiences with a number of ad objectives.

In order to create a retargeting campaign on Facebook, you need to carry out three steps:

1. **Create a list of existing contacts**: In HubSpot, create a list based on their life cycle stage and their interests based on the topic of their most recent download. When this list is sufficiently large, move to the next step. If it's not, rethink your segmentation and/or type of retargeting to implement.

2. **Add list to Facebook's Audience Manager**: After the number of contacts in the list is sufficient, export the list to a CSV file and import it to the Facebook's Custom Audience manager to match up email addresses with Facebook profiles. (There are other third-party platforms that also sync these lists on social media and across the web, so feel free to pick which upload/sync option works best for your company.)

3. **Determine your destination URL**: To create a new campaign on Facebook, enter your Ad Manager area, then hit the green **Create** button in the top-left corner of the ad platform home screen.

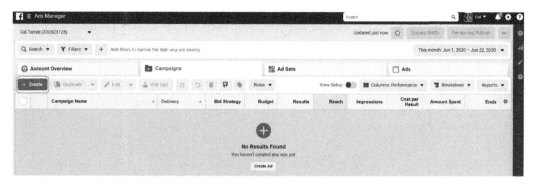

Figure 7.27 – Ad creation on Facebook

Facebook gives you the option to choose the type of campaign you want to create from three different types of campaigns: awareness, consideration, and conversion.

On Facebook, you can use an internal form or add a UTM tracking URL that will help you track the people that come from this campaign and eventually the success of your campaigns.

If using an external URL, the next step is to give your campaign a name, which will be inserted underneath the URL textbox. Keep your campaign names simple and clear. After naming, add your ad segmentation in order to reach specific audiences. Finally, set the budget for this campaign, and you're done.

Analysis of ad campaigns

With HubSpot's Ads tool, you have the ability to track the following metrics:

- Number of impressions
- Cost per click
- Cost per contact
- Cost per customers
- Total budget spent
- ROI

You can then choose to deep dive and understand exactly which ads are performing better than others and exactly how many contacts each ad is generating across each platform.

Figure 7.28 – Ad analysis

On the ad screen, you can see all the information, but you can also make changes, such as extending the budget, schedule, and creative assets.

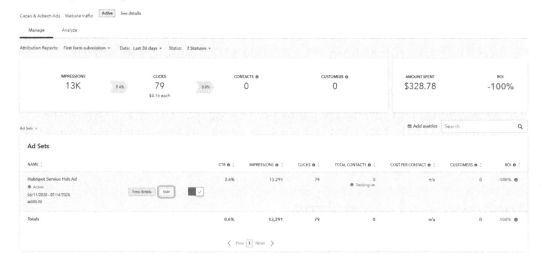

Figure 7.29 – Editing ad sets

Clicking on the **Edit** button opens a new pop-up page with all the metrics you can edit.

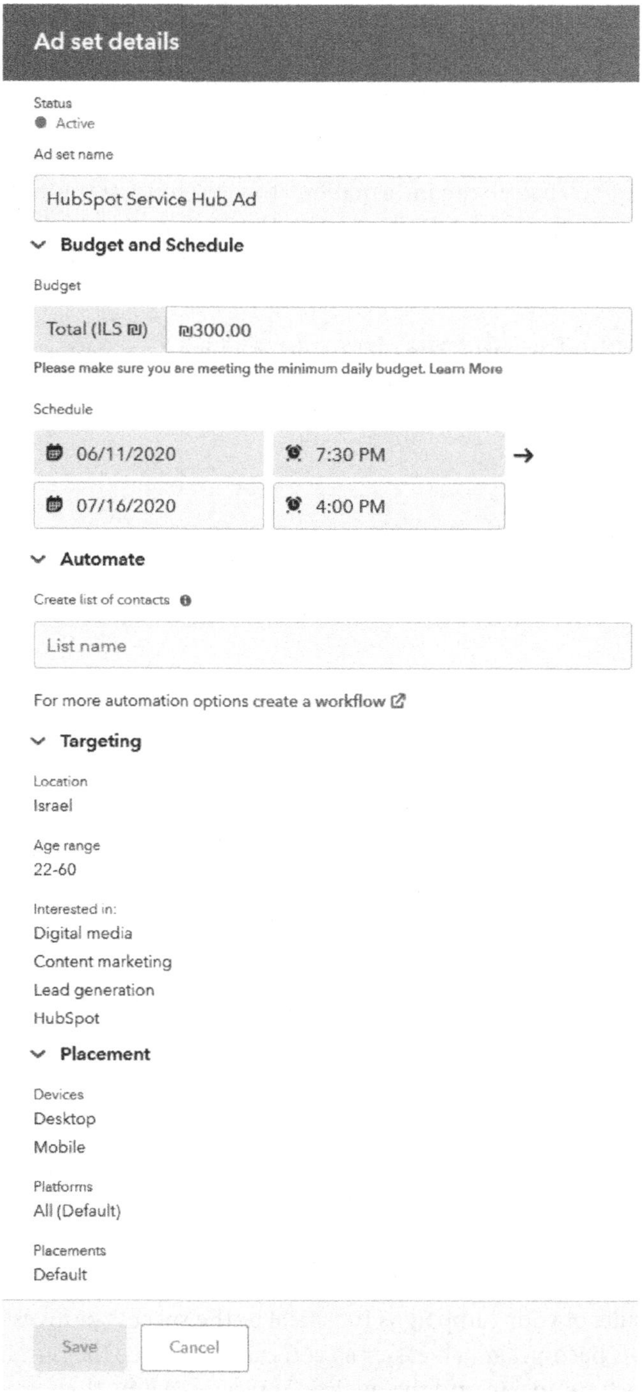

Ad set details

Status
● Active

Ad set name

HubSpot Service Hub Ad

∨ **Budget and Schedule**

Budget

Total (ILS ₪)	₪300.00

Please make sure you are meeting the minimum daily budget. Learn More

Schedule

📅 06/11/2020   ⏰ 7:30 PM   →

📅 07/16/2020   ⏰ 4:00 PM

∨ **Automate**

Create list of contacts ℹ

List name

For more automation options create a **workflow** ⅃

∨ **Targeting**

Location
Israel

Age range
22-60

Interested in:
Digital media
Content marketing
Lead generation
HubSpot

∨ **Placement**

Devices
Desktop
Mobile

Platforms
All (Default)

Placements
Default

Save   Cancel

Figure 7.30 – Different ad metrics to edit

Analyzing the ads report

Your ads are running great; you are doing A/B tests and you made sure to invest your money in the right places, but in order to justify your promotions and money spent, it's important to analyze the report.

You have a few ways to analyze the information. To view your ad campaign data, navigate on the top menu to **Marketing | Ads**. In the first **Campaigns** tab, you'll see all the information about your campaigns from impressions, clicks to total contacts, and even the number of customers you got from these campaigns.

The page is built with a few parts. The first report is a high-level report and the table beneath it is a breakdown of the information per campaign. On the **Analyze** tab, you get more detailed dashboards.

Figure 7.31 – Ad campaign reports

Analyzing the results of your campaigns is critical to the success of investing in paid ads. With HubSpot, this becomes much easier as you can clearly see the number of contacts generated from each campaign and the quality. You can see how they progress through the funnel from lead to marketing qualified lead, sales qualified lead, opportunity, and customer.

Summary

With the competition that companies have today, they must think and plan their paid ads strategy in order to have an edge and be ahead of the competition. SEO and organic contacts are a good and essential part of the strategy, but it's not enough. In this chapter, we covered all the information you need in order to create a strategic plan and paid campaigns on social media for your business. We focused specifically on how the HubSpot ads tool can help you be more effective and efficient in managing and implementing your paid ad campaigns. Remember to start with connecting your accounts to HubSpot, create an audience, create the campaigns (A/B tests), and, of course, analyze the information to ensure you get the highest possible returns on your investment.

In the next chapter, you'll understand the value of implementing live chat as well as a chatbot on your website and learn how easy it is to set up these features using HubSpot—no coding necessary!

Questions

To help you remember some key concepts and tips discussed in this chapter, here are a few review questions to consider:

1. Which permission levels are necessary to connect an ad account to HubSpot?

2. Can you connect a Google Ad Manager account to HubSpot?

3. What must be the audience size when creating an audience in HubSpot to push to LinkedIn?

Further reading

- *The Ultimate Guide to PPC Marketing*: https://blog.hubspot.com/marketing/ppc

- *How to Generate Quality Leads From Your PPC Campaigns*: https://blog.hubspot.com/marketing/9-strategies-to-improve-lead-quality-b2b-ppc-campaigns

- *How to Perfectly Manage a PPC Campaign [Template]*: https://blog.hubspot.com/blog/tabid/6307/bid/33882/how-even-you-can-master-ppc-campaign-management-template.aspx

8
Conducting a Portal Audit

If you are a current customer of HubSpot, by now, you must have realized there is a whole lot more you can do with your portal than sending emails. Although HubSpot initially began as a marketing automation tool, today, it is described as a CRM platform with complete marketing, sales, and service capabilities. Its goal is to help small, medium, and enterprise companies scale efforts and reach revenue targets. The problem is that even though most companies may have the correct licenses, they aren't utilizing all the functionalities within their respective portals.

On the other hand, some companies may fully utilize the various tools in their portal. Still, maintaining the data or generally keeping the CRM clean isn't optimal. For this reason, it is recommended to at least do a portal audit every 6 months or so to identify any issues and perform the cleanup necessary to get proper reports and insights.

Remember the rule of thumb for good data hygiene – garbage in, garbage out. And the most effective way to measure if your portal is optimized is to check if you can rely on the reports that have been generated. If you still have to depend on Excel sheets for your reports, you need to consider doing a portal audit.

In this chapter, we will cover the following topics:

- Identifying issues in your HubSpot portal
- Step 1 – Implementing structure and order in your portal
- Step 2 – Mapping your customer journey
- Step 3 – Performing a technical audit
- Step 4 – Conducting an audit for your Marketing Hub
- Step 5 – Conducting an audit for your Sales Hub portal
- Step 6 – Prioritizing which problems to fix first

Note that the goal of this chapter is not to get you to use all the functions available just for the sake of using them. Instead, this chapter aims to highlight some of the options that may already exist in your portal that you may not be fully utilizing and can help you achieve some of your business goals.

To make this chapter most relevant, we will focus on the HubSpot Professional and HubSpot Enterprise licenses.

Let's get to it!

Identifying issues in your HubSpot portal

Like most things in life, you often don't know you have a problem until something disastrous happens. HubSpot users are often anxious to begin using the platform and prove a **return on investment (ROI)**, as discussed in *Chapter 2, Generating Quick Wins With HubSpot in 30 Days*, so that they can justify the budget they asked from CEOs to get the platform. This means they often don't take time to plan how they will organize the portal and optimize the tools at their disposal.

Therefore, some of the most common issues customers face after using HubSpot for some time without proper planning are as follows:

- They can't find or understand anything in your portal. If you find yourself with too many lists or workflows and don't remember why they were created or can't understand the reason why they were created, this means you did not maintain a proper log of your assets. Even if you find yourself scrambling to find the last email you sent out, or the last landing page you created for a webinar 3 months ago so you can clone it for the next upcoming event, this is a clear sign that you need to consider better naming conventions for your assets.

- They're sending the wrong emails to the wrong contacts. This is a sign your database hasn't been segmented correctly.

- Your leads haven't been entered correctly in your CRM from your website or campaigns. You may have an issue with your technical setup.

- Them not being able to rely on the reports. This is often a sign that the data hasn't been captured correctly in the right properties.

- They don't understand the contacts in your database and their status. This signals a lack of understanding of effectively using lead status stages and/or life cycle stages.

- Your email deliverability and open rates are below the industry average. This highlights an opportunity for better segmentation and even personalization.

- Your sales managers are still running their reports and team meetings primarily using Excel. This indicates a low adoption rate of CRM among sales reps.

- Your marketing, sales, and service teams still have too many meetings to get updates on leads. This shows that the leads are not updated in the CRM and that there is no clear handover process within the departments.

- Your management team is asking for daily updates on the status of potential leads and customers. The reports aren't making sense to them.

- You are considering adding more platforms to your MarTech stack, but not sure if they integrate with HubSpot or even if it's necessary. This signals the need to revisit the tools HubSpot offers and look at their integration app list to check how easy it would be to use this new tool with HubSpot.

…and the list can go on and on. However, now that we understand the nature of the symptoms, let's explore the cure.

Step 1 – implementing structure and order in your portal

Similar to a financial audit, the goal of a portal audit is to go over every detail of your portal to understand where the gaps may exist. The following are a few scenarios that you can begin with when performing a HubSpot portal audit:

- **Access to platform**: Double-check who currently has access to the platform and what level of access they have. This is a great time to review all the users on your platform and make sure you understand who everyone is, their role, and how they are expected to use HubSpot to determine their level of access. For instance, do all the people with super admin access need such access? This access generally gives such users the ability to edit, delete, and view everything and anything about your portal. One of the most crucial things they can do is delete everything in your portal and not note that deleted items can't be recovered. So, you will want to pay special attention to who has super admin access. Another group of people you may want to pay attention to is your external vendors. Sometimes, a web developer has access to your portal to help build out some customized landing pages or website pages for your brand. Although they do need access to the development tools within HubSpot, they do not need access to your contacts' data. So, ensuring that their visibility is set to **View** – None, **Edit** – None, and **Delete** – None will safeguard your data.

- **Naming conventions**: An important aspect of maintaining your portal's cleanliness is being able to establish naming conventions to quickly identify your assets. One suggestion for structuring such a naming convention is `Type of Campaign |MM/YY|Name of asset`. So, for example, `Nurture Campaign|08/22 |Email 1` or `Webinar Campaign|May 2022|Invitation Email` or `Customers List|2022`.

- **Folder structure**: Another system that helps keep your items organized is folders. Most assets in HubSpot can be grouped into folders. For example, lists, files, emails, and workflows can all be organized into folders, which should follow a similar pattern as your naming convention.

Step 2 – mapping your customer journey

Now that you have implemented some form of structure in your portal, the next step is to map out the customer journey that a contact typically follows in your business to become a customer. This is often overlooked but is critical as, by now, you would realize that after using your portal for some time, you have a variety of contacts in your system, and you aren't always sure how to deal with them.

At this stage, we recommend that you have a plan for the five scenarios most contacts will typically encounter in your business:

- **Entry path**: In this scenario, you want to make sure you have defined a process for how new leads are treated. For example, you may want to consider what their lead status and life cycle stage should be. Most times, these fields would be updated to **Lead status** - New and **Lifecycle stage** – Subscriber (if they simply filled out their email to subscribe to your newsletter) or Lead (if they filled out a form to download a piece of content).

- **Success path**: As outlined previously, the goal is to make most of the contacts in your database customers if they are relevant to your business. So, you would want to map out various paths a contact could take to move along the journey of becoming a customer. For example, you may need to consider what will move a contact from a lead to a **marketing qualified lead** (**MQL**). Is it when they download a specific type of content that is more middle of the funnel, such as a white paper and not just a checklist? Or is it when they sign up for a webinar and give their company emails and do not use generic email systems such as Gmail or Yahoo? And then what will make them a **sales-qualified lead** (**SQL**)? Must they fill out a form to request a demo or ask to speak to a salesperson through the contact us form? Or would it be sufficient that they satisfy all the criteria that identify them as an ideal client? Such criteria include the right job title, right company size, right country, and whether they've visited more than three website pages and attended one webinar. Does this make them a SQL and can you hand them over to sales for a follow-up? Whatever your decision, these paths must be mapped out and built into the system using workflows.

- **Fast track path**: You then need to consider how *hot leads* are treated. These include contacts who came to your website and immediately requested a demo. They could also be people who spent a lot of time combing through your website, visiting multiple pages. For these types of leads, you will want to consider how to notify sales immediately by email or text to let them know these are "hot" leads and should be treated with priority. As discussed in *Chapter 13*, *Leveraging the Benefits of the Marketing Flywheel*, you may consider using a specific lead status and life cycle stage combination such as **New | MQL** so that the sales team will prioritize these contacts over other leads that may have come in on that day.

- **Dead end path**: The reality is that not all contacts that come into your CRM are relevant. Oftentimes, this happens when research students come across your ebook and download it. Even your competitors may be interested in taking a sneak peek at your content. So, how you prevent these leads from reaching your sales teams is another factor you must consider. To manage such leads, you can build a workflow that has enrollment triggers. For example, if the job title is student, professor, unemployed, or any of the gibberish you sometimes see people enter into your forms, then set this contact with a lead status of *unqualified*. Note that sometimes, these contacts' life cycle stages may have already progressed because they took a specific action, such as requesting a demo, and you may have a previous workflow that set them a SQL. It's okay that their life cycle stage is advanced because you want to track how many contacts reached these stages only to be deemed unqualified. This would help inform you of the gaps in your campaigns so that you can tighten the reins there.

- **Recycled path**: In this case, some leads may have reached out to the sales teams and had several discussions, but they were not ready to buy yet. These leads should be returned to the marketing team so that they can be nurtured accordingly until they are ready to buy. Even contacts that were active opportunities, but eventually turned out to be lost sales, should be identified so that marketing can also help nurture them. One way to build this recycled path is to place a condition in the deal stages for the sales reps to choose a reason when the *Closed lost* deal stage is chosen. For example, the stages could be competitor, budget, project postponed, missing feature, price, champion left, no longer relevant, and other. Then, depending on the reason, the marketing team would have predefined sales nurtures set up that would automatically enroll these contacts to the respective nurtures. This could keep your business in the contact's mind for when your product or service becomes relevant to them again.

Taking the time to map out these five possible paths that contacts can take when entering your database will help you set up more successful campaigns as you will have a better understanding of the contacts in your database.

Next, let's look at the most important technical things you must check in your portal as you conduct your audit.

Step 3 – performing a technical audit

As we described in *Chapter 1, Overview of HubSpot – What You MUST Know*, several technical aspects are needed when you're setting up your portal for the first time. This includes connecting your domain, connecting your website, connecting your social media account as well as your paid ad accounts, and even setting up all your branding assets such as logos, brand colors, and more. If you need further tips on how to do this correctly, I suggest that you revisit *Chapter 1, Overview of HubSpot – What You Must Know*. In this section, we will focus on how to audit the most critical aspects of your technical setup, which are as follows:

- Checking that your domains are connected
- Checking that your website is connected (especially if you rebranded recently)
- Checking that your branding has been updated in the correct places
- Checking that the pages that allow your subscribed contacts to unsubscribe are working correctly
- Checking that your social media and paid ads channels are connected

Let's learn how to perform an audit on each of these elements and fix them at the same time.

Are your domains connected?

The first thing you must double-check is whether your domains are connected. Your domains are the URLs where your company website sits, as well as where your company emails are based. Connecting your domains to HubSpot is critical if you wish to host your content on HubSpot. For example, you should build your blog or landing pages where the URLs will be branded with your company domain name, not HubSpot's. You can do the same if you wish to send emails from HubSpot using your company email addresses.

So, if you are having difficulty with any of these things, follow these steps:

1. Go to **Settings** at the top right-hand corner of your portal.
2. Scroll down on the left-hand side menu and choose **Website | Domains and URLs**.

Once you're there, you should see green dots on the various domains you've connected, such **Blog** and **Landing pages**. You can always connect additional domains if you want to create additional sub-domains to host specific types of content, such as events:

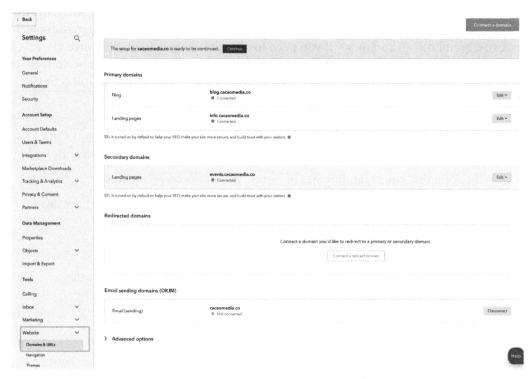

Figure 8.1 – Connecting your domains to HubSpot

3. Note that if you do not see a green dot on one of your supposedly connected domains, such as what's shown in the preceding screenshot, then you will need to reconnect this domain. To do this, you must have super admin access to your HubSpot portal and access to the platform where you purchased the domain, such as GoDaddy, 123reg, or something else. You may need to work with your IT administrator to get this access.

4. Once you've gained the relevant access, simply click **Continue** on the blue banner that appears at the top of the page and complete the steps that follow.

Again, if you get stuck, we have outlined step-by-step instructions in *Chapter 1, Overview of HubSpot – What You MUST Know*, so feel free to revisit this content.

Is your website connected to HubSpot?

You likely completed this step while updating your portal for the first time, but sometimes, this is often overlooked in a rebranding exercise. It is often only much later, when leads don't come into the CRM, that you notice there is a problem. But how do you know if there is a problem? There are two telltale signs in your portal.

First, you can check the **Traffic Analytics** report by going to **Reports | Analytics Tools | Traffic Analytics** to see if there has been any data for the last few days. If you see no traffic over a period, but there has been traffic before, it means there might be a problem with the connection. The following screenshot shows an example of this type of report:

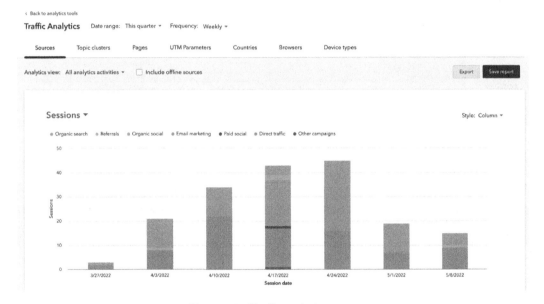

Figure 8.2 – Traffic analytics report

Another health check to do is to fill out a few forms on your website and see if the data is coming into your CRM. If you see the information, then everything's fine. You can also go to **Marketing | Lead Capture | Forms** to see if the website forms appear there.

Note that if you have not changed the forms on your website to HubSpot forms yet and your site is built on WordPress and using gravity forms, you will typically see your forms listed as #gform_1, #gform_2, and so on.

Checking your branding

In HubSpot, there are two places you can update your brand assets.

First, you can go to **Settings | Account Defaults | Branding | My brand kit**, as shown in the following screenshot. You can update this brand kit to choose these options and create public-facing content such as emails:

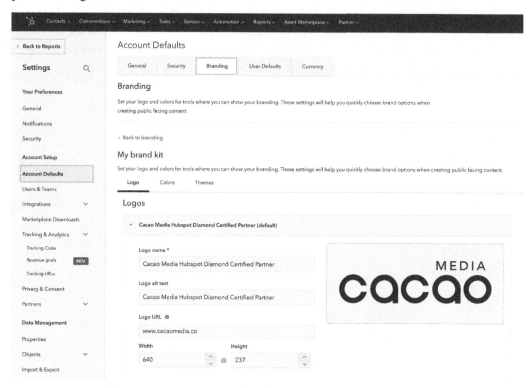

Figure 8.3 – Setting up your brand assets for public-facing content

You can also update your branding by going to **Settings | Website | Pages | Branding**, as shown in the following screenshot. This is where you update your logo for your pages such as blogs, landing pages, and unsubscribe pages. By default, when you do update your logo here, the size is usually 2,500 x 500 px. Therefore, you will need to adjust it to something more reasonable, such as 640 x 237 px, so that it doesn't take over the entire page when loaded. I'm sure that if you click the unsubscribe button in your emails, you will be surprised to see that your logo is very large here. So, this is the place to fix it:

Figure 8.4 – Setting up brand assets for pages in HubSpot

This brings us to the next most overlooked setup in HubSpot – unsubscribe pages.

Checking your unsubscribe pages

One of the most overlooked but easiest points of reconversion is the unsubscribe page. By law, every marketing email that's sent out must have an unsubscribe button. By default, HubSpot has already added this button to your marketing emails. But you may want to make some adjustments when you see this page.

To access this page, go to **Settings**. Then, via the left-hand menu, scroll down to **Marketing | Email | Subscriptions**, as shown in the following screenshot. Once there, you will see three options:

- **Subscription preference pages**: This page allows users to decide which of your subscription types they wish to stay subscribed to or unsubscribe from.

- **Subscription update confirmation page**: This page confirms to the unsubscriber that they have successfully unsubscribed from your emails.

- **Unknown contact submission preferences**: This page is the first page that contacts who wish to unsubscribe will see when they click on the unsubscribe button. It will prompt them to enter their email addresses so that they can be unsubscribed.

These options can be seen in the following screenshot:

Figure 8.5 – Subscription pages in HubSpot

You can customize and rebuild these pages by clicking **Edit Page**. This will take you to HubSpot's CSS platform. However, if you aren't into coding, feel free to ask your designer to create a design that's on brand and then have a developer develop it for you.

Checking your social media and paid ads connection

The last thing I would suggest that is critical to check are your connections with your social media channels and paid ads channels. As part of their privacy policies, most social media channels' integration with third-party tools expire. Sometimes, they expire every 3 months or every year or at their discretion. So, you will want to double-check that all the respective social media channels and paid channels are connected:

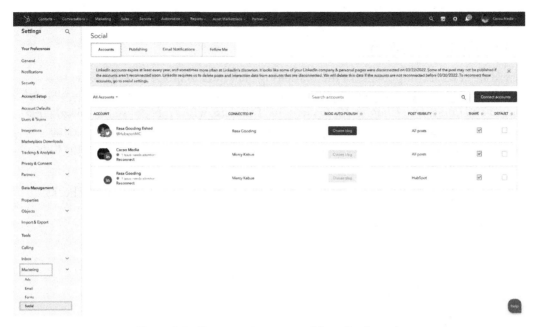

Figure 8.6 – Reconnecting your social media channels

To check if any of your channels are disconnected, go to **Settings**. Then, via the left-hand side menu, scroll down to **Marketing | Social** and click on **Accounts**.

As shown in the preceding screenshot, you will see which accounts need attention; then, you can click the **Reconnect** button. As always, you will need to have super admin access to HubSpot and be an admin on the social media channels you are trying to connect.

Now that you have the most critical technical elements of HubSpot set up, the next step is to carefully do a marketing and sales audit and then identify which actions you should prioritize to fix.

Step 4 – conducting an audit for your Marketing Hub

There are several components of the Marketing Hub in HubSpot. For a detailed description of how to use them, you can explore *Chapter 6, Geting Known through Social Media on HubSpot,* to *Chapter 10, Revive your Database with HubSpot's Email Marketing Tools.* In this section, we will focus on the most common and important aspects that should be checked for every HubSpot portal, regardless of the types of campaigns they are running.

When performing a marketing audit, there are five critical elements you must check:

- Contact fields and segmentation
- Lead source
- Email campaigns
- Lead management
- Reporting

There are, of course, many more items to check, such as landing page optimization, forms, tracking URLs, and much more. But for now, let's take a look at what it takes to ensure these five elements are running properly in your portal.

Contact fields and segmentation

This part of the audit involves checking what percentage of your contacts have the fields filled out that you have deemed critical for understanding your database. For instance, every contact in your database should have a valid email address. To check this, you must create an active list with the **Email address is unknown**, **Email hard bounced reason is known**, **Unsubscribed email is equal to True**, or **Opted out of all email marketing information is known** filters. This can be seen in the following screenshot.

If you take this number and divide it by the total number of contacts in your database, then multiply it by 100, you will get the percentage of the invalid entries in the database:

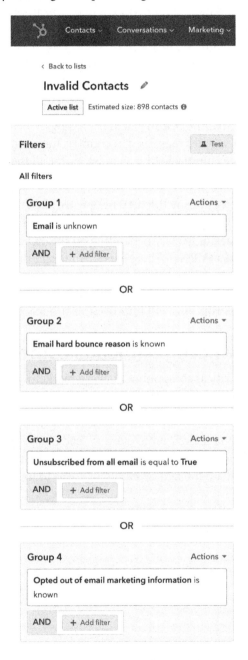

Figure 8.7 – Filters for building a list to check for invalid contacts in your database

You should repeat this process to understand how many contacts don't have job titles, whether the country is unknown, or any other criteria necessary for you to understand who is who in your contact database. Generally, having this information helps you understand how to segment your database to send them relevant information or enroll them into specific nurture content. During your audit, you will find out which fields are lacking information, so you could decide on tighter restrictions or implement additional workflows or integrations with platforms such as Zoominfo to fill in any missing contact information.

For example, if you notice that the country field is missing, which is necessary to assign the contacts to the respective sales reps for that country, then you have a few options. The first is to make sure that the country field is mandatory for all the forms on your website and campaigns.

You can also build workflows to copy the **internet protocol** (**IP**) country to the country field, as the IP country is always automatically captured when a contact submits your form. However, the drawback of heavily depending on this field is that some companies use **virtual private networks** (**VPNs**). This helps them falsify their location to protect their network. So, if it is a much-needed field to ensure your sales reps follow up on qualified leads and you notice that it is generally missing during the audit, then implementing either of these options will improve this process going forward.

Understanding where your leads come from

The lead source is often a critical component in every marketing strategy. It helps marketers understand which channels bring the best leads so that they can increase the resources toward that channel and optimize lead generation.

HubSpot automatically captures the source of every lead in a property called **Original Source**. This field cannot be updated and captures the first channel that brought a lead to you. The seven sources that are tracked by HubSpot are as follows:

- **Organic search**
- **Direct traffic**
- **Organic social**
- **Paid social**
- **Referrals**

- **Email marketing**

- **Other campaigns**

- **Offline sources**

You can see these sources when you go to **Reports | Analytics Tools | Traffic Analytics** and scroll down a bit until you see the table shown in the following screenshot. Remember that if you don't see any information here, you may want to check if your website is connected to HubSpot properly:

	SOURCE	SESSIONS	SESSION TO CONTACT RATE	NEW CONTACTS	CONTACT TO CUSTOMER RATE	CUSTOMERS	BOUNCE RATE	SESSION LENGTH
✓	Direct traffic	9,934	2.91%	289	11.07%	32	67.66%	2.6 minutes
✓	Organic search	8,316	0.82%	68	11.76%	8	81.29%	49 seconds
✓	Paid social	7,369	8.47%	624	0.16%	1	79.12%	26 seconds
✓	Referrals	1,780	4.49%	80	1.25%	1	55.84%	124 seconds
✓	Organic social	1,373	7.5%	103	2.91%	3	71.38%	59 seconds
✓	Email marketing	1,143	3.24%	37	5.41%	2	53.54%	61 seconds
✓	Other campaigns	193	0%	-	0%	-	91.71%	7 seconds
✓	Paid search	1	0%	-	0%	-	0%	37 seconds
✓	Offline sources	-	0%	2,977	10.51%	313	0%	-
	Report Total	**30,109**	**13.88%**	**4,178**	**8.62%**	**360**	**73.31%**	**84 seconds**

Figure 8.8 – Sources of traffic

Notice that the source that often brings the most contacts and customers is **Offline sources**, and this can mean many things. Offline sources capture leads that are manually created in the system, uploaded via an Excel spreadsheet, or created via integrations such as email integration, or with any other tool that's integrated with HubSpot. Therefore, it is often necessary to break down this source so that you can understand where these leads come from. One way to do this is to build a custom lead source that itemizes the major buckets where leads are generally coming from, then build workflows that will associate these various lead sources with your custom lead source.

Auditing your email campaigns

When it comes to your email campaigns, the quickest way to audit your activities is to check your email health in your portal. To access this feature, navigate to **Marketing | Email** and click on the **Health** option:

Figure 8.9 – Email health summary

This tool gives you an email health summary and a breakdown of how your emails are performing on average. It looks closely at your open rate, click-through rate, hard bounce rate, unsubscribe rate, and spam report rate compared to your chosen industry average. Clicking on **See details** for any of the options for email health breakdown gives you further details and suggestions on how to improve any email-related metric that is underperforming against the industry's benchmarks.

Besides these typical benchmarks, you will also want to consider if there are any emails you should be denylisting. Or, more importantly, how to manage the burnout rate of contacts so that they don't get too many emails from you. Another factor to consider is which contacts should be enrolled or unenrolled from nurtures when they no longer fit the criteria.

These are all things you should consider when performing an audit on your email operations. However, should you need further resources on this, feel free to review *Chapter 10, Revive your Database with the HubSpot's Email Marketing Tools.*

Effective lead management

Lead management is one of the primary reasons marketers often choose HubSpot. Using the workflow tool, leads can be managed quickly, getting them to the right people at the right time. Some of the most common issues you should be checking for when auditing your portal for effective lead management are as follows:

- **Setting lead owners for new contacts**: Are your contacts assigned to a contact owner? As contacts come into the database, they should be assigned to the relevant person, depending on the path that was previously defined in your strategic planning.

- **Qualifying leads**: Do you clearly understand which leads are qualified and are ready to talk to your sales team? Using properties such as lead status and life cycle stages is a good way to highlight which contacts are qualified.

- **Handover from marketing to sales**: Is there a clear handover process between marketing and sales so that the sales reps know exactly which leads they are now accountable for? With lead scoring, as will be discussed in detail in *Chapter 9, Converting Your Visitors to Customers*, marketing teams can implement a method to qualify leads automatically and hand them off to sales to begin working on them.

- **Onboarding new customers**: Does your team have a clear handover process to the finance team and customer success team for new customers so that the entire onboarding process for new customers runs smoothly? If there are still gaps in this process, you may want to consider automating some of these handoffs. For example, it may help speed up the onboarding process if, from the moment a customer signs their agreement, an automated email is sent to customer success teams and finance, informing them that a new customer just signed up so that they can begin the onboarding process.

- **Reporting gaps**: Reporting is usually the place in your audit where you see all the problems in your portal because, usually, either your reports make very little sense or you simply cannot rely on the data. *Chapter 11, Proving That Your Efforts Worked Using These Reports*, provides an in-depth overview of how to build reports. But you must remember that even though you may be able to build the report, it is still dependent on the data in the system. So, ensuring all the previous steps are optimized as best as possible will make your reports more reliable.

Now that you understand how to conduct a marketing audit on your portal and fix the crucial issues, let's look at how to do a sales audit and fix some of those issues at hand.

Step 5 – conducting an audit for your Sales Hub portal

As you know by now, you have the option to choose which HubSpot hubs you will use within your company. At the time of writing, HubSpot has five hubs, including the CRM – Marketing, Sales, Service, CMS, and Operations. Most companies use one of the hubs individually or some together. In this section, we will focus on Sales Hub Professional and how to perform an audit on this part of your portal if you've been using it for some time.

Remember that the goal of the audit is to be aware of the gaps that may exist in your processes or data so that they can be fixed for your portal to produce reliable reports. Your CRM system should be your single source of truth for your business and this can only happen if the data in the platform is being maintained.

Sales Hub is meant to be used in close conjunction with the CRM so that it can help your sales team convert qualified prospects into paying customers. Therefore, there are a few crucial elements you will want to pay attention to, to ensure you have correctly implemented and optimized your Sales Hub instance. Some of the features we will pay attention to are as follows:

- Custom fields
- Deal pipeline and stages
- Sales tools such as connected inbox, meetings, templates, sequences, and more

Let's take a look at what symptoms these features exhibit to indicate that there is room for improvement.

Custom fields

Similar to Marketing Hub, you can create specific fields related to your sales process. However, sometimes, when setting up a portal – in the first instance or even using it over time – duplicate fields tend to be created as new users are added to the system, and time isn't taken to check what was created before. For example, when you examine the list of properties that have been created, you may see several properties for the *Country* field. This happens because, in the first instance of setting up the portal, the *Country* field was single-line text and once data was imported, the field became uneditable. So, later on, when the field was used to create a form, another property for *Country* was created to make the field a list of dropdown options so that users couldn't fill in whatever they wished. Instead, they have a list of options to choose from. Cases like these are often the root cause of problems in reporting, so you need to double-check how your fields are constructed.

Another problem with fields built for sales teams is that the field needs to be built in the **Deal properties** object, not **Contact properties** if they are to be used in **Pipelines** or specific sales reports. If the field needs to be used across contacts and pipeline properties, it would need to be duplicated, and in this case, you will need to use workflows to keep the fields updated on both object properties.

Now that you understand what to pay attention to, let's look at the deal pipeline and stages and some of the problems that may exist there.

Deal pipeline and stages

The most common issue that occurs across most portals is how the deal stages were set up in the first place. Often, when HubSpot was first set up, the deal stages were not set up as action-oriented stages that objectively signal what the potential buyer had done. Therefore, there are often stages in the pipeline that may say *Follow up* or *Unqualified*, which should either be action items or state why the deal was closed.

Remember that the deal stages in the pipeline should reflect the exact stage a prospect is at to give you an idea of how many more steps are needed to close that deal. If you need to ask your sales rep what it means when a prospect is in that stage, then you don't have a clear pipeline. You can read more about best practices when setting up your pipeline in *Chapter 3, Using HubSpot for Managing Sales Processes Effectively.*

Your audit process is also a good time to revisit any improvements or changes that may be needed to the initial setup of your pipeline with your sales managers. Another common scenario that you will often come across is how to get the sales teams to input critical data on an opportunity they are working on. For example, most sales managers need to know the date a **Proof of Concept** (**PoC**) or pilot project started, so they will need that field to be populated each time an opportunity is moved to the PoC/pilot stage. To ensure sales reps fill this out, a condition can be set up in the pipeline to make these prompts appear each time a deal is moved to a different stage. This ensures that the sales reps are reminded to populate it.

To set up this feature, follow these steps:

1. Go to **Settings**, then scroll through the left menu to **Objects** | **Deals**.
2. A new page will appear. Click on **Pipelines** via the top menu bar, select the relevant pipeline, and then hover over the stage you wish to add a condition to.

3. Then, select **Edit properties** and choose the field you wish to populate. You must have created the field as a deal property first to select it from this list:

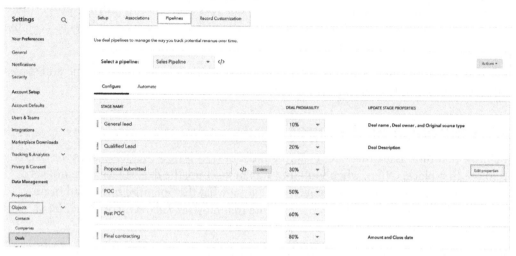

Figure 8.10 – Edit properties

So, this is one way HubSpot helps you optimize sales experience and get the reps to enter more data about the current opportunities they are working on. It is important to highlight that this feature is available to everyone, but only Sales Professional account users can make it mandatory. For free users, this feature is optional.

Next, let's look at the sales tools that are available – and that most users don't even know exist in their portals for free – and should be used regularly.

Sales tools

Sometimes, HubSpot users aren't aware of all the free tools that are available within their portal that can optimize the way sales reps work. In *Chapter 5, Increasing Online Visibility Using HubSpot's SEO Tool*, we discussed all of these tools thoroughly, so I suggest going back to that chapter for a refresher. But for now, we will focus on a few tools that we think are critical:

*   **Connected inbox**: If your sales teams have not done this yet, you must get them to do this. This free tool, which is available to all levels of HubSpot customers, will give you insights into what kind of communication your sales reps are having with prospects and the questions that are being received. This information can be useful to marketers as it provides the content that's needed for playbooks or sales presentations for the sales teams. Of course, do this within the legal restrictions under which your business operates.

- **Templates**: This is another free tool that allows your team to share best practices of emails that work to get prospects to book meetings or move forward in the deal. It allows other teammates to copy the text straight into their email inboxes.

- **Sequences**: This is automation for sales reps as it can allow your sales reps to send out a series of emails to prospects until they take action. It is only available to sales professional users, but it can save a lot of time chasing customers for a follow-up after that demo call, or after you've sent a contract.

- **Meetings**: This free tool allows you to create a meeting link where users can see your availability and book time with you directly.

- **Calling**: You can call prospects directly from your laptop or phone and record the call in your portal so that other sales reps can hear the best practices of that call.

- **Call transcriptions**: Previously, this was a tool that was only accessible to sales enterprise users, but HubSpot has now made it available to Sales Professional users so that they can transcribe calls. This can often be of great help to sales teams and marketers as they can repurpose text to improve sales training or collateral.

This is just the tip of the iceberg of the sales tools that are available within HubSpot (at the time of writing), but I would suggest that you at least start with these in your audit to ensure your sales teams are using them correctly.

Now that you have performed a detailed analysis of your portal and found areas of improvement, you may be overwhelmed with how many things you need to do. But, where should you begin? We will outline a few tips to help you get started in the next section.

Step 6 – prioritizing which problems to fix first

There is nothing scarier than a to-do list. This is why we suggest using this formula to decide which of the tasks from your portal audit are urgent, important, and nice to have. But how do you decide which tasks fit into each of these categories? The rule of thumb is to start by asking yourself which tasks will get your flywheel spinning faster (more on that in *Chapter 13, Leveraging the Benefits of the Marketing Flywheel*), but to simplify it, these are some of the questions you will need to answer:

- Which tasks, if done, will improve customer experience significantly?

- Which tasks, if done, will reduce the stress on the sales teams and make them more efficient?

- Which tasks can be done in a short amount of time and produce quick wins for our customers and internal team?

- Which tasks will take longer and maybe need additional resources but will make our lives easier?

Once you have understood the answers to these questions, you can begin tackling your lists accordingly. Remember, the goal is not to fix everything at once or to get your portal at 100% capacity. But being able to move the needle a bit so that you are 10% or 20% better off than where you were pre-audit can make a huge difference.

Summary

Conducting a portal audit can seem to be a monumental task that requires significant experience to complete. Although you must have some experience in HubSpot and understand your functions as a marketer or sales rep, you can still perform at least some of the actions described in this chapter without being an expert.

The goal of the audit is not to focus on finding what's wrong but instead to find places where there are inefficiencies or where things could be done better and made easier. Always remember that the goal when working with any CRM platform is to measure if this platform is meeting the needs of your company and customers or providing more friction.

If you are in doubt about performing the audit yourself, or you would simply prefer to hire an expert, you can always work with one of the many HubSpot partners that exist within the ecosystem. Many of them offer portal audits as part of their services. In the next chapter, you'll master how to create landing pages, forms, and workflow strategies and how to nurture programs to engage with their leads and customers.

Questions

Let's now see whether the concepts in this chapter have resonated with you:

1. Why is it important to do a portal audit?

2. If leads are not coming from your website to your HubSpot portal, what should you check?

3. If you cannot generate reliable reports from your portal, what should you focus on fixing?

Further reading

To learn more about the topics that were covered in this chapter, take a look at the following resources:

- *How to audit your HubSpot Portal*: `https://events.hubspot.com/events/details/hubspot-madison-presents-how-to-audit-your-hubspot-portal/`

- *HubSpot Partner Directory*: `https://ecosystem.hubspot.com/marketplace/solutions`

9
Converting Your Visitors to Customers

Running a successful business involves not only being able to attract new visitors but also the ability to convert these visitors into meaningful business opportunities and, eventually, customers. The concept of **inbound marketing** was built on this premise. This enables you to connect with potential customers and prospects, and then eventually convert them to paying customers by giving them relevant and valuable content to inform their decision.

HubSpot is designed to help you reach your potential customers, build meaningful relationships with them as they become relevant opportunities, and then turn them into a customer and—eventually—your biggest promoters. It has several tools—for example, smart content, emails, and workflows—to help you achieve this.

In this chapter, we'll show you how to use HubSpot to create lasting relationships with prospects and customers through email nurture plans and workflows. We will also explore the use of conversion tools such as **calls to action** (**CTAs**), forms, and lead flows to capture the information of prospects visiting your site.

We'll cover the following topics in detail:

- Creating forms and using their features
- Creating a landing page in HubSpot
- Building lead-nurturing workflows

By the end of this chapter, you will have learned how to use HubSpot's conversion tools to personalize your communication with prospects and increase the number of qualified contacts handed over to sales.

Technical requirements

To get the most out of this chapter, you will need the following:

- A HubSpot Marketing Professional account
- Super admin access to your HubSpot portal

Creating forms and using their features

Forms are a critical part of any marketer's strategy as they are the most popular way to capture a lead's details. Every website page, campaign, and social media ad eventually leads the prospect to give you their details using a form. Therefore, the more control you have over adjusting fields or optimizing the **user experience** (**UX**) when filling out a form, the higher the likelihood of capturing more contacts. Remember—the goal is to make filling out forms as painless as possible and to ask the right questions at the right time. It is often said that filling out a form is like going on a first date. There are some questions you ask on a first date and others you leave for second or future dates.

Unlike regular website forms, using HubSpot forms for your website and campaigns allows you to capture vital information without making the user feel overwhelmed at having to fill out too many fields. Here are five features of HubSpot forms that can help you convert more leads:

- **Choose from a variety of forms**: From website forms to standalone forms, exit pop-up forms, or slide-in forms, HubSpot allows you to create any type of form, without coding, to increase the chances of capturing a visitor's information.

- **Add custom fields**: You can choose to add any fields or questions to forms.

- **Optimize your form experience with dependent fields or progressive fields**: This feature allows you to decrease the length of your form by keeping certain questions hidden until a user has answered previous questions.

- **Ensure data privacy with built-in General Data Protection Regulation (GDPR) text**: Stay compliant with this feature by explicitly showing visitors how their information will be stored and used when filling out a form.

- **Continue the conversation by sending a follow-up email**: As most form submissions require some way to follow up, you can build a follow-up email within the **Forms** tool if needed.

In the following sections, we will explain in depth how to use each of these features, but first, let's understand how to access the **Forms** tool in HubSpot.

To access forms in HubSpot, go to **Marketing | Lead Capture | Forms**, as shown in the following screenshot:

Figure 9.1 – Accessing the Forms tool in HubSpot

Now, we can look at the five features of the HubSpot **Forms** tool.

Choosing your form type

By clicking **Create Form** on the top right, you will soon arrive at a dialog box showing six different types of forms you can create within HubSpot, as illustrated in the following screenshot:

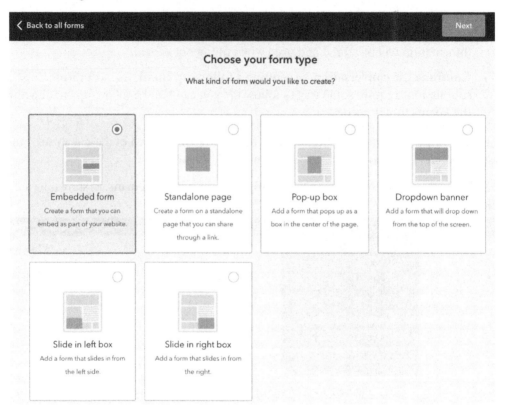

Figure 9.2 – Types of forms in HubSpot

The types of forms you can choose are explained as follows:

- **Embedded form**: These are forms you would typically use on your website or a landing page.

- **Standalone page**: These are forms you would like to use just as a form without any additional text or design around it. Think of it as **Google Forms** when you just want people to fill out the information.

- **Pop-up box**: These are for exit forms that can be placed on the site when someone is leaving your website.

- **Dropdown banner**: These are forms that are placed on the top of your website or landing page to make a specific announcement or lead to another place.

- **Slide in left box**: These are forms that can be placed on a specific page and slide in from the left so that they can prompt the visitor to click and be redirected to another place on your site. This technique is often used on blog pages so that users can then download a higher-converting asset such as an e-book or a case study.

- **Slide in right box**: This is very similar to the **Slide in left box** form type just described, with the only difference being that it slides in from the right.

In *Chapter 2, Generating Quick Wins with Hubspot in the First 30 Days*, we explained how to use **Pop-up box** as a quick win to convert more leads. **Slide in left box** and **Slide in right box** are relatively new features released by HubSpot. They are like a pop-up form and can be used as a quick-win technique as well to improve conversions. So, in this chapter, we will focus on how to optimize the use of the **Embedded form** and **Standalone page** forms. They both operate the same way; technically, only their use cases are different.

Once you click on **Embedded form** and **Next**, you will then be taken to another page that prompts you to select a template, as shown in the following screenshot:

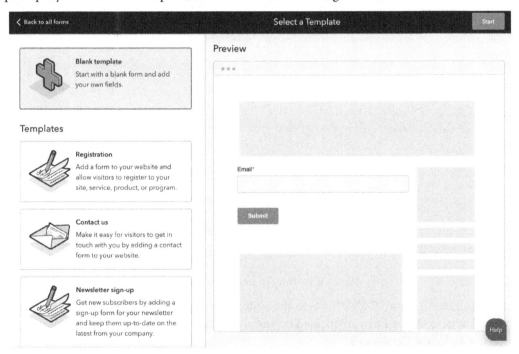

Figure 9.3 – Selecting a template for your forms

HubSpot offers some pre-made templates to help you decide on the most important fields for the various types of forms you might be considering. Choosing any of them can also be a great start in creating your form. In this example, however, we will begin by clicking on **Blank template** and then **Start**.

Adding fields to a form

You will notice once you arrive at the next page that **Email** is already a mandatory field in the form. This is because it is the minimum information you will need to collect about a contact. Also, as HubSpot is an inbound platform mostly focused on online communication, it only uses email to identify a unique contact and not something else, such as a phone number.

Now, let's say we are creating a webinar form for an upcoming webinar event. The first step is to consider the minimum information you would need to collect from a contact registering for it. Besides email, you may want to consider **First Name** and **Last Name** fields, and if you aren't insisting on a company email address, then you may want to add a **Company Name** field.

So, let's first see how to add these fields. Have a look at the following screenshot:

Figure 9.4 – Understanding form fields

As you can see in *Figure 9.4*, all fields in the system are on the left-hand side, while fields that will appear on the form are located on the right side. To add a field to the right side, you need to follow these steps:

1. Search for the name of the field using the search bar on the top left.

2. Click on the field you want to choose. It will then appear on the right side.

3. Rearrange the fields in the order you want them to appear on the form. You can see an illustration of this in the following screenshot:

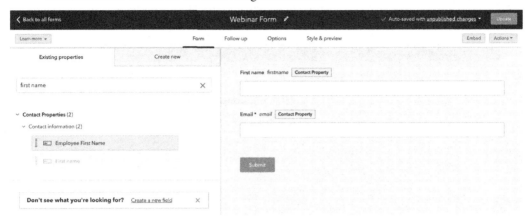

Figure 9.5 – Building fields in a form

Should you wish to add more fields to your form that do not exist in the list of options, click on **Create new** on the top left-hand side of the screen, as illustrated in the following screenshot:

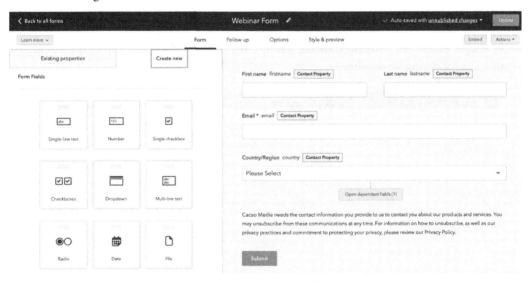

Figure 9.6 – Creating additional fields

Should you wish to add text—for example—to your form, you will need to select the **Header Text** option. The text will then appear on the top of the form, and you can add any text you wish by clicking on this sample text that appears. You can see an illustration of this in the following screenshot:

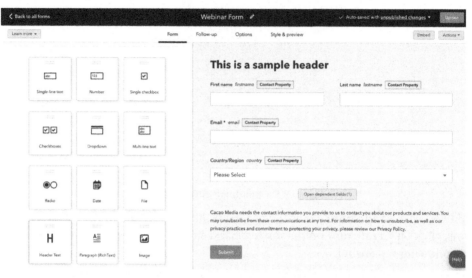

Figure 9.7 – Adding header text

Once you've edited the text, click **Done**, and the text will appear at the top of the form, as seen in the following screenshot:

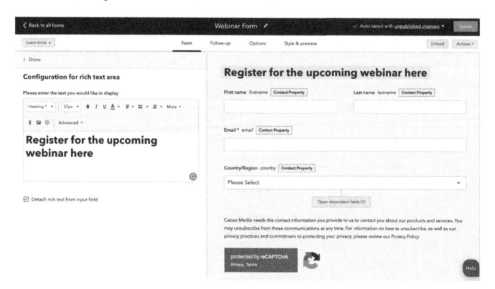

Figure 9.8 – Editing the header text

Completing these steps will allow you to have a completed form, as seen in the following screenshot:

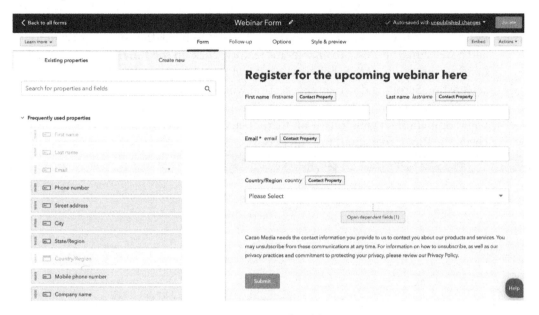

Figure 9.9 – Completed form

The next step is to find ways to optimize the form and make it easier for people to fill it out.

Optimizing the form by adding dependent or progressive fields

Although most online users are accustomed to filling out forms, this does not mean they enjoy doing it. Most drop-offs from websites and campaigns occur when a contact reaches a form and, for some reason, decides not to complete it. The most popular reasons for not completing a form are that the form is too long or asks for information the visitor is not yet ready to share. However, marketers are often measured by how many of these contacts they can get to fill out a form while ensuring these contacts are qualified.

Next are three important features HubSpot forms offer to ensure conversions are not hampered:

- **Collecting business emails instead of generic emails**: To get users to enter their business email address in a form, you would need to block the ability for them to add a free email address. To enable this feature, click on the **Email** field in the right-hand section, and another box on the left will pop up, as shown in the following screenshot. Scrolling down on this section, you will eventually arrive at a box that says **Email domains to block**. Here, you have the option to add domains, such as your competitors if you don't want them to access this event. Or, you can simply check the **Block free email providers** box:

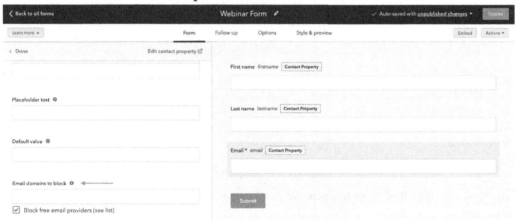

Figure 9.10 – Blocking free email providers

> **Note**
>
> Once you've chosen to block all free email domains, it is best to remove **Company Name** from the form. Asking this question is redundant, as HubSpot can then automatically fill this in using the contact's domain provided in the email address.

- **Using dependent fields to ask more questions without making the form lengthy**: Another consideration when creating a form is to think about questions that can be answered depending on the previous answer in a field. For example, let's say I added **Country** to the list of form fields, and then, if a contact chooses **United States**, only then would they see another field asking to choose a **State** value. To build this logic, you would need to use a feature called **Dependent Fields**. Follow these steps to execute it:

  - Add the field you want to be first filled out to the form. In this case, it's **Country/Region**.

- Click on the field, and then the box on the left changes, as shown in the following screenshot. After this, click on the **Logic** tab:

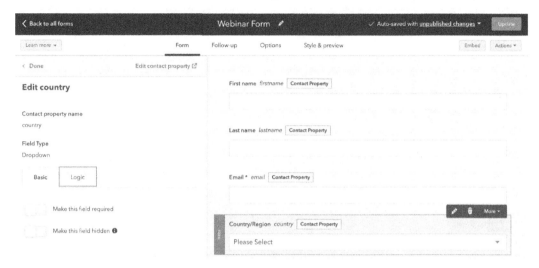

Figure 9.11 – Building logic into fields

- Scroll until you see **Dependent fields**, as shown in the following screenshot. Once there, complete the logic, which in this case is *If country contains any of United States, then show State/Region field*. The purpose of this function is that the **State/Region** field will remain hidden in the form from visitors who never choose **United States** as their country. Only visitors who choose **United States** as their country will see the **State/Region** field after:

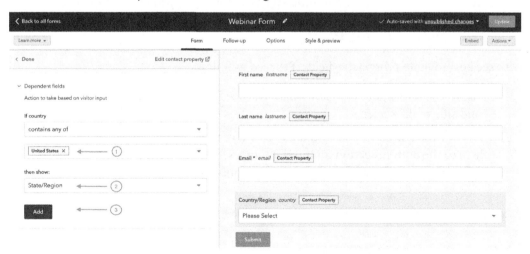

Figure 9.12 – Building dependent fields in a form

- Once this is completed, the dependent field appears in the form, as seen in the following screenshot, and will operate accordingly:

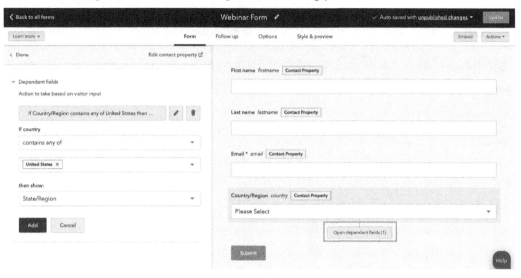

Figure 9.13 – Dependent field in a form

- **Being able to use the progressive forms feature**: Progressive forms allow you to change the fields displayed on a form for returning visitors so that you can capture more interesting information from the contact. As mentioned earlier, you can think of it very much like dating. You don't want to ask your date every time you meet them what their first name, last name, and email address are. Instead, you want to get to know them better every time you meet them. So, you may consider asking questions such as "*What is your job title?*", "*What is your phone number?*", or "*Are you currently using a CRM?*".

Let's see how to build progressive fields. Proceed as follows:

1. Ensure you are back to the view where you see **Existing Properties** on the top left-hand side of the screen.

2. Look for the questions you would like to ask of returning visitors and drag and drop them to the bottom section on the right, in a section called **Queued Progressive Fields**. Your form should then look like the one shown here:

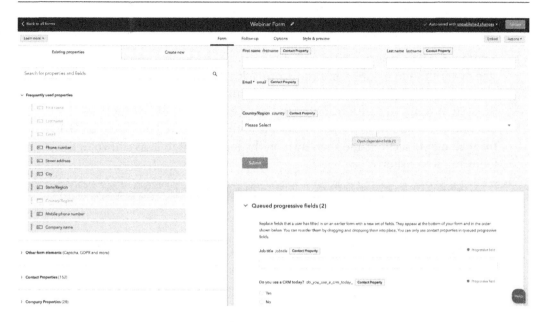

Figure 9.14 – Successfully adding progressive fields to a form

Remember that these progressive fields will only be shown to returning visitors whose information you already have in your **customer relationship management** (**CRM**) database. New visitors who have not yet converted or given you their information will see regular fields, such as **First Name**, **Last Name**, **Email**, and **Country**.

Preventing spam submissions and ensuring data privacy

Now that your forms are optimized, the next consideration is to add elements that would prevent bots and spam from submitting information to your forms and to ensure your forms are **GDPR**- and **California Consumer Privacy Act** (**CCPA**)-compliant. Adhering to these regulations allows you to store the information of your contacts and reach out to them in the future without being exposed to fines and penalties.

To set up these features, follow these steps:

1. **Set up reCAPTCHA**: reCAPTCHA encourages users to go through one more step of verification before submitting forms. It could be to rewrite a combination of letters and numbers or to identify all the traffic lights in a picture. This helps the system verify you are a real user and not a bot. To turn this feature on in HubSpot, scroll down to the left-hand side of the page until you reach the **Other form elements** section, and then turn on the toggle next to it, as shown in the following screenshot:

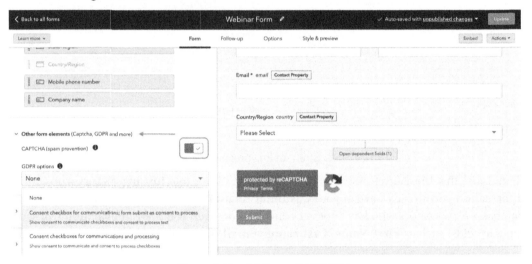

Figure 9.15 – Adding reCAPTCHA

2. **Adding GDPR notices to your forms**: Data privacy has become a central issue among online users, and therefore it is highly recommended to always have some type of GDPR notice on any forms that exist on your website or campaigns. This ensures users are fully informed of your interest to store their data and contact them in the future. This is particularly important if your target audience is primarily located in Europe and the **United States (US)** (the US equivalent of GDPR is CCPA).

To activate this feature, you simply need to choose one of the three pre-built options of GDPR notices in HubSpot. To access them, you will find a box called **GDPR options**, just below **CAPTCHA (spam prevention)**. Clicking on it gives you three options from which you can choose. Once chosen, it will appear right after the last field on the form so that visitors can comply before clicking **Submit**. See the following screenshot to view this in more detail:

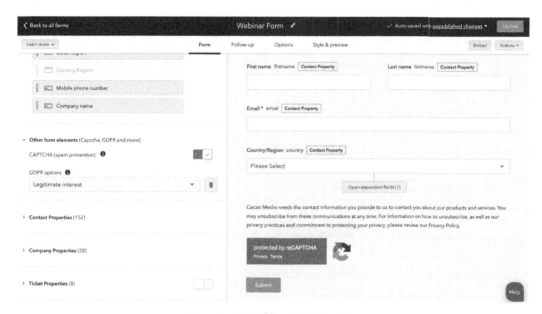

Figure 9.16 – Adding GDPR notices

Adding these two features to your form often helps to improve the quality of the leads you attract, since—as we will discuss later in the chapter—you would like to nurture these contacts a bit further before they get on a call with you.

Adding a follow-up email

Now that we have all elements of the form in place, the next step is to ensure there is some confirmation for contacts when they have submitted a message. HubSpot forms make this easy by providing an option to create a follow-up email within a form. To access it, click on **Follow-up** on the top navigation bar in the form module, as shown in the following screenshot:

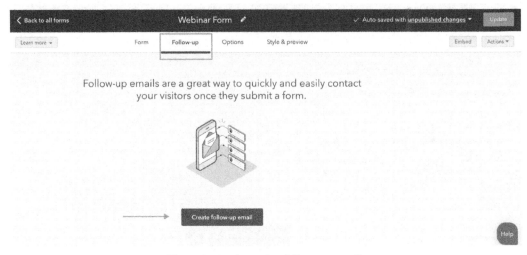

Figure 9.17 – Accessing follow-up emails

Once there, click on **Create follow-up email** and begin creating an email. Note that for this particular webinar form, you won't necessarily need to create a follow-up email. The email will automatically come from the platform hosting your webinar—Zoom or GoTo Webinar. But for illustration purposes, we have created an email as it can be used for other scenarios such as a **Contact us** form or a **Downloading the content** form. The process is illustrated in the following screenshot:

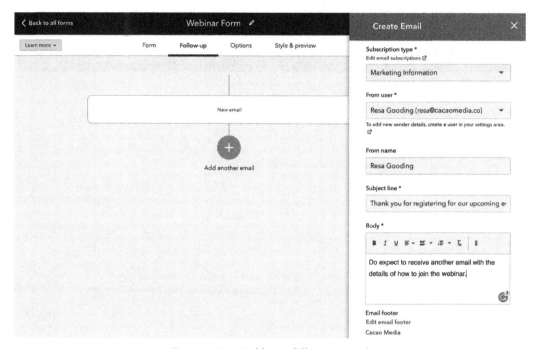

Figure 9.18 – Building a follow-up email

A follow-up email is created, as seen in the following screenshot, but note a few restrictions when creating this email. For example, personalization tokens are not accessible in this simple form email template, as well as the ability to edit the footer address to a single line or two not being possible. If these are features important to your follow-up email, I suggest building a regular automated email and then adding it to the workflow. Later in this chapter, we will demonstrate how to do this. In the meantime, the following screenshot demonstrates an example of what a follow-up email would look like when created in a form:

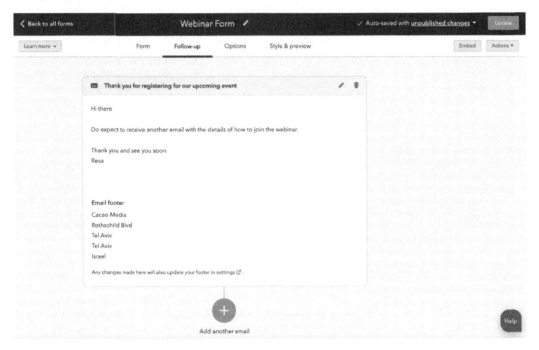

Figure 9.19 – Example of a follow-up email

Once a follow-up email is created, the next option is to define what should happen next when a user submits the form and who should be notified, as well as whether these contacts should be set as marketing contacts and be created as new contacts in your CRM.

Defining the next steps once a form is submitted

I'm sure you've filled out a form online before and recall one of the following two things happening:

- You saw a thank-you message appear after you clicked **Submit**.

- You were redirected to another page where a thank-you message appeared, along with some other assets.

To execute either of these actions in HubSpot, you must first click on **Options** on the top navigation bar of the form, and then the first section allows you to determine which of these actions you would like to occur. To display a thank-you message, simply click on this option and create a message you would like to appear. Notice in this textbox that you can add hyperlinks, so if you created this form to download an asset (for example), you can give access to the asset from this message. You can see an illustration of this in the following screenshot:

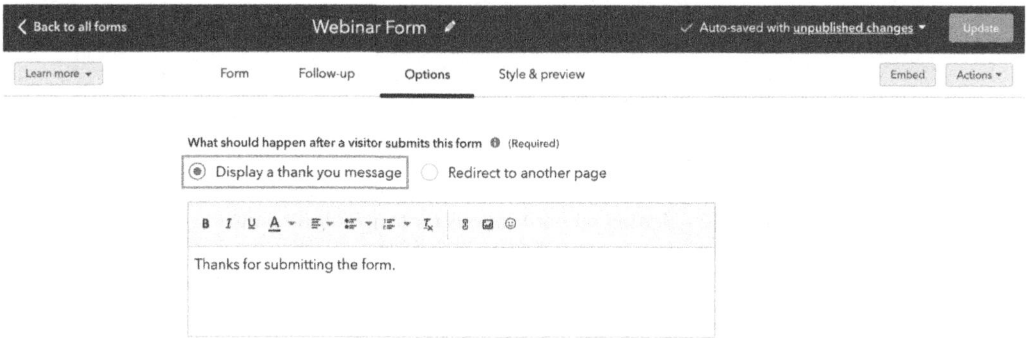

Figure 9.20 – Setting up a thank-you message after a contact submits a form

On the other hand, if you wish to redirect users to another page to display more information, you can do so by checking the **Redirect to another page** option, as seen in the following screenshot:

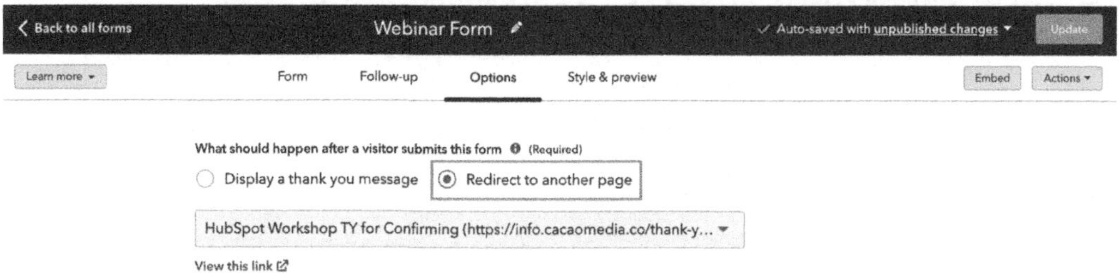

Figure 9.21 – Setting up a redirect link after a contact submits a form

The next setting you may like to configure for form submissions is who should get a notification once a form is submitted. By default, whoever creates the form is notified, but this isn't often the case. For example, if you have set up a demo form, you would usually like the owner of the lead to be notified; or, you may choose to notify additional users within the system so that other team members will know a contact has requested a demo.

To set up notifications for the owner of a contact to be notified, ensure you are still on the **Options** tab of the **Form** page. Then, scroll down a bit and check the **Send submission email notifications to the contact's owner** box, as seen in the following screenshot; and to add additional contacts to notifications, add their email address to the **Send submission notifications to** section:

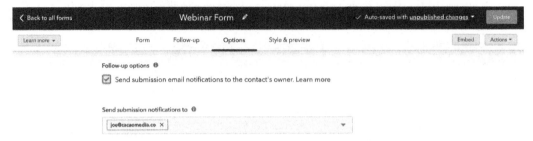

Figure 9.22 – Setting up notifications for form submissions

So, now what's left? Designing the form, of course.

Designing the form

HubSpot has made it possible for everyone to have the option to style and design forms as they wish. You can do so by accessing the **Style & preview** section within the form module, as shown in the following screenshot:

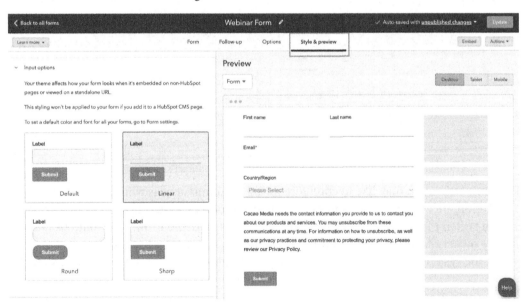

Figure 9.23 – Styling forms

In the **Input options** section of the form builder, you can decide whether your form fields should be boxes with squared edges or round edges or lines, as seen in the following screenshot:

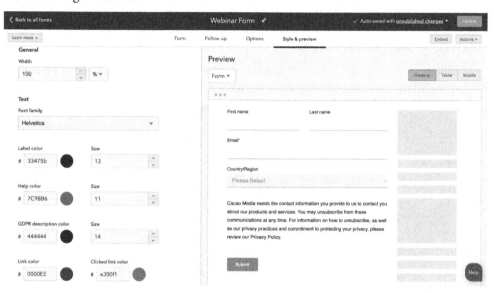

Figure 9.24 – Changing the font and size of form fields

You can also choose the font of form fields, the label color, the help color, and GDPR description notice colors, as shown in the following screenshot:

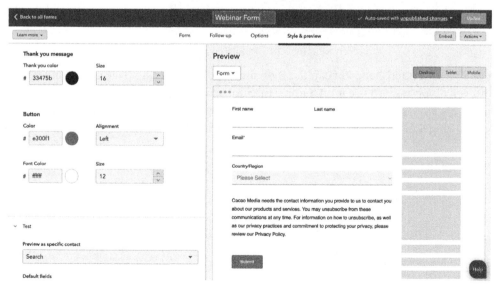

Figure 9.25 – Changing the thank-you message and button design

In addition, if you wish to change the size and color of the thank-you message, the option exists to do so, as seen in *Figure 9.25*.

After completing these previous steps, you are now in a position to publish your form.

Setting your form live

To publish your form, simply click on **Update** in the top right-hand corner of your page and click **Publish**, as shown in the following screenshot:

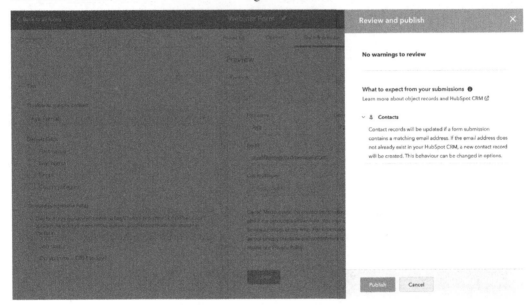

Figure 9.26 – Publishing a form

Once a form is published, you can use it on any HubSpot landing page or website page. However, if you wish to use it on a non-HubSpot asset such as your website, you will need to copy the embed code that appears on the final page after you click **Publish**, as shown in the following screenshot:

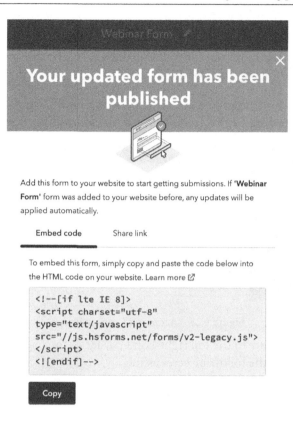

Figure 9.27 – Using the embed code to set a HubSpot form live on a non-HubSpot asset

Following these eight steps will help you successfully create, optimize, and use a HubSpot form on your website or your landing page.

Next, let's examine how to create a landing page in HubSpot. We'll also see how you can connect a form and the thank-you page.

Creating a landing page in HubSpot

Landing pages are dedicated web pages usually focused on getting users to take one specific action, which is usually to fill out the form on the landing page. Each landing page should have the following:

- A headline text
- An explanatory subtext
- A form
- An image or a video

In most cases, there is no navigation bar on a landing page.

HubSpot's cloning and drag and drop features make it easy to create and reuse landing pages. To create a landing page, follow these steps:

1. Access the **Landing pages** tool by going to the top navigation bar and clicking on **Marketing | Landing Pages**, as illustrated in the following screenshot:

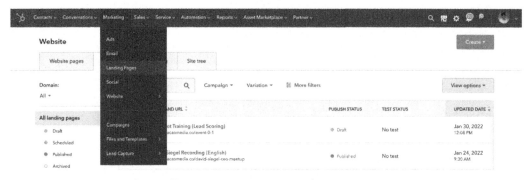

Figure 9.28 – Accessing Landing Pages

2. Then, click on **Create** in the top right-hand corner of the page and choose **Landing page**, as shown in the following screenshot:

Figure 9.29 – Choosing Landing page

3. A pop-up box will then appear, prompting you to select a subdomain and enter a **Page name** value, as shown in the following screenshot:

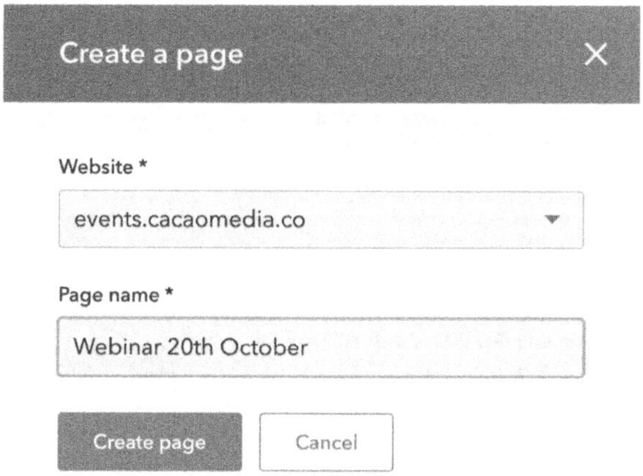

Create a page   ✕

Website *

events.cacaomedia.co   ▼

Page name *

Webinar 20th October

Create page   Cancel

Figure 9.30 – Choosing a subdomain and a page name

4. Click **Create page**, and then choose one of the templates that will appear, as illustrated in the following screenshot. Note you can always design your own template and apply it in HubSpot:

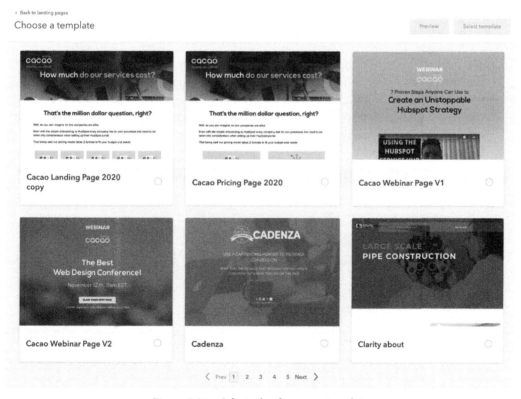

Figure 9.31 – Select a landing page template

5. Once you have chosen a template, you can update the text via the modules that will appear on the left-hand side, as shown in the following screenshot:

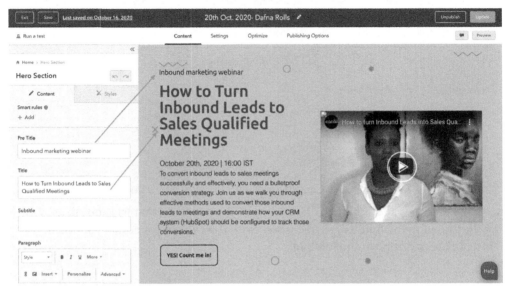

Figure 9.32 – Editing the text on the landing page

6. The next step is to add the form you previously built to the landing page by selecting the form from the options on the left side. Click **Choose a form**. At this point, you will also be asked whether you want to redirect the users to a thank-you page or to display an inline thank-you message. Whichever option is chosen here will override the options set previously when building the form. The process is illustrated in the following screenshot:

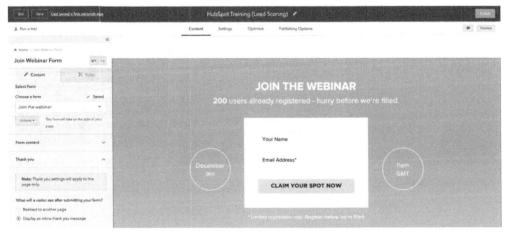

Figure 9.33 – Adding the form on the landing page

7. Once you are satisfied with the content that visitors will see on the landing page, the next step is to configure the settings. Clicking on **Settings**, found on the top navigation bar, will take you to the backend of the landing page. Here, you can first choose an internal name for the page and a page title, as shown in the following screenshot. Note that the **Internal page name** value is for your records only so that you can find the page in the future in HubSpot, so it's good to keep some type of naming convention here. The **Page title** value is what visitors will see as the name of the page in search engines, and so on:

Figure 9.34 – Choosing a page name and title

8. Next, update the **Page language** setting to your preferred language. Then, choose the correct subdomain and add a **Content slug** value, which is usually the name of your page. Next, add a **Meta description** value. See the following screenshot for an illustrative example of each of these points:

Figure 9.35 – Choosing a page name and title (continued)

9. The next set of options invites you to attach a campaign to the landing page so that you can track the results of this campaign. You should also insert an image so that if the page is shared on social media, there would be a dedicated image that would show up and it would make your page optimized for sharing. Remember to add the name of the webinar as the alternative text of the image as this helps with **search engine optimization (SEO)**, as we will discuss in the next step. The process is illustrated in the following screenshot:

Figure 9.36 – Adding campaigns and featured images

10. Once the page settings are complete, the next action would be to check the SEO optimization of the page. You want to ensure, at the very least, the following main items are optimized: a page title exists, the title is fewer than 70 characters, search engines can display the page in search results, and the page has a meta description. The bottom line is the more green checkboxes you have on the left, the more optimized your page will be for SEO. The process is illustrated in the following screenshot:

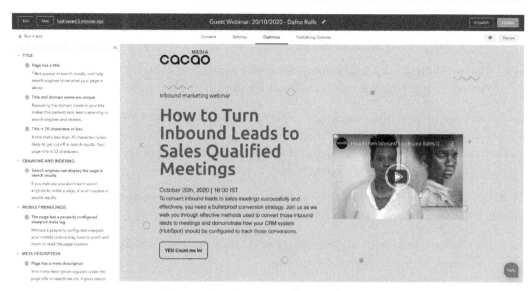

Figure 9.37 – Optimizing the page for SEO

11. Once these steps are completed, all that is left to do is to publish your page by clicking **Publish** or **Update** in the top right-hand corner.

So, now that we have built forms and landing pages, the next step is to ensure that leads are getting timely emails to follow up once an action is taken and a form submitted. In this example, the next expected action when the form is submitted would be to get a confirmation email with details of how to join the webinar. In other cases, it could be a link to download an asset or confirmation that someone will be in touch with you. These latter cases can be dealt with by using the form options, as described previously, but for an event such as a webinar, we would need to use the workflow function to get this step done.

Building lead-nurturing workflows

Workflows are the holy grail of the HubSpot portal. A workflow is the most commonly used tool in Marketing Hub as it allows marketers to build drip campaigns and maintain the internal organization of the CRM. In this section, we will specifically look at how to build a nurturing workflow for a webinar.

However, before getting into the workflow itself, we must first map out what is required from a webinar workflow. Which actions would you like this workflow to perform? Here are some scenarios to consider:

- The workflow should send a confirmation email with details of how to join the webinar to contacts who submitted the form.

- The workflow should send a reminder to contacts who registered for the webinar, maybe a day before and an hour before.

- The workflow should send a summary of the webinar to contacts who attended the webinar. Those who missed the webinar should get its recording.

These three are basic actions you would expect for a webinar event. Of course, there might be more internal actions you may want to add, such as converting attendees into **marketing-qualified leads** (**MQLs**) and sending them off to the sales team. We will consider these scenarios in the next section.

At this point, let's break this down into steps to understand what we need to convert these actions into a workflow. This is what we'd need to do:

1. Send a confirmation email to contacts who submitted the form. In order to send this email, we would need the following:

   - The form that users will be submitting to join the webinar

   - Integration to the webinar platform chosen to host the webinar so that a confirmation email could be sent to those contacts

2. Send a reminder email to contacts who registered a day before and an hour before the webinar. In order to send this email, we would need the following:

   - Date and time of the webinar

   - A reminder email with details of how to join the webinar

3. Send a summary email to attendees and non-attendees with a recording of the webinar. In order to send this email, we would need the following:

   - A list of attendees and non-attendees

   - A recording of the webinar

   - A post-webinar email with a link to the recording

> **Note**
> Ensure this email does not go out before the recording is available.

A few more points you may want to consider are set out here:

- Are there any contacts that should never be enrolled in this workflow?

- Should contacts be allowed to re-enroll in this workflow?

- How to prevent contacts from enrolling in the workflow *after* the event has occurred.

This exercise should be performed for any type of workflow you are building, especially for nurturing workflows that will affect the information your contacts will receive.

Now that we understand what's needed, it's time to execute the actions.

Building a nurturing workflow for an upcoming webinar

To build a nurturing workflow for a webinar, there are a few steps to follow, as outlined here:

1. **Integrate HubSpot and your preferred webinar platform**: HubSpot integrates seamlessly with Zoom or GoTo Webinar, two of the most popular webinar platforms for businesses. To integrate either of these platforms to HubSpot, go to **Settings | Integrations | Connected Apps**, then click on **Visit App Marketplace**, as illustrated in the following screenshot:

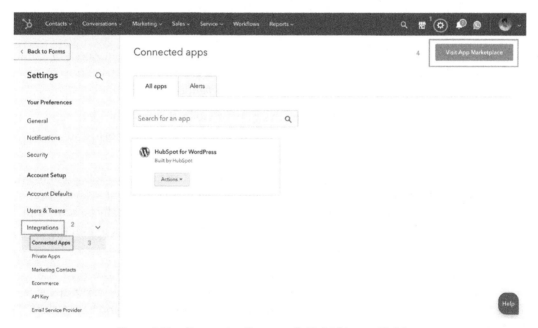

Figure 9.38 – Connecting Zoom or GoTo Webinar to HubSpot

You will then be redirected to another page where you can insert a webinar in the search bar and see all the webinar tools that exist and are integrated with HubSpot. Choose your preferred platform. The process is illustrated in the following screenshot:

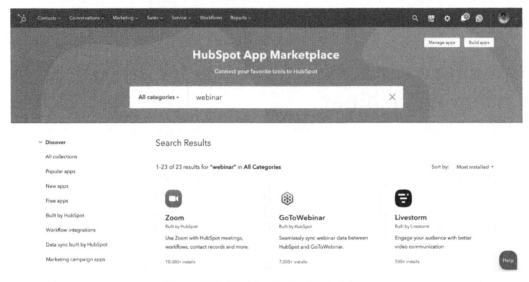

Figure 9.39 – HubSpot's App Marketplace

2. **Set up a webinar**: First, be sure to upgrade to the webinar package in Zoom or GoTo Webinar in order to complete your setup there. To see the steps of how to set up a webinar in Zoom or GoTo Webinar, go to *Appendix A* of this book.

    Once the webinar setup is completed in Zoom or GoTo Webinar, the next step includes building all the assets we referred to earlier for creating a form and landing page.

In addition to forms and landing pages, you would want to create an invitation email to be sent out to your database and a *last chance to register* email that can be sent a day before the webinar date. Note that your reminder emails to registrants will typically be sent from Zoom or GoTo Webinar itself, as each registrant will receive a unique link to join the webinar so that you will know who attended and for how long.

Once these assets are created, you must then build a workflow to connect the form, the invitation emails, reminder emails, and post-webinar emails. To build this workflow, go to the top menu of your portal and choose **Workflows**. In some cases, if you have **Sales Professional (Sales Pro)**, you will see **Automation** on the top menu of your portal; from there, choose **Workflow**.

Click **Create Workflow** in the top left right-hand corner of your portal.

The next page that appears gives you several options. First, you need to choose the type of workflow you wish to create—**Contact-based**, **Company-based**, **Deal-based**, or **Ticket-based**. Each of these options will depend on which properties you are trying to access within the HubSpot portal. For a webinar workflow, choose **Contact-based**.

Your next option is to choose how you want the workflow to start. Once again, you have several options, as outlined here:

- **Blank workflow**: This means your workflow is completely blank and can be used for any function you would like.

- **Schedule**: This type of workflow helps you set up recurring actions or send out recurring emails or messages to your prospects, customers, or team. For example, if you want to send out holiday greetings every year for Christmas, this workflow can be used.

- **Specific date**: This type of workflow helps you set up a chain of actions that will happen on a specific date. This is the "eBay workflow" for events such as webinars and conferences, so there will be no errors of prospects signing up for your event after the event date and receiving a confirmation email even though the workflow was left on after the date had passed.

- **Contact date property**: This type of workflow allows you to send emails or set up an action once that date property has arrived. This is generally useful for sending out a welcome email to a new customer or to send a notice to the onboarding team once a new customer is assigned.

The preceding options are shown in the following screenshot:

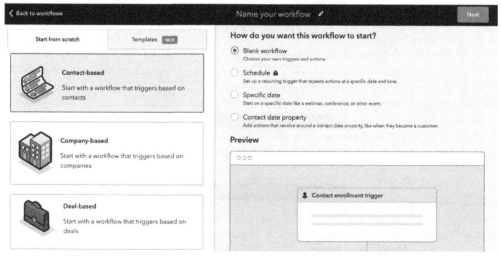

Figure 9.40 – Types of workflows

Now that we know we need to choose a specific date workflow, we click on this option and set the date of the webinar, and then click **Next**, as shown in the following screenshot:

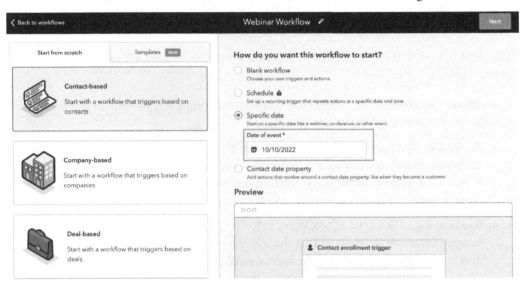

Figure 9.41 – Building a specific date workflow

On the next page, you will see the outline of the workflow. The first stage is to choose an enrollment trigger. This is a list of contacts from your database you wish to invite to the webinar. You can see an illustration of this in the following screenshot:

Figure 9.42 – Adding a list of contacts to receive invitation emails

Once a list of contacts is chosen, the next step would be to choose the next action and the date on which you would like it to take place. It is typical to promote a webinar between 4 and 6 weeks before the webinar, so in this step, it is recommended to add the first invitation email that you would like your prospects to receive. Click **Save** once the date is entered, as seen in the following screenshot:

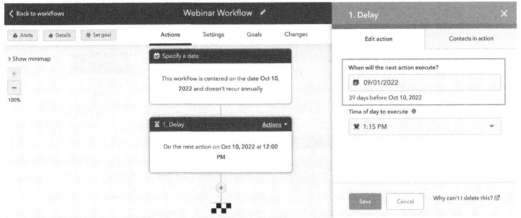

Figure 9.43 – Selecting a date and time you would like contacts to receive the first email

After choosing a date, you will then want to attach the first invitation email contacts should receive about the webinar. To do this, click the + sign again and choose **Send email** in order to select an invitation email that was created previously, as illustrated in the following screenshot:

Figure 9.44 – Choosing the Send email option for external communication to send out an email invitation

Choose emails from the list of emails that will appear once you click the **Send email** option. Then, once you choose the relevant email, click **Save**, as illustrated in the following screenshot. Note that you must create an automated marketing email and ensure it is published for you to see it as an option in workflows:

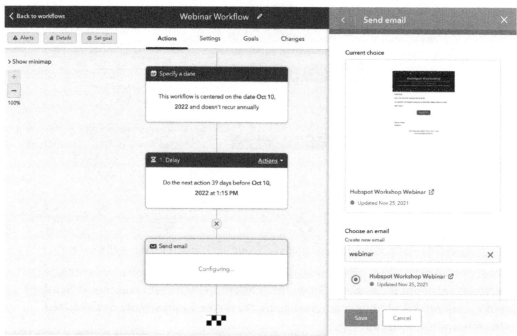

Figure 9.45 – Choosing an automated email from the list

Next, click the + sign and choose the **Delay** option to choose a time you would want the second email to go out. Next, you will want to split your actions so that only people who did not click on the webinar link in your email will get the second email, as it is assumed those people haven't signed up yet. To create an if/then case, click on **If/then branch**, as shown in the following screenshot:

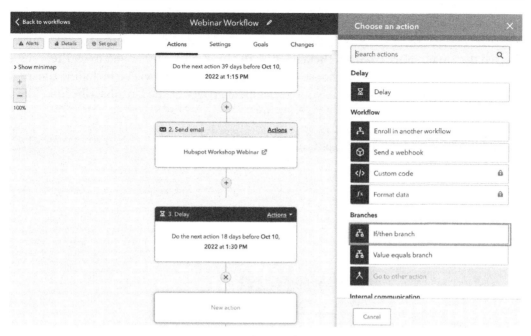

Figure 9.46 – Selecting If/then branch

Next, choose the **Marketing emails** option, as illustrated in the following screenshot:

Figure 9.47 – Selecting the Marketing emails filter type

Select the previous email sent to the list of contacts—in this case, **HubSpot Workshop Webinar**—so that the system can check who clicked the links in those emails. Once you've selected the email, select **Contact clicked a link in email**, and select a link to register for the webinar. Note that if you choose the **Any link** option, you will be including those people who also clicked the links to your social media pages or the **Unsubscribe** link. The process is illustrated in the following screenshot:

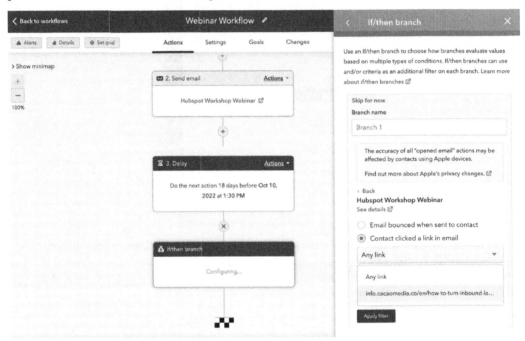

Figure 9.48 – Selecting a link that contacts should click to join the webinar

Once you've set up this *if/then* option, the next step is to insert a second email you would like to send to those who did *not* click on the link to receive. You can repeat these steps until all of your invitation emails have been included in the workflow. The process is illustrated in the following screenshot:

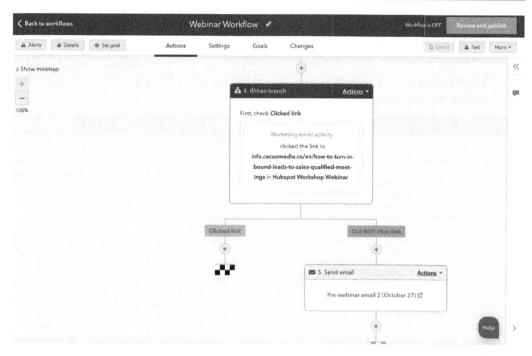

Figure 9.49 – Adding a second email to the relevant branch

Before turning on this workflow, though, there are some scenarios you must consider to check how the workflow will affect each contact in your database, not just the ones enrolled into the workflow as you intended. Some scenarios that you may want to consider are noted here:

- **Whether contacts should be re-enrolled**: If you would like contacts to be re-enrolled in the workflows, click on **Enrollment triggers** and select **Re-enrollment**, as illustrated in the following screenshot:

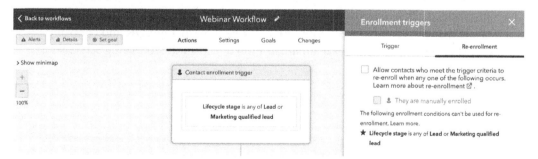

Figure 9.50 – Re-enrollment function of workflows

- **Whether some contacts should never get into this workflow at all**: If you would like certain contacts to never be enrolled in the workflow, even if they fulfill the action, click on **Settings** at the top of the workflow menu. Then, choose **Unenrollment and Suppression** and add the list of contacts to the suppression tab, as shown in the following screenshot:

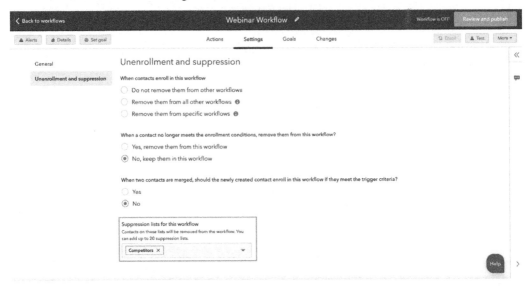

Figure 9.51 – Suppression function of workflows

- **The point at which contacts should get out of this workflow**: The point of the workflow is to get contacts signing up for the webinar. So, once they have taken this action, they should be taken out of the workflow to prevent them from receiving further emails. In order to do this, you must set a goal for the workflow that, once met, will unenroll contacts from the workflow. To set a goal, simply click on **Set Goal** in the top left-hand corner and choose a goal based on the properties available. In this case, the goal of this workflow is for the contact to submit a form. Note that you can always set more than one goal by clicking **OR** and choosing another property. You can see an illustration of this in the following screenshot:

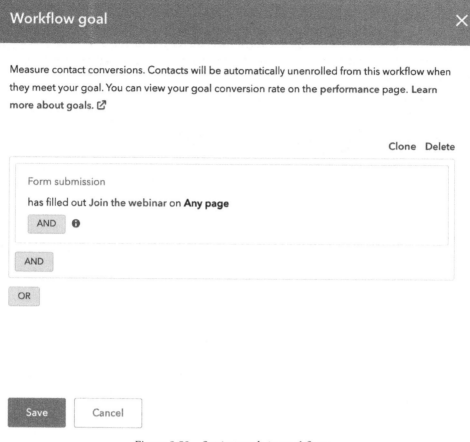

Figure 9.52 – Setting goals in workflows

There are a few other workflow features that might come in handy for this workflow or any other workflow you may build in the future—for example, sending emails out only during specific days and times or not sending them out on specific days, such as weekends or holidays. Other features, such as **Remove them from specific workflows**, also help you to remove contacts from workflows they may have previously been enrolled in so that they are not inundated with too many emails. The best practice when building workflows for lead nurturing is to spend some time brainstorming and mapping out exactly what these workflows should do and accomplish and then utilize the features to make it happen. After considering all scenarios, you can move on to the next step, which will ensure contacts get webinar confirmation emails from the chosen platforms.

Build a separate workflow to ensure registrants receive a confirmation email from Zoom or GoTo Webinar. It is recommended not to connect these steps to the previous workflow since contacts could reach the form for registering for the webinar in various ways. Therefore, the enrollment trigger for this type of workflow should be the form used on the landing page and not a list, as seen in *Figure 9.51*. Note the type of workflow used for building this process is **Blank workflow**. The process is illustrated in the following screenshot:

Figure 9.53 – Selecting a form as the enrollment trigger

Once you've selected an enrollment trigger, your next step is to connect the webinar created in Zoom or GoTo Webinar to the workflow. You can use one of the following options:

1. To connect the webinar in Zoom to the HubSpot form, you must look for Zoom's webinar **identifier (ID)**. Then, click the + sign and choose the **Add Contact to Zoom Webinar** option, then place the webinar ID below it, as indicated in the following screenshot:

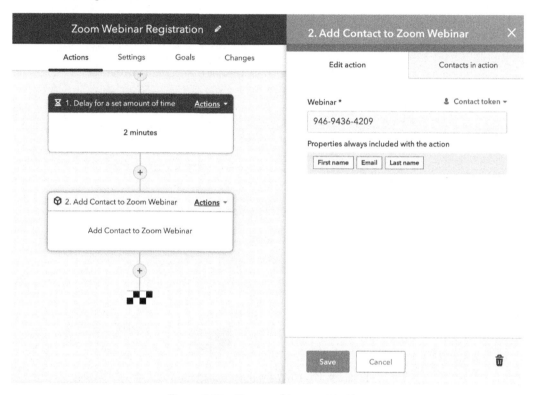

Figure 9.54 – Zoom webinar registration

2. To connect the webinar to GoTo Webinar, we recommend you build the workflow with an enrollment trigger, using the form on the landing page. Then, click the + sign and choose the **Add Contact to Webinar** option. A box will appear from which you can choose a name for the webinar and fields you wish to integrate with the webinar, as shown in the following screenshot:

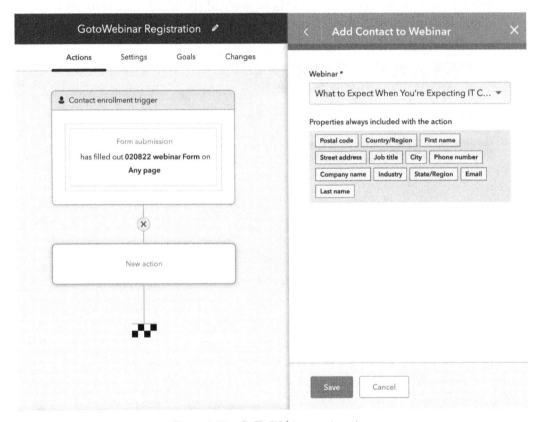

Figure 9.55 – GoTo Webinar registration

Following these steps will ensure that contacts who sign up for your webinar receive a unique confirmation email from either of these platforms to join the webinar. Note that if you use a regular meeting link from Zoom or GoTo Webinar to host a webinar, you will lose the ability to track who attended the event versus those who did not attend, as neither of these platforms retains this data when an event has ended if it was set up as a meeting since everyone used the same link to join the event. It is for this reason that it is highly recommended to use the **Webinar** add-on feature on Zoom or GoTo Webinar.

Summary

Understanding how to convert leads into qualified contacts that turn into meaningful opportunities is every marketer's challenge. Therefore, having a suite of easy-to-use tools that allow you to achieve this is what each marketer seeks in a platform.

HubSpot offers a variety of such tools all in one platform. From forms to landing pages to workflows, these tools become a marketer's secret weapon as they allow a myriad of tasks to be done quickly and efficiently to achieve the main goal of improving conversions. Therefore, it is imperative that you take the necessary time to understand how each of these features works in order to ensure you get the best results from your campaigns.

In the next chapter, we will look more closely at how the email marketing tool in HubSpot can help you build meaningful relationships with your customers by sending them personalized and relevant information.

Questions

Have a go at answering the following questions:

1. Which feature in HubSpot helps prevent spam submissions and ensures data privacy?

2. What are the five features most landing pages should have?

3. How do you prevent contacts from re-enrolling in your workflows?

Further reading

-   *Understanding Workflows in HubSpot*: https://academy.hubspot.com/lessons/understanding-workflows-in-hubspot

-   *Using Workflows to Power Your Inbound Strategy*: https://academy.hubspot.com/lessons/Using-Workflows-to-Power-Your-Inbound-Strategy

-   *How to Implement Workflows in Each Stage of the Flywheel*: https://blog.hubspot.com/customers/implement-workflows-hubspot

-   *56 Ways Customers Use Workflow Integrations*: https://blog.hubspot.com/customers/56-ways-customers-use-workflow-integrations

-   *5 Biggest Workflow Mistakes (and How to Avoid Them)*: https://blog.hubspot.com/customers/5-biggest-workflow-mistakes-how-to-avoid-them

10
Revive Your Database with HubSpot Email Marketing Tools

Email marketing is one of the most fundamental tactics within the inbound marketing toolkit. It is also one of the oldest forms of communication since the invention of the internet. Regardless of the many new shiny tools that have surfaced as customers became more sophisticated shoppers, it remains one of the most effective means of converting a prospect. Therefore, it is imperative for marketers and sales teams to understand how to effectively use this tool in order to maintain authentic conversations with their audience and, at the same time, not abuse this privilege by sending spammy content.

In this chapter, you will learn about the following topics:

- Building an effective email marketing strategy
- Setting up an email successfully in HubSpot
- Analyzing the results of an email
- Optimizing the email for best performance

To get the most out of this chapter, you will need access to the HubSpot marketing emails, which are available in the Free, Starter, Professional, and Enterprise versions.

Technical requirements

To get the most out of this chapter, you will need to have the following:

- Marketing access to HubSpot to create emails
- Access to reports in order to analyze the email results

Building an effective email marketing strategy

When was the last time you received an email from an unfamiliar source and were excited to open it? Even if you vaguely remembered subscribing to a blog or interacting with a company after a few days of getting an email from them, were you in a rush to prioritize reading the content received or did you simply click open to get rid of the number of unread messages in your inbox? And for more savvy inbox users, I guess you either simply open another generic email used for collecting such content or filter them into folders never to be seen again, right?

Well, guess what? Your contacts are probably doing the same thing. In this section, we will teach you how to build the right strategy in order to create an email campaign that will deliver useful and helpful content to your contacts at the right time:

1. **Define your goals**: The first step of any successful email campaign is understanding your goals. Are you trying to get people to open your newsletter, sign up for a webinar, or simply receive updates from you about new products or services you offer? Understanding your goal helps to define the metrics by which you will measure your success.

2. **Build your email lists**: In order to send an email, you must have contacts within your database to send it to. So, you must think of ways to capture people's email addresses. Some popular ways are to give free offers of something of value, such as an e-book to capture these emails.

3. **Segment your lists**: Once you have built your emails, the next step is to make sure your lists are segmented so that the correct people are receiving relevant emails. Taking the time to do this will help you to avoid high unsubscribe rates or reports of spam and, therefore, protect your email deliverability.

4. **Make a send schedule**: Understanding the best time to reach your target audience is crucial to email marketing success. According to Campaign Monitor, 53% of people open their emails on weekdays during the hours of 9 a.m. and 11 a.m. However, after sending thousands of emails on behalf of my clients, I have found that the best time to send emails depends on the type of email. For example, when sending event emails, the best time to send them is often after work hours or on weekends. This is because people are, generally, browsing through their emails at that time and are more inclined to sign up for an event during their downtime, as they don't think about how busy they are. Additionally, for newsletters or general content emails, the best time to send them is during weekends and holidays, as people are more likely to read content to help improve their work or business.

5. **Create the content of the emails**: Content is crucial to emails. Without it, there is no point in sending the email. However, it is important to remember to keep the length of those emails reasonably short. People no longer have the attention span to read lengthy emails. So, in order to get your contact to take action, keep it to 3–4 lines maximum.

6. **Format the content of the emails**: Formatting your emails is important so that they can be easily scanned. Having a line space of at least 1.5, a font size of at least 11, and a font color that is legible makes a big difference. Of course, ensuring your emails are optimized for different devices and email clients, as we shall discuss in later sections, is also important.

7. **Send the emails**: Pressing the send button is always nerve-wracking. But there comes a point when you simply must press send. The important thing to check before sending is that there are no spelling errors, the links work as they should, and the email displays correctly on both mobile and desktop devices.

8. **Track and monitor your success**: Now that your contacts have received your emails, it is time to see who has actually engaged with it. Understandably, you will want to check the open rates and the click-through rates. However, it is also just as important to check the quality of the contacts that are opened and clicked on. So, doing some deep diving into understanding the contacts that engaged in your email can help you justify the results.

Now that you understand how to build a successful email strategy, the next step is to understand how to actually set up an email in HubSpot.

Setting up an email in HubSpot

HubSpot's email marketing tool has a host of features to ensure that you can reach your target audience and optimize your email campaigns for maximum results. To set up an email in HubSpot, follow these steps:

Navigate to **Marketing | Email** in the top-level menu and click on **Create email**:

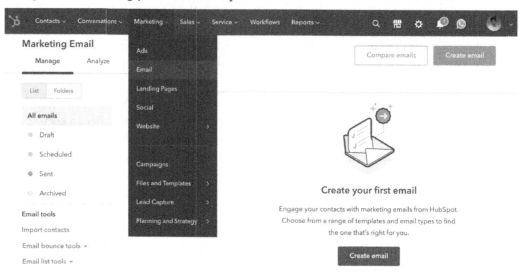

Figure 10.1 – Creating your email

Following this, you will be prompted to choose the type of email you wish to create. A regular email can be used for sending emails just once, for instance, a newsletter or an announcement. Automated emails are used when you wish to send a series of emails through the workflow function. In comparison, blog/RSS emails are emails you wish to automatically publish whenever you publish a blog:

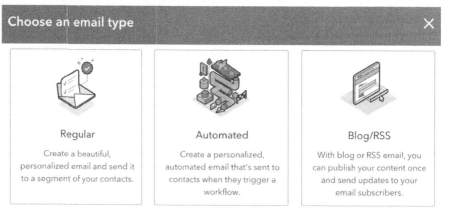

Figure 10.2 – Different types of emails in HubSpot

Choosing **Regular** or **Automated** has the same steps described next to create an email. In this example, we choose **Regular**, and then you are prompted to choose a template under the **Drag and drop** section. The **Custom** tab allows you to design and create your own template to match your brand.

In the free version or starter version of HubSpot, you will only have access to the basic templates, but for those with HubSpot Professional or Enterprise, you will have access to more templates. In this example, we will choose the **Simple** template in the **Basic** section:

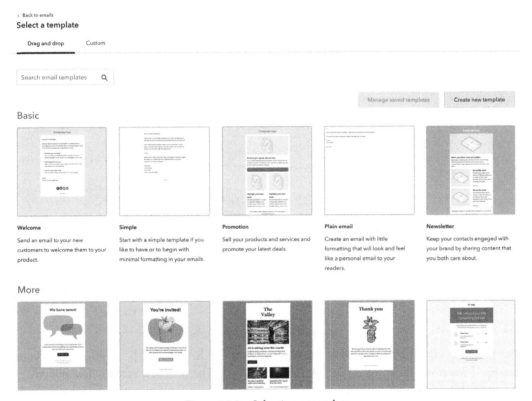

Figure 10.3 – Selecting a template

Once you've selected a template, in this case, **Simple**, you will be taken to the **New email** screen. This allows you to build and customize your template as you wish. The right-hand side of the screen includes modules for adding images, text, CTA buttons, videos, social icons, and more that you can simply click on and drag and drop to the desired position in the email:

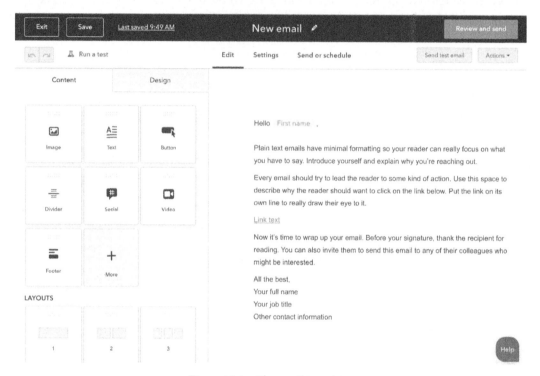

Figure 10.4 – The email template

For instance, clicking on the image icon allows you to add an email header on top of your email. If you don't have any design skills, don't worry. The next few steps will show you some shortcuts to overcome this.

To add an image without having a designer, click on the **Select Image** button and a box will appear, prompting you to add an image or design with Canva, as shown in the following screenshot:

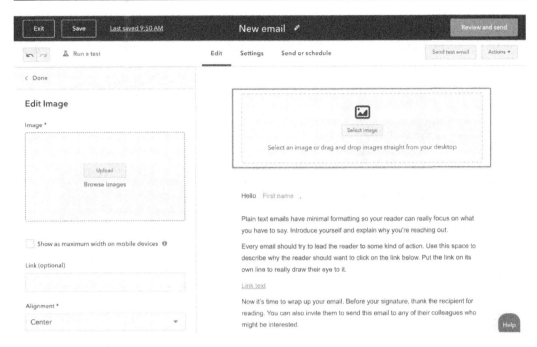

Figure 10.5 – Adding an image module to your email

Clicking on the **Design with Canva** option allows you to connect with your Canva account or create one for free if you don't yet have one.

Then, search for the email header option and click on it. It will direct you to the Canva platform:

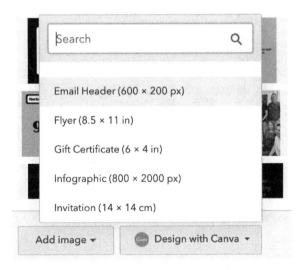

Figure 10.6 – Accessing Canva to create images within your email

You will be redirected to the Canva platform where you will see a host of email header designs to choose from, as shown in the following screenshot. Choose any template you wish and customize it to your needs:

Figure 10.7 – Choosing an email header template

Customize the image by adding your own images, changing the colors, and adding new text as needed. Once you are done, click on **Save** in the upper-right corner. You will be redirected back to the HubSpot platform:

Figure 10.8 – Designing your email header in Canva

Once you have been redirected to HubSpot, click on the image that is saved in your library and it will appear in the email header space, as shown in the following screenshot:

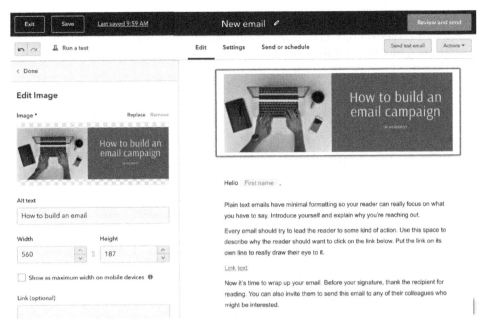

Figure 10.9 – Adding the email header to your HubSpot email

Pay attention to the completion of the sections in the module to will help your readers have a more optimized experience. For example, adding alt text allows your email to be found online if there is a web version applied to it. Also, adding a link to the content you would like your readers to access ensures that if they click on the image, they will have another entry point to the content:

Figure 10.10 – Filling out the Alt text and Link sections

The next step is to decide which other modules you would like to add to the email, for instance, a **call-to-action** (**CTA**) button. To add any modules, just click on them and drag and drop them to the place in the email where you want them to appear:

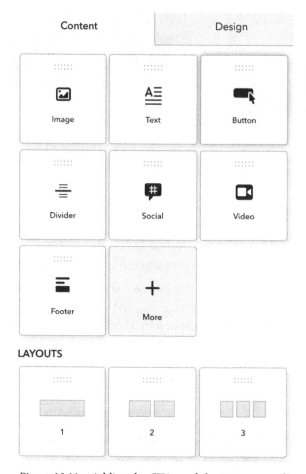

Figure 10.11 – Adding the CTA modules to your email

Once the CTA module has been added, a box will appear on the left-hand side where you can customize the CTA, as needed. Add a URL that users can be redirected to once clicked. Change the text to whatever action is needed; for example, `Download Now`, `Sign up Here`, and more. Customize the color of your button, text, type of font, font size, and font color for posting, as shown in the following screenshot:

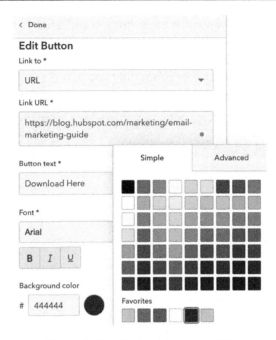

Figure 10.12 – Customizing your CTA

Once this has been completed, your CTA will be included in the email, as shown in *Figure 10.11*. Now, you can proceed to edit the text in order to complete the content of your email:

Figure 10.13 – Adding your CTA to the email

The last part of creating your content is to ensure you add a footer to your email. For marketing emails, you will need to include your company's address and an **Unsubscribe** button at the bottom of the emails. To include your company's address, click on the footer section of the email. A box will appear prompting you to include your company's physical address. Click on **Save Changes**:

Manage Footer

Company Name *

Cacao Media

Address *

Rothschild Blvd

Address Line 2

City *

Tel Aviv

State *

Tel Aviv

Zip Code

Country

Israel

Phone

Save Changes

Figure 10.14 – Editing the footer of your emails

Once this is complete, you can add the **Unsubscribe** and **Manage Preferences** buttons to your email. At this stage of your business, you generally should not open more than one type of email since it is already difficult to get people to subscribe to your emails, and every different type of email will require contacts to subscribe to it in order for them to receive your emails. Therefore, it is advised to just use the default marketing email subscription type that already exists within HubSpot. Therefore, there is no need to include the option for **Manage Preferences** in the footer of your email. So, by clicking on the footer, you can change the option from **Both** to just **Unsubscribe**:

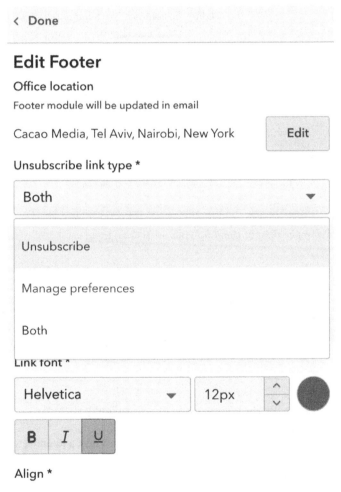

Figure 10.15 – Selecting your subscription type

Now that the content of your email is ready, the next step is to add the sender and subject lines and preview the text. To do this, click on the **Settings** tab in the middle section of the email. Here, you can decide where the email should be sent from. By default, it will be set to be sent from the person creating the email, but this can be easily changed by clicking on the **From name** and **From address** boxes and choosing or adding new senders. It is important to note that it is always better to send these emails from a real person instead of `info@companyname.com` or `marketing@companyname.com`. You can also add the subject line and preview the text the reader will see before they open the email:

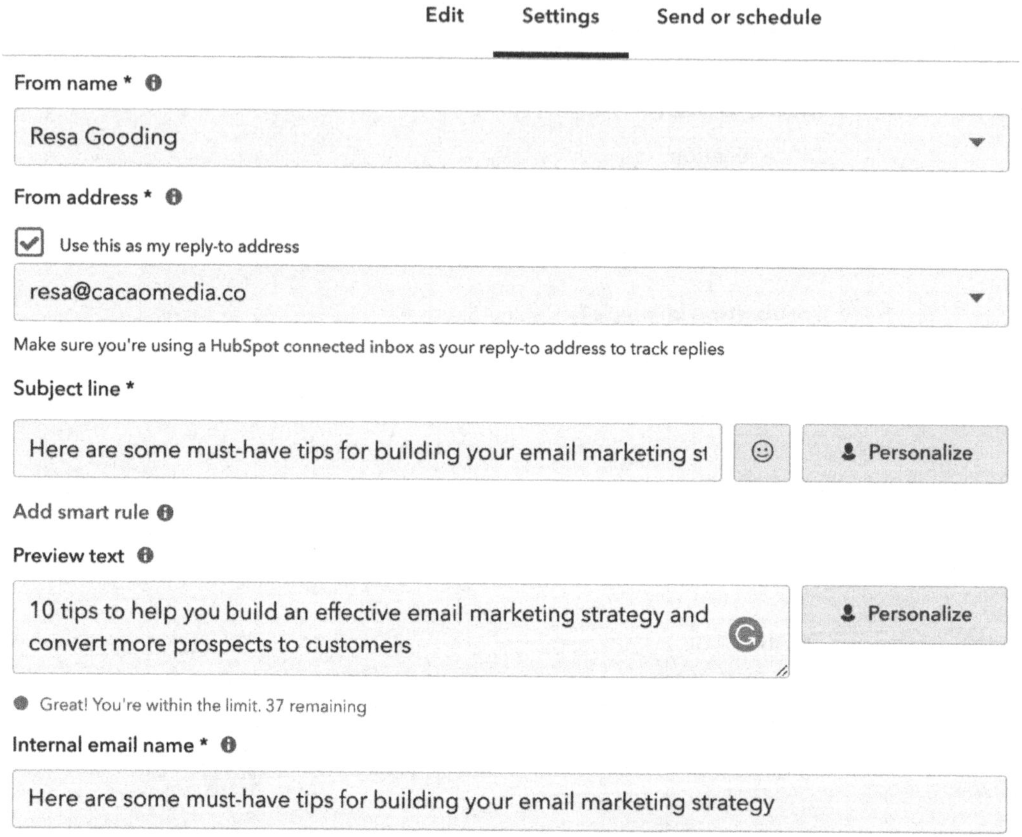

Edit   Settings   Send or schedule

From name * ⓘ

Resa Gooding   ▼

From address * ⓘ

☑ Use this as my reply-to address

resa@cacaomedia.co   ▼

Make sure you're using a HubSpot connected inbox as your reply-to address to track replies

Subject line *

Here are some must-have tips for building your email marketing si   ☺   👤 Personalize

Add smart rule ⓘ

Preview text ⓘ

10 tips to help you build an effective email marketing strategy and
convert more prospects to customers   ↻   👤 Personalize

● Great! You're within the limit. 37 remaining

Internal email name * ⓘ

Here are some must-have tips for building your email marketing strategy

Figure 10.16 – Setting the sender's name and email, subject line, and previewing the text

With the settings and content complete, your next step is to decide on the contacts that should receive the email. To do this, click on the **Send or Schedule** tab in the middle section of the email screen and choose the lists of contacts that should receive this email. You also have the option to choose contacts or a list of contacts you do *not* want to receive the email. This is often a good feature to use when you wish to exclude customers or current opportunities from the list:

Recipients

Send to* ⓘ

Select recipients   ▼

Don't send to ⓘ

Select lists or contacts   ▼

☐ Don't send to unengaged contacts (398) ⓘ

Figure 10.17 – Selecting recipients for the email

Before clicking on the send button, check how the email looks on a desktop and mobile and even how it will appear to different email clients. You can do this by clicking on **Actions** in the upper-right corner of the email and then clicking on **Preview**:

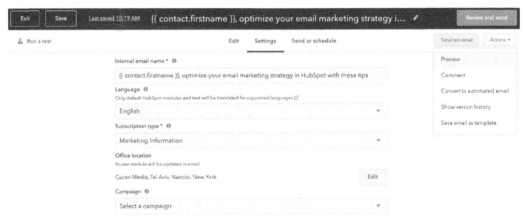

Figure 10.18 – Previewing your email on a desktop and mobile

Following this, you will be redirected to the desktop and mobile version, as shown in the following screenshot. Here, you can see the layout of the content to ensure the flow is exactly as you intend:

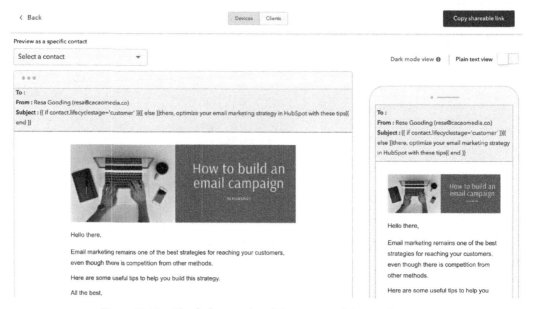

Figure 10.19 – The desktop and mobile preview of the email content

For users with a HubSpot Professional or Enterprise account, you can also see how the emails look on different email clients such as Outlook and Gmail alongside different mobile devices such as Samsung, iPad, and iPhone. To access this feature, click on the middle banner that says **Clients**, select the different email clients and devices from the left-hand side that you wish to test, and then click on **Test my email now**:

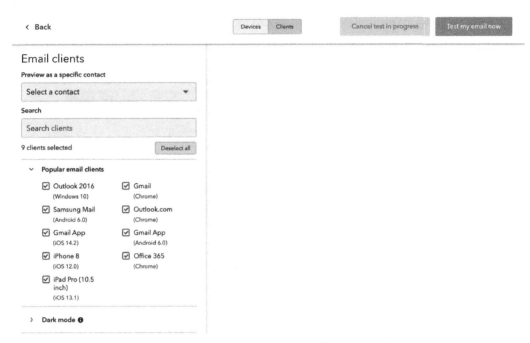

Figure 10.20 – Testing your email on different email clients

Once this is done, you can click through to see what your email will look like according to the different email clients you chose. Note that if any changes are required, you will need to go back to the edit section of the email to make any changes. In addition, it is important to note that the goal is not to optimize for every single type of email client but, instead, to optimize for the top three or so email clients and devices that are the most popular among your contacts.

Figure 10.18 shows an example of what it would look like on Outlook Windows 10:

Figure 10.21 – The Microsoft Outlook email preview

In comparison, *Figure 10.19* shows the mobile version of what the email will look like on Gmail App on the iOS platform version 14.2 (yes, it's that precise):

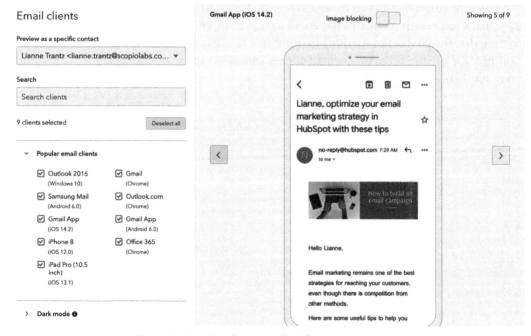

Figure 10.22 – Gmail App on the iPhone email preview

After ensuring your email's content and layout are ready, it's time for distribution. Using some of the initial tips mentioned at the beginning, we will ensure the emails are going out to the right contacts at the right time by using the following features.

First, click on the top-level menu and select **Send or Schedule**. The next step is to choose a list of contacts to whom you would like to send the email. In this section, notice that you also have the option to select a list of contacts that you do not want to receive the email. So, for example, if it's a promotional email you are sending and you wish to ensure that none of your existing customers receive it, you can exclude them.

The next step is to choose whether you wish to send it immediately or to schedule it to be sent at a later date and time. If you choose the latter, be sure to choose a date and time in the future. Additionally, note that you will also have the option to ensure that the email arrives at a specified time according to the time zone of the recipients. For instance, if you chose to send the email at 11:33 am, it will be sent at 11:33 a.m. across all the time zones of the recipients:

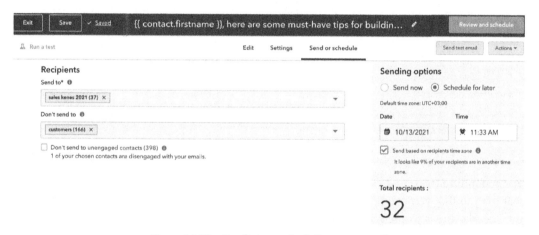

Figure 10.23 – Sending or scheduling your email

Once you've sent your email, the next nail-biting moment is to check the results. Often, you will be anxious to know the open rate and the click-through rate of your email and exactly who has opened and clicked on it. HubSpot offers all of these analytics and more so that you can then take any necessary actions for future email sends.

Analyzing the results of your email

To see the results of your sent email, simply return to the email under **Marketing | Email** and click on the email that was sent. The **Performance** page will appear with the following charts.

The following chart shows your open rate, click rate, and even the reply rate. Generally, for most industries, the benchmark lies around a 30% open rate and a 3% click rate:

Figure 10.24 – The overall performance rate of the email

The following chart shows the delivery rate. Here, you want to pay attention to any unsubscribes or spam reports to ensure you remove those email addresses from your database:

Delivery

SUCCESSFUL DELIVERIES	BOUNCES	UNSUBSCRIBES	SPAM REPORTS
147	0	2	0
100%	0%	1.36%	0%

Figure 10.25 – Delivery rates

Understanding the statistics described so far is important, but HubSpot also presents a heat map so that you can better understand how your content has performed. The heat map clearly shows where readers have spent the most time. So, for future emails, you can determine where to place the most important information.

On the right-hand side of the heat map, as shown in the following screenshot, you can also see which links were clicked on the most and which contacts were the most engaged. Both are measured by the number of times they opened your email along with the number of times they clicked on your emails:

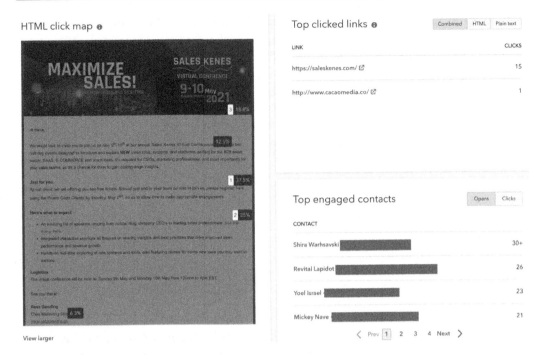

Figure 10.26 – Heat map for email engagement

Next, we would want to better understand the level of engagement your contacts had with the email. The following graph shows how many people actually read the email compared to those who skimmed it or just took a glance at it. This statistic allows you to gauge the interest level of the content that was sent:

Time spent viewing email

READ ❶	SKIMMED ❶	GLANCED ❶
32.3%	51.6%	16.1%

Figure 10.27 – Time spent viewing the email

In comparison, the engagement over time graph, as shown in the following screenshot, allows you to better understand the timeframe in which your emails extracted a response. You can change the filters to see the results either within the first 24 hours or for longer periods, as follows:

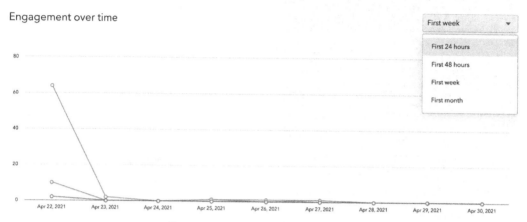

Figure 10.28 – Engagement over time

One of the most important, but often overlooked, statistics is understanding not just which devices opened your emails but which email clients were the most popular for opening your emails. This guides your process for optimizing your email layout, as described in the previous section:

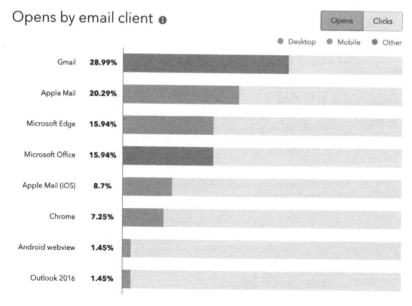

Figure 10.29 – The number of opens by email client

The next step is to go a bit deeper and gain a better understanding of exactly which contacts in your database were engaged with your content. By clicking on the **Recipients** bar at the top, you shift from just seeing overall numbers to seeing the details of every contact who received your email, opened it, and clicked on it along with those contacts who unsubscribed or whose email might have bounced.

The value of having this level of detail allows you to collect these contacts in specific lists so that you can use this information in the future. For example, should you wish to resend the email to contacts who didn't open the email, you can make a list of contacts who opened the email and then resend the email to all contacts in your original list, excluding those who have already opened it:

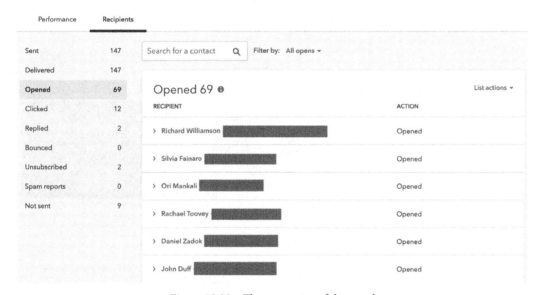

Figure 10.30 – The open rates of the email

After analyzing the statistics of your email, you might still be wondering how you can improve your results. How do you get more people to open your emails and take action on the content you've sent them? In the next section, we will discuss the different tools within HubSpot that can help you to optimize your results.

Optimizing the email for best performance

When it comes to email marketing, there are only a handful of techniques that can be used to optimize the performance of an email:

- Improving/testing the subject line, click rate, and click-through rate
- Simplifying the content

- Creating more targeted content for specific audiences

- Personalizing the content

- Improving/testing sending times

In HubSpot, you have the ability to do all of these optimizations using the tools explained in the following sub-sections.

A/B testing

The A/B testing tool allows you to test the open rate, click rate, and click-through rate of your emails over a specific period of time. To run an A/B test, go to the email, and from the upper-left corner, click on the **Run a Test** button:

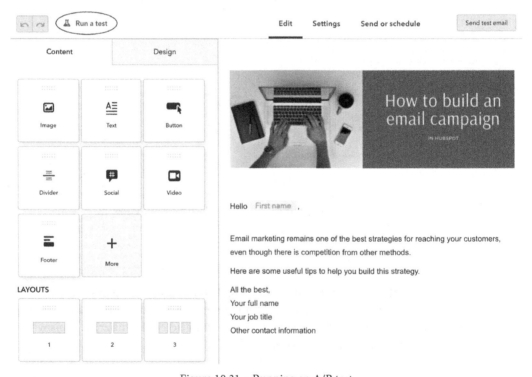

Figure 10.31 – Running an A/B test

Clicking on this button reveals a pop-up box that prompts you to first choose another subject line that will be used for the second version of the email. Then, you can choose which metric you wish to test for, such as the open rate, click rate, or click-through rate, and, finally, the length of time that you wish to test for. Once this is complete, click on **Create test**:

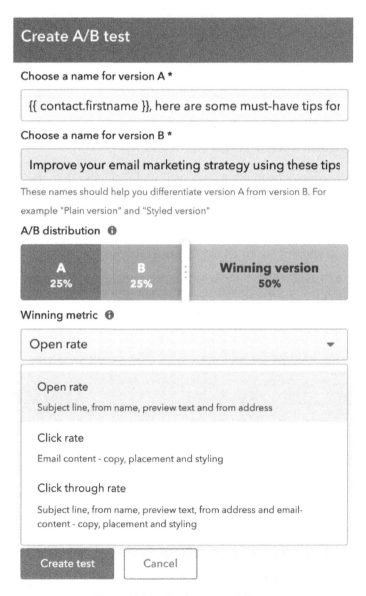

Figure 10.32 – Setting up an A/B test

Once the test has been created, you now have two versions of the email that can be accessed by clicking on the upper-left subject lines and switching between them. This allows you to edit both versions of the email so that you can test different elements of the email. In *Figure 10.29*, you can see the option of switching between each of the emails in the A/B test:

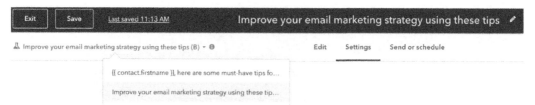

Figure 10.33 – Setting up two versions of the email

Some suggestions of items to test are listed as follows:

- Changing the content by making one email slightly longer than the other
- Changing the colors of the CTA button
- Changing the placement of the CTA button
- Making one version of the email in plain text without any images:

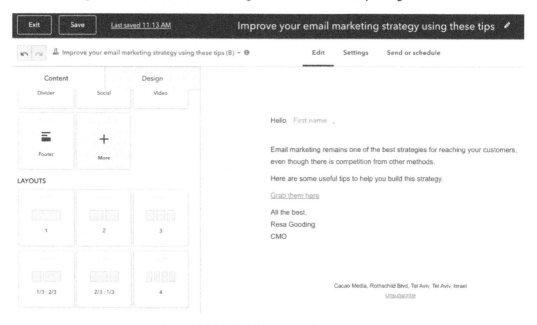

Figure 10.34 – A plain text email as version B

After your email has been sent, the A/B testing tool will return the results of your email and determine which version of your email performed better for the metric you tested. Here's what the test results look like:

Figure 10.35 – The A/B test results

A/B tests are essential to your strategy, as they allow you to improve the conversion rates, which can make a difference to your bottom line.

The smart module

Another tool to test within the emails is the smart module. In HubSpot, the smart module allows you to send different versions of your subject line to different types of contacts. To access the smart module, go to **Settings** in your email settings, and click on **Add smart rule** right below the subject line:

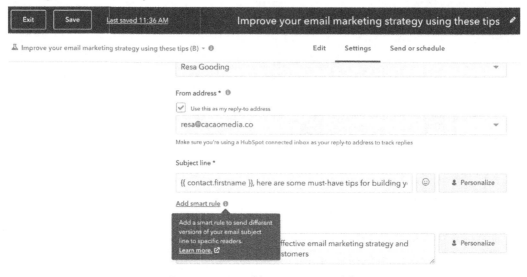

Figure 10.36 – Adding a smart module

Clicking on **Add smart rule** will reveal a pop-up box that prompts you to choose a group of people that will see different content. You can choose them based on **Contact list membership** or **Contact lifecycle stage**:

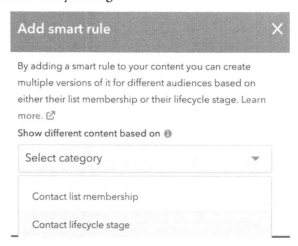

Figure 10.37 – Choosing a category

Choosing either category prompts another filter option to appear, allowing you to choose between the list you want and the life cycle stage. Once you have made your choice, click on **Create**:

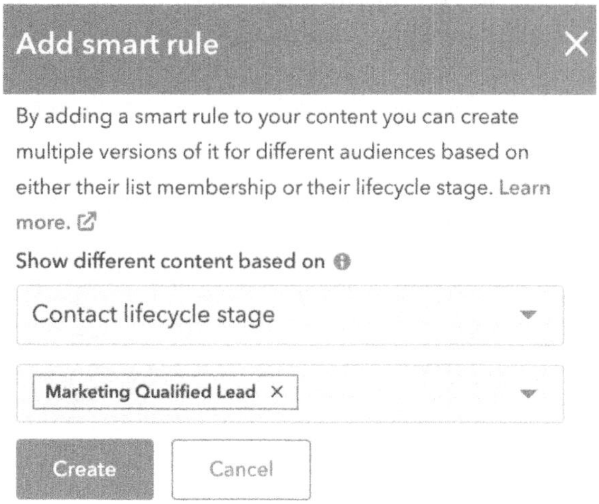

Figure 10.38 – Choosing the sub-category

You will then be returned to the **Settings** section of the email where you will be prompted to enter another subject line:

Figure 10.39 – Entering the subject line that the separate segment of contacts can receive

Smart rules are one of those tools that are often overlooked in HubSpot, but when implemented right, they can make a significant difference as it often gives readers the feeling that the content has been personalized.

Personalizing the content

Personalization is the art of using your contact's data within the email itself. It gives you the feeling that the message has been written specifically for them. In HubSpot, to access the personalization feature, you can click on the personalize buttons shown in the email body, or the subject lines, and choose to include any of the fields that collect personal information about the contact. Some of the most commonly used fields are the user's first name, company name, and more:

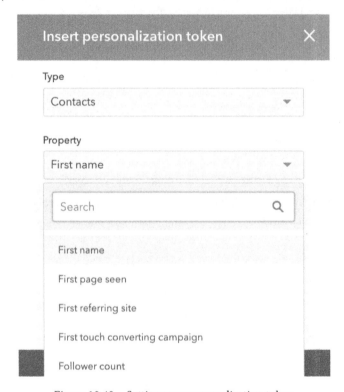

Figure 10.40 – Setting up a personalization token

Additionally, you have the option to choose a default token in cases where the information does not exist. For example, if the first name is missing, then it won't appear blank. Or worse still, the personalization token might appear but a generic alternative such as *there* or *colleague* will be shown instead. To set up the default token, click on **Settings | Marketing | Email**, scroll to the bottom of the page, and then click on **Edit defaults** for **Contact property defaults** or **Company property defaults**:

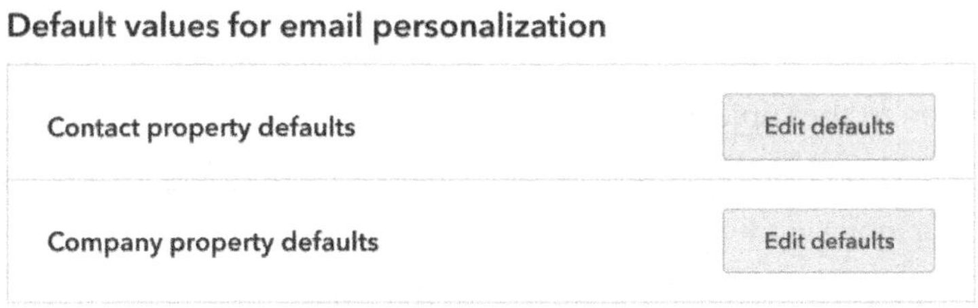

Default values for email personalization

Contact property defaults	Edit defaults
Company property defaults	Edit defaults

Figure 10.41 – Email personalization tokens

Following this, you choose a generic default name you wish to insert if the information is missing. So, for example, if the first name is missing, the word "there" can be used as the default. Then, click on **Save**:

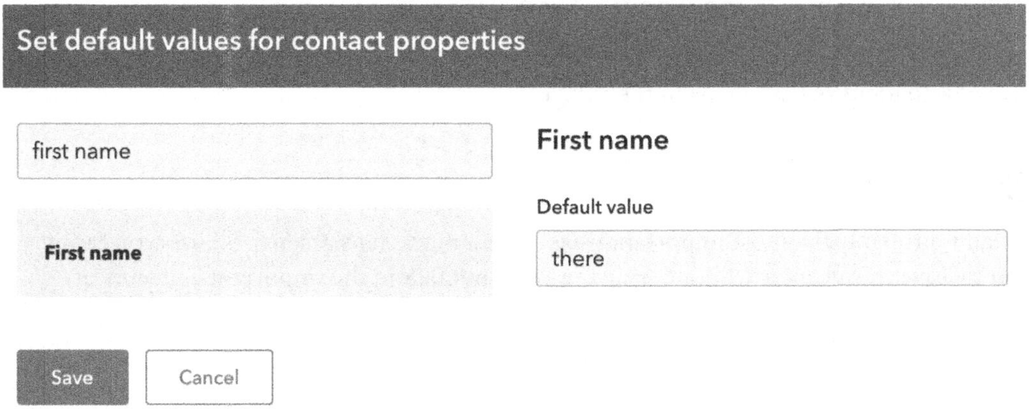

Set default values for contact properties

first name

First name

First name

Default value

there

Save   Cancel

Figure 10.42 – Setting up a generic default

No one ever sends an email campaign that gets great results each and every time. Therefore, your strategy must include some element of optimization so that you can always make your campaigns better. One simple and quick way to implement a strategy in each email campaign is to resend the emails to contacts who did not open the emails the first time around by using a different subject line.

Summary

As you can see, for a successful email marketing campaign, a lot of thought and trial and error must be exercised in order to achieve the results you seek. Implementing just one or two of the tips mentioned earlier should help you see improvements in your email campaigns.

Here are a few reminders to pay attention to:

- Pay attention to the subject lines and ensure they are short but click-worthy.

- Keep the content short. Any email that is over 60 words must offer great value and not just be a long-winded sales pitch.

- Use personalization wherever possible – in the subject line, in the preview of the text, in the body of the email, and, of course, in the salutation.

- Try not to add too many links to the email, which take users to different content. Ensure the links are relevant to the action you want the contacts to take.

As often as possible, ensure the emails are coming from a person and not a generic email such as `marketing@companyname.com` or `info@companyname.com`.

In the next chapter, you will learn how to create reporting and tracking within HubSpot and how to identify key trends in their data.

Questions

Email is probably the most important weapon in a marketer's arsenal. So, we won't want you to leave this chapter without ensuring you understand the important concepts of gaining great results from your email campaigns. Let's recap with a few short questions:

1. Which elements do you need to consider when building an email strategy?

2. Can you design images within HubSpot for your email campaigns?

3. What are two best practices you can implement right now to improve your email campaigns?

Further reading

- *The Modern Guidebook to Email Marketing*: `https://www.campaignmonitor.com/resources/guides/modern-guidebook-email-marketing/`

- *The Ultimate Guide to Email Marketing*: `https://blog.hubspot.com/marketing/email-marketing-guide`

- *23 Simple Email Marketing Tips to Improve Your Open and Clickthrough Rates*: `https://blog.hubspot.com/marketing/make-emails-more-clickable-list`

11
Proving That Your Efforts Worked Using the Reports

Today's marketers are required to bring measurable results. Every campaign, every activity, and every dollar spent can now be measured and accounted for so the ROI of marketing efforts can be measured. HubSpot reports are, therefore, an integral part of the system to ensure marketers can show the results of their efforts and what worked and what didn't.

In this chapter, you will learn about the following:

- Creating marketing reports to track your success
- Creating sales reports that help your sales teams close more deals
- Knowing which reports your management team cares the most about
- Using the data from the different analytics reports in HubSpot to boost your campaigns
- Exploring third-party tools that can give further insights into your reports

By the end of the chapter, you'll know how to prepare reports that show how the marketing department's activities directly contribute to the bottom line of a company.

Technical requirements

To get the most out of this chapter, you will need the following:

- Access to HubSpot Marketing Professional or Enterprise
- Access to the reports tool
- At a minimum, view-only access to contacts, companies, and deals data

Creating marketing reports to track your success

There are three categories of reports or dashboards you will want to create:

- Traffic analytics to measure how many visitors are coming to your website
- Engagement reports to measure how many visitors are converting to leads or downloading assets
- Funnel reports to show how leads are moving through the funnel

Let's take a look at how to build traffic reports.

Building traffic reports

In HubSpot, on the top menu, clicking on **Reports** and **Traffic Analytics** takes you to a dashboard of prepared reports:

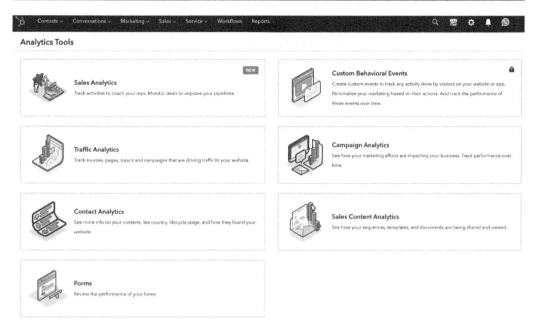

Figure 11.1 – Analytics tool

Clicking on the **Traffic Analytics** option brings you to a dashboard that shows the number of visitors coming to your website:

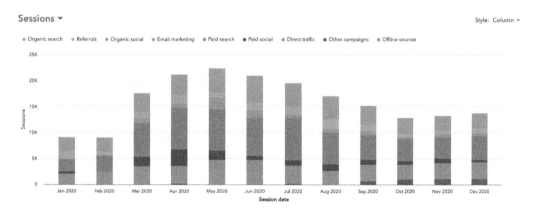

Figure 11.2 – Graph of traffic sources

This report shows you the nine sources of traffic that HubSpot automatically tracks:

- **Direct traffic**: Contacts who came to your website from a website link that was sent to them

- **Email marketing**: Contacts who came to your website after receiving an email from your company or one that was forwarded to them from another source

- **Organic search**: Contacts who came to your website after inputting a query on a search engine, such as Google or Bing, which gives one of your website pages as an option

- **Offline sources**: Contacts who were manually inserted into the system or added via integrations of external platforms

- **Organic social**: Contacts who visited your online assets via organic posts on social media

- **Other campaigns**: Contacts who visited your online assets via campaigns promoted by you on external platforms

- **Paid search**: Contacts who came to your online assets via Google Ads.

- **Paid social**: Contacts who came to your online assets via ads on social media platforms such as LinkedIn, Facebook, and Twitter

- **Referrals**: Contacts who came to your online assets via other websites that mentioned you and gave you a backlink

The following table shows the breakdown of these traffic sources, which is a similar view to Google Analytics with the exception that you can now see the exact contacts that were created via each source:

	SOURCE	SESSIONS	SESSION TO CONTACT RATE	NEW CONTACTS	CONTACT TO CUSTOMER RATE	CUSTOMERS	BOUNCE RATE	SESSION LENGTH
☑	Paid search	66,963	2.28%	1,527	0.39%	6	82.69%	36 seconds
☑	Organic search	43,251	1.17%	504	6.15%	31	71.72%	87 seconds
☑	Direct traffic	39,794	2.03%	809	5.19%	42	65.94%	122 seconds
☑	Referrals	15,060	0.72%	109	4.59%	5	88.61%	36 seconds
☑	Paid social	13,002	24.08%	3,131	0.73%	23	79%	43 seconds
☑	Other campaigns	4,946	5.8%	287	3.48%	10	91.23%	12 seconds
☑	Email marketing	4,896	11.79%	577	0.52%	3	60.29%	61 seconds
☑	Organic social	4,654	6.92%	322	5.9%	19	71.7%	56 seconds
☑	Offline sources	-	0%	9,512	3.17%	302	0%	-
	Total	192,566	8.71%	16,778	2.63%	441	76.36%	66 seconds

Figure 11.3 – Table of traffic sources

Note, **Offline sources** captures everything that does not fall into the other eight categories, for example, contacts created manually, contacts created because of the sync with each of your team members' personal inbox, contacts uploaded through Excel, contacts created via integration to another platform, and so on. To understand exactly where each contact came from with respect to online sources, you will need to look at two other fields, **Original source drilldown 1** and **Original source drilldown 2**.

You will also notice that clicking on any of the sources will give your further details of the exact source that brought the lead. For example, in *Figure 11.4*, clicking on **Paid social** will show a breakdown of the social media networks that brought the lead:

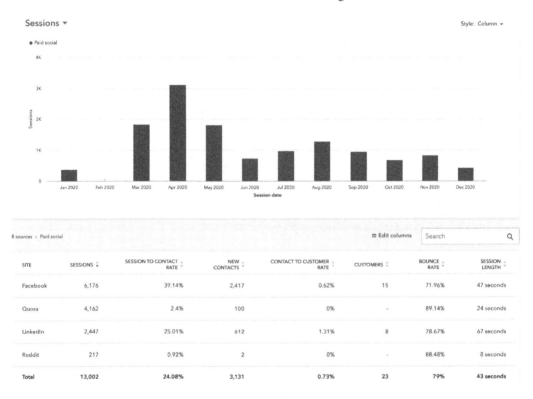

SITE	SESSIONS	SESSION TO CONTACT RATE	NEW CONTACTS	CONTACT TO CUSTOMER RATE	CUSTOMERS	BOUNCE RATE	SESSION LENGTH
Facebook	6,176	39.14%	2,417	0.62%	15	71.96%	47 seconds
Quora	4,162	2.4%	100	0%	-	89.14%	24 seconds
LinkedIn	2,447	25.01%	612	1.31%	8	78.67%	67 seconds
Reddit	217	0.92%	2	0%	-	88.48%	8 seconds
Total	13,002	24.08%	3,131	0.73%	23	79%	43 seconds

Figure 11.4 – Paid social

This is **Original source drilldown 1** as mentioned previously. And, clicking once again into each of the social media networks will give you the exact campaign that brought the lead, as shown in *Figure 11.5*. In the preceding table, there are several headings that are automatically calculated by the system. Here's what they represent:

- **SESSIONS**: This is the number of times someone came from this channel to your website. Note, it does not include unique contacts so it could include one person coming 6,000 plus times. Also, if you have not excluded your team members from the traffic, your team's visits will also be included in these numbers here.

- **SESSION TO CONTACT RATE**: This calculation is based on how many times your new contacts visited your website measured as a percentage. The formula used here is *New Contacts/Sessions x 100*.

- **NEW CONTACTS**: This measurement refers to the number of contacts that were converted by submitting a form on your website.

- **CONTACT TO CUSTOMER RATE**: This calculation looks at the percentage of customers that were created from new contacts. The formula used is *Customers/New Contacts x 100*.

- **CUSTOMERS**: This number represents the number of contacts with closed deals in this period.

- **BOUNCE RATE**: This number represents how many visitors came to your website but did not proceed to another page. Generally, you want this number to be as low as possible.

- **SESSION LENGTH**: This number represents how long visitors stayed on your website.

All sources > Organic social > LinkedIn

CAMPAIGN	SESSIONS	SESSION TO CONTACT RATE	NEW CONTACTS
Unknown campaign	47	17.02%	8
uk webinars	2	50%	1
social media	5	0%	-
content marketing	1	0%	-
webinar series israel	1	0%	-
new hires	9	0%	-
free hubspot workshops	1	0%	-
Total	**66**	**13.64%**	**9**

Figure 11.5 – Campaigns associated with Organic social networks

On the top navigation bar of the **Traffic Analytics** report, you will see many other parameters that can be tracked, for instance, page views, countries, and devices, to name a few:

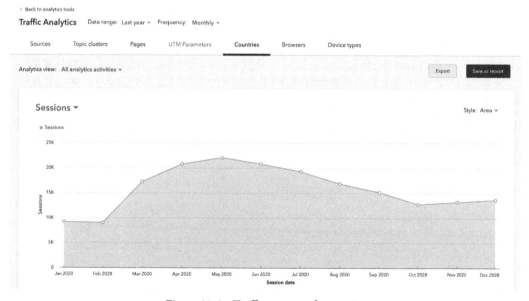

Figure 11.6 – Traffic sources of countries

Each graph is accompanied by a table, as seen next. These analytics are collected from the integration of HubSpot with your website and you will notice some familiarity with Google Analytics with the parameters being measured, for instance, the number of new sessions, bounce rate, and so on:

All countries ›   ⊞ Edit columns

	COUNTRY	SESSIONS	% NEW SESSION	SESSION TO CONTACT RATE	NEW CONTACTS	CONTACT TO CUSTOMER RATE	CUSTOMERS	BOUNCE RATE	SESSION LENGTH
☐	United States	68,281	78.01%	2.65%	1,811	2.82%	51	80.21%	49 seconds
☐	Israel	36.961	51.81%	1.52%	563	1.95%	11	69.32%	96 seconds
☐	United Kingdom	14,315	78.23%	3.45%	494	1.01%	5	79.24%	47 seconds
☐	Germany	12,436	82.94%	3.82%	475	2.11%	10	80.9%	42 seconds
☐	India	11,238	70.24%	2.76%	310	5.81%	18	73.05%	88 seconds
☐	Singapore	10,824	64.98%	3.17%	343	0.87%	3	77.99%	50 seconds
☐	Canada	4,922	73.73%	4.82%	237	4.64%	11	74.46%	63 seconds
☐	France	2,091	73.27%	2.01%	42	4.76%	2	71.45%	91 seconds
☐	Netherlands	1,758	74.18%	1.93%	34	8.82%	3	71.62%	59 seconds
☐	South Korea	1,715	65.83%	1.75%	30	3.33%	1	69.68%	101 seconds

Figure 11.7 – Breakdown of contacts and the different countries they came from

Note, there will be a difference between the numbers seen in these reports and Google Analytics as there is a lag between the information being synced to HubSpot. It is, therefore, recommended to use these reports to measure two main things: the number of new contacts and the number of new customers that originated from these sources. Clicking these numbers highlighted in blue will give you the exact list of contacts that came from each source, which is something Google Analytics cannot give you, and this is the main benefit of using HubSpot reports to measure your traffic.

Let's now look at which reports will show you how contacts are engaging with your content.

By once again clicking on **Reports | Analytics Tools**, you will see a section called **Forms**:

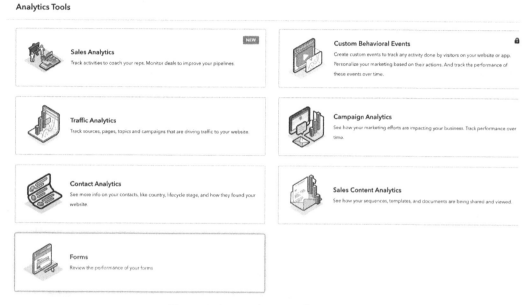

Figure 11.8 – Analytics Tools – Forms

Forms analytics allow you to understand the view-to-submissions rate (or your conversion rate) of your landing pages so you can measure the effectiveness of your content and the questions that are asked on the forms:

Figure 11.9 – Forms analytics

According to the 2021 Conversion Benchmark Report produced by Unbounce, each industry has various conversion rates, as seen in *Figure 11.10*. If your company's conversion rate is below the industry's average, there are a few things you can consider checking.

The first place to begin is to make sure your forms aren't too long. Asking too many questions on a form that provides access to content can be a turnoff. For instance, if you wish to collect more subscribers to your blog, then asking for an email address is sufficient for this type of content. If you've taken the time to produce a valuable long-form piece of industry-worthy content such as an e-book or white paper, then asking a few more questions (such as name, job title, and business email) is acceptable. However, if it's important for you to get more information from your leads, then consider using tools such as progressive forms, which allow you to collect more information from a lead on their next visit to your content. Further details on this can be found in *Chapter 9, Converting Your Visitors to Customers.*

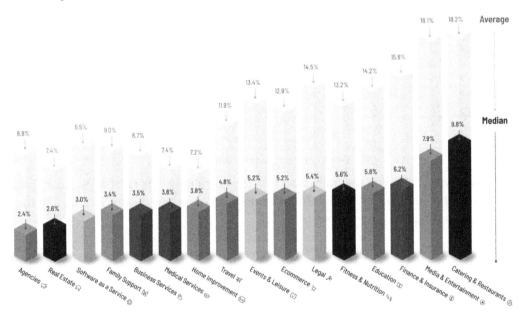

Figure 11.10 – Conversion rates by industry (source: Unbounce)

Another type of report that can help you measure your engagement and the effectiveness of your marketing efforts further down the funnel is **Campaign Analytics**. To access this report, navigate once again to the top menu, and click on **Reports | Analytics Tools**. You will see a section called **Campaign Analytics**, as shown in the following figure:

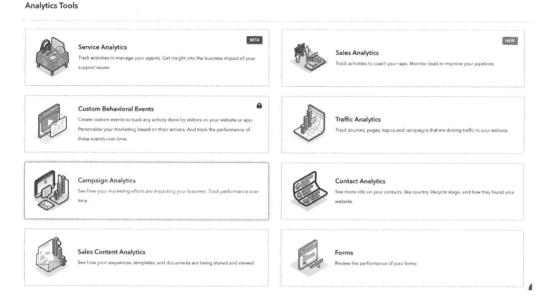

Figure 11.11 – Campaign Analytics

Figure 11.12 shows the campaign analytics. They help you to measure how effective your campaigns were in bringing you relevant leads, opportunities, and revenue. There are a few metrics you would want to pay attention to when using this campaign tool:

CAMPAIGN	SESSIONS	NEW CONTACTS (FIRST TOUCH)	INFLUENCED CONTACTS	CLOSED DEALS
AI for Connected Vehicles Webinar	4,674	136	3,041	0
The MLOps Live Webinar Series #14	1,591	117	2,866	2
The MLOps Webinar Series #13	2,020	94	2,486	1
The MLOPs Webinar Series #12	1,176	85	2,443	1

Figure 11.12 – Measuring the number of sessions, new contacts, and influenced contacts of campaigns

The first is **INFLUENCED CONTACTS**. This helps you understand which contacts engaged or interacted with any assets related to your campaign. Whether it's a social media post that they liked, shared, or left a comment on, an email they opened, or a form they filled out, any asset that you have associated with the campaign will be tagged and tracked accordingly.

The second metric is **SESSIONS**. This measures how much traffic each asset related to your campaign attracted.

Then, you would also want to measure **NEW CONTACTS (FIRST TOUCH)**, which lets you know how many new contacts your campaign generated because they visited a URL associated with your campaign.

NEW CONTACTS (LAST TOUCH) is also an interesting metric. This metric lets you know which contacts converted after visiting an asset related to your campaign. That is, they submitted a form in the same session while visiting an asset within your campaign.

Then finally, you will want to measure **CLOSED DEALS**, which lets you know which campaigns the contacts touched before they became an opportunity or customer.

The last set of reports that you will want to create in this series is what is popularly known as **funnel reports**. Admittedly, these reports are often the most difficult to create simply because most companies do not correctly use the life cycle stages within HubSpot correctly and these reports depend on this. In this chapter, we focus on how to build the reports and interpret the data from them.

First, let's explain what a funnel report is. The goal of a funnel report is to show a general flow of how contacts convert from one stage to the next. For example, most contacts that enter the system for the first time will be tagged as a **lead**, and as they progress and more information is collected about them that matches the company's ideal client profile, they will eventually convert to a **marketing-qualified lead** (MQL) and **sales-qualified lead** (SQL).

There are two types of funnel reports in HubSpot – the contact life cycle stage funnel and the deal stage funnel. To create these funnel reports, navigate to the top menu and click on **Reports** and then **Reports** again:

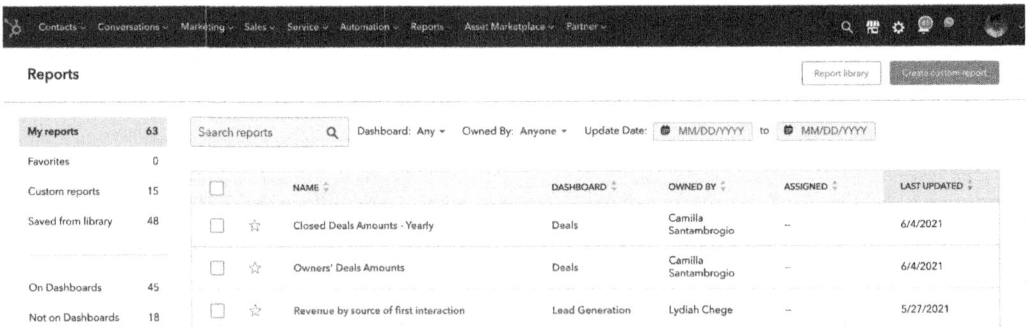

Figure 11.13 – Accessing the report library

Then, on the top-right corner, click on **Report library** and navigate to the left-side menu and check the box called **Funnels** and the two reports will appear:

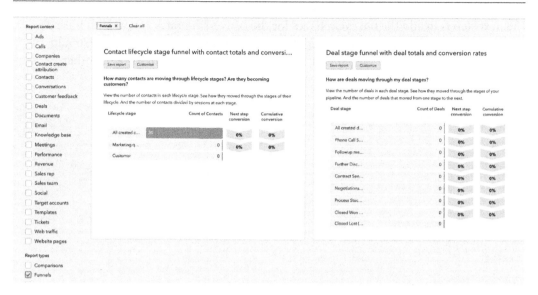

Figure 11.14 – Accessing the funnel reports

Once you've reached the reports, clicking on the gray **Customize** button allows you to change the filters of the fields you wish to see in the report, as seen in the following figure:

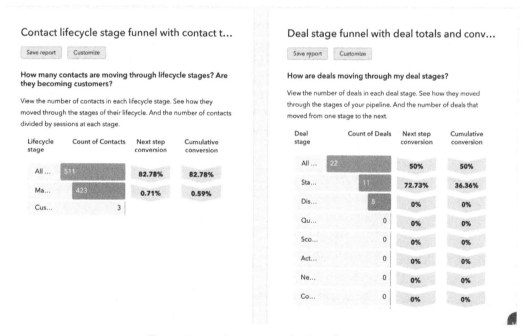

Figure 11.15 – Customizing the funnel reports

The next step is to add the life cycle stages for the conversion rates you wish to measure. Be careful to also put them in the order they should be in, for example, a lead should be placed before the MQL stage since a lead converts to an MQL and not the other way around.

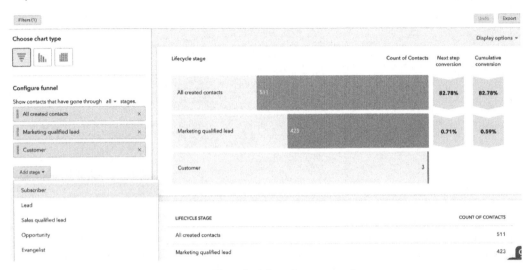

Figure 11.16 – Adding the life cycle stages to the reports

Once you've added all the life cycle stages as seen in *Figure 11.17*, you will then want to decide whether you wish to measure the conversion rates for contacts who went through *all* of the stages (meaning they must be first a lead, then an MQL, and then an SQL), or to measure the conversion rate of contacts who went through *any* stage, meaning they might have come into the system and been immediately tagged as an MQL because they fit the description of your **ideal customer profile (ICP)**. Choosing one of these options over the other will greatly influence your report as you will see the numbers change drastically:

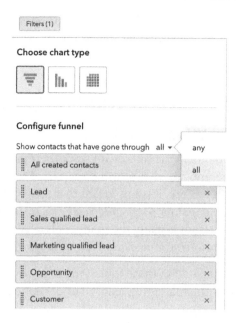

Figure 11.17 – Deciding whether to look at contacts who went through all stages or any stage

Your last decision to make in these reports is to decide which date range to measure. Clicking on **Filters** at the top will allow you to choose exactly which period you wish to examine these conversion rates:

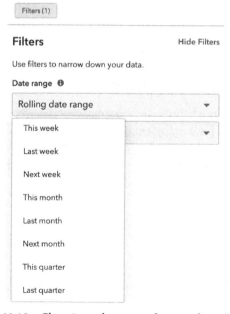

Figure 11.18 – Choosing a date range for your funnel report

Once the date range has been chosen, you are now able to see the conversion rates of your contacts moving from one life cycle stage to another if you chose the **all** option, or contacts in any life cycle stage if you chose the **any** option.

Creating sales reports that help your sales teams close more deals

In order to create reports that help the sales team track their progress on deals, it is important to remember that most of the information related to sales lies in the deals object or activities object. Therefore, it is important that the pipelines be set up and in use (refer to *Chapter 3, Using HubSpot for Managing Sales Processes Effectively*, for tips on how to do this) and that the sales team is using the many tools available within HubSpot, as discussed in *Chapter 4, Empowering Your Sales Team through HubSpot*.

Once the information is populated in these topics, the following reports can be useful to your managers as well as for the marketing team to understand the success of their efforts:

- Activity leaderboard
- Deal leaderboard
- Opportunities by Original Source
- Deals won by source
- Closed Lost Reasons

Let's take a look at what each of these reports represents.

Activity leaderboard report

The activity leaderboard report shows how many activities were done by each sales representative. It measures how many emails were sent to contacts, how many replies were received from these emails, how many meetings were booked, and how many calls were made. Note that the emails here are not marketing emails but emails sent by each representative via their personal email account.

The activity leaderboard report looks like the following figure:

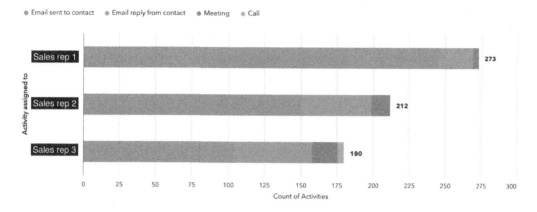

Figure 11.19 – Activity leaderboard – Sales representatives

These reports can be customized as needed to show only specific members of the team, specific activities, and a specified date range.

Deal leaderboard report

The deal leaderboard report shows how many opportunities were won by each sales representative during a specific time period. Here's what it looks like:

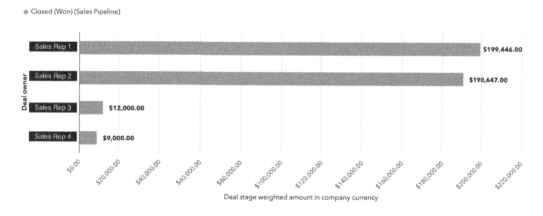

Figure 11.20 – Deal leaderboard – Sales representatives

To build this report, you will need to add a filter for **Deal Stage** and choose **Deal Stage |**
Closed (Won).

Opportunities by Original Source

This report helps you to understand which channels brought you the most opportunities so you can expand your efforts in these areas:

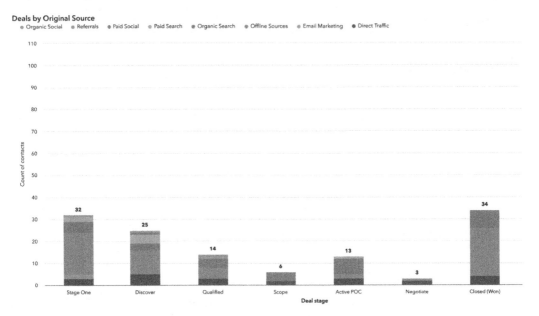

Figure 11.21 – Deals by Original Source

You may see in this report that **Offline Sources** created the most deals because there might be many contacts created via imports or by the sales representatives directly. To better understand the breakdown of these offline channels, you can add **Original source drilldown 1** as another filter in these reports.

Deals won by source

Complementary to the previous report, you may also want to specifically explore which channels contributed to the revenue of the company. In the following example, it is clear that **Organic search** is one of the most important sources of generating customers for this company, which means they should invest more in SEO:

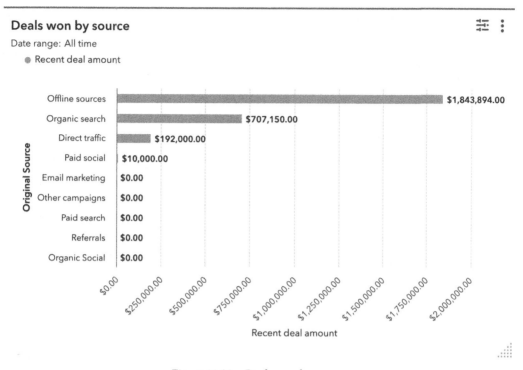

Figure 11.22 – Deals won by source

In addition, paid social advertisements placed on LinkedIn or Facebook have potential, so this channel can be optimized more.

Closed Lost Reasons

Often overlooked is this report, Closed Lost Reasons. It is a default field in HubSpot that is a multi-line text. However, to make sense of the information placed in this report, it is often recommended to convert it to a drop-down menu and add the most common reasons your sales teams typically lose deals. Once this field is prepared, place it as mandatory in the deal stages so once a representative moves an opportunity to the closed-won stage, they must update this property.

Figure 11.23 shows a graph of the reasons that deals were closed-lost, which were recorded each time a sales representative moved a deal to the closed-lost stage:

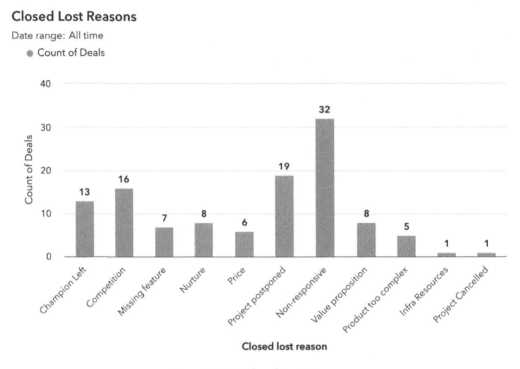

Figure 11.23 – Closed Lost Reasons

One of the benefits of building such a report is that you often realize the price is not the main reason for customers not choosing your product or service. Therefore, it helps you to improve in the areas that are more compelling. In the preceding example, the top three reasons deals are lost are contacts suddenly disappearing, the project being postponed, or the prospect choosing to go with one of your competitors. Therefore, this insight prompts the marketing team to offer support such as building nurtures for contacts that went cold to see whether they would eventually return. In addition, for projects that were postponed, the sales team can set up sequences to touch base with the prospect once every month or even 3 months to see whether there have been any changes. The point is that this report can help you reactivate deals that were seemingly lost.

Note that there are dozens of other reports pre-built in the HubSpot tool to help both marketing and sales teams understand the results of their efforts. So, I implore you to spend some time rummaging through the report library and sales analytics reports to see which other reports can be useful to you and your team. And remember, whatever doesn't exist can be built as a custom report.

The reports your management team cares the most about

Now that we understand which reports better serve marketing and sales teams, it is time to understand which reports truly matter to your management team. To know which reports they really want to see, I suggest the following two methods:

- **Ask them**: Yes, simply ask them which types of reports they would like to see. Most times, they won't be able to articulate the exact name of the report but a sufficient explanation of the data they are looking for is often more than enough to begin.

- **Start with revenue**: If in doubt, always remember that managers generally care about the bottom line. They want to see reports that show them how well they are doing financially and what's contributing to this success or failure.

After setting up hundreds of HubSpot accounts, these are the five reports most commonly requested or appreciated once they are built:

- Revenue forecast
- Deal time spent in each stage
- Number of opportunities created
- Deal velocity
- Deal revenue by source

Let's take a look at what each of these reports signals to the management team.

Revenue forecast

This report predicts for management how much revenue they can expect to receive in any period. It uses a property called **Forecast category**, which allows the sales team to manually update how likely a deal is to close and, therefore, gives the management team a high-level overview of where the majority of deals stand in the pipeline. *Figure 11.24* shows how this type of report is typically reflected in HubSpot:

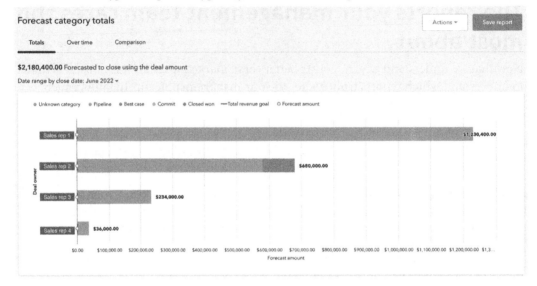

Figure 11.24 – Forecast revenue

One of the ways to help populate this field instead of asking the sales team to fill out yet another property is to build a workflow that will assign the forecast category based on the various stages in the pipeline. For example, let's say there is a stage in your pipeline called **proof of concept**, then you can build a workflow that will assign the forecast category as **Best case** since most deals in Proof of concept are most likely to close.

Deal time spent in each stage

This report helps the management team to understand how long a deal is taking to progress through the various stages and, more importantly, where they are getting stuck:

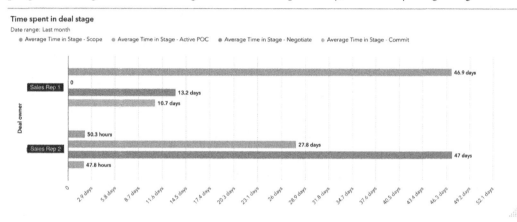

Figure 11.25 – Time spent in deal stage

In the preceding example, there appears to be a big difference in the number of days that deals stay in the **Negotiate** stage for **Sales Rep 2** compared to **Sales Rep 1**. Therefore, it can be a good indication to the VP of sales to train **Sales Rep 2** on the methods **Sales Rep 1** uses for negotiation to shorten the timeline.

Number of opportunities created

The goal of this report is to show you which months are typically the strongest and which are the weakest to know where the teams are needed the most in order to maintain a healthy pipeline. This report can be found in **Reports | Analytics Tools | Sales Analytics** if you are using Sales Professional. In the following example, it is clear that January, March, and December are the weakest months:

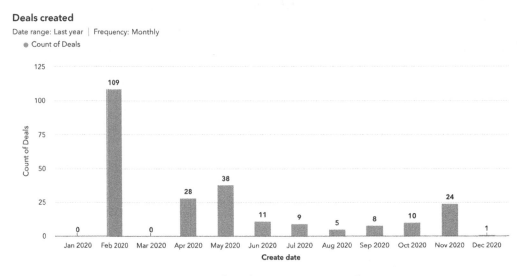

Figure 11.26 – Number of opportunities created in 2020

For December and January, this is understandable as most of the world is on holiday during this time for Christmas and New Year, and typically, budgets are being closed and reset so it's difficult to get companies to be interested in anything during this time. However, the peak in February shows that once companies are back in the game and have the necessary budgets in hand, they are ready to explore the products or services they need. So, there is nothing too worrying until this point. However, March is a weak month for this company, and it might signal that the sales teams, after placing all their efforts to close deals in February, began slowing down in March. But, a closer look at the data shows that this was March 2020, the beginning of the global pandemic of COVID-19. Therefore, the world became paralyzed as companies were unsure of their futures, so most were not spending during that particular month. But, it is seen that once the activities of this company continued, they were able to pick up more deals in months to follow.

For management to explore that their assumptions had some merit, it would be worth looking at the opportunities created in the following year. In the following example, it shows that the pipeline recovered, especially during the months of January and March, which were previously difficult months for the company:

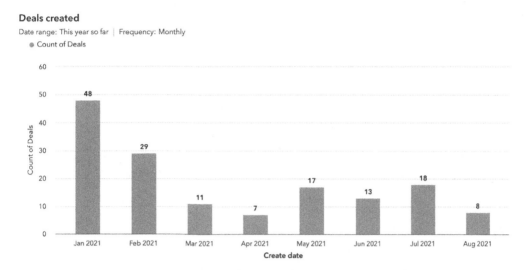

Figure 11.27 – Number of opportunities created in 2021 to date

The point is that it is often not enough to look at the data without comparing it to something else. The best insights come from being able to look at trends over a period of time so expectations must be set once you are building these reports.

Deal velocity

Deal velocity measures how long on average it takes your sales teams to close a deal. This metric is important for management teams as it helps forecast the revenue stream. In the next example, it shows that on average, it takes 69 days to win a deal between both reps. This means that every 2 months or so, you can expect to close a deal that is in your pipeline.

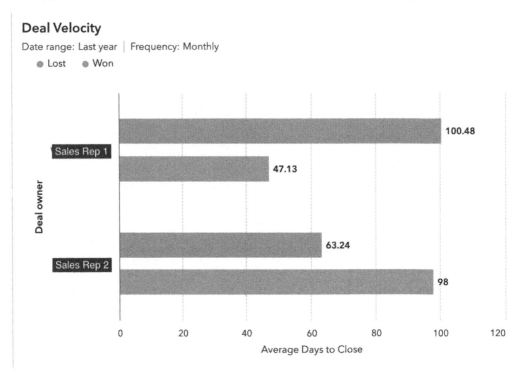

Figure 11.28 – Deal Velocity

The power of this report is that it helps you understand the average sales cycle of your deals so you can predict how often you can expect to close a deal.

HubSpot dashboards

Once you've built these different categories of reports, you will typically want to place them on a dashboard for easy viewing. To build a dashboard, you simply go to the top menu and click on **Reports** | **Dashboards**:

Figure 11.29 – Accessing the reporting dashboards

Then, click on **Create dashboard**:

Figure 11.30 – Create dashboard

And then, choose either a pre-made dashboard with eight reports already suggested for you or start from scratch. Remember, each dashboard can only hold a maximum of eight reports.

You can then choose to email a dashboard at a predefined time to various stakeholders so they can receive the details in their emails instead of logging into HubSpot.

Best practices for building reports

As mentioned previously, there are many reports already pre-built for you within your HubSpot portal. With some slight customization, you can see reports relevant to your business and gain meaningful insights.

Here are some best practices to keep in mind when building reports:

- Think of the story you want to tell and see how the data can support that story.
- Be mindful of the audience, that is, who are you building the report for. Different stakeholders will have different interests.
- Take time to understand the information being presented in the report, as you will be asked to explain it.

- Use the reports to fill out missing information in your data. You should not see too many values in categories such as **No Value**, so double-check why this data is missing and fill it out.

- Use the data to examine your assumptions and plan accordingly. If you have an inclination that the summer months are slow months for sales, then use this time to meet with sales to determine how you can further assist them and create the collateral needed.

Remember, the goal is to keep your reporting simple, repeatable, and meaningful. As a wise person once said, *Just because the data is available, does not mean you have to use it.*

How to use the data from the different analytics reports in HubSpot to boost your campaigns

As reiterated throughout this chapter, to be an effective marketer in today's world, it is important to make your decisions based on data. Many of the reports highlighted in this chapter can boost the results of your marketing campaigns if the insights from these reports are interpreted correctly.

For example, when looking at the **Traffic Analytics** report in *Figure 11.31*, it is tempting to think that more money should be invested in **Paid social** (Facebook and LinkedIn adverts) as this channel bought the most leads. However, a closer look shows that most customers were generated from **Organic search** and, therefore, SEO should be given more resources as this source as well as leads generated from direct traffic (suggesting the brand is well known) had the best conversions.

	SOURCE	SESSIONS	SESSION TO CONTACT RATE	NEW CONTACTS	CONTACT TO CUSTOMER RATE	CUSTOMERS	BOUNCE RATE	SESSION LENGTH
☑	Paid social	7,280	13.94%	1,015	1.08%	11	86.15%	26 seconds
☑	Organic search	39,399	1.16%	458	6.55%	30	70.05%	87 seconds
☑	Direct traffic	30,495	1.21%	369	3.79%	14	61.4%	140 seconds
☑	Paid search	30,876	1.07%	329	3.04%	10	85.05%	30 seconds
☑	Referrals	36,940	0.3%	110	1.82%	2	94.82%	14 seconds
☑	Organic social	3,253	3.2%	104	8.65%	9	74.52%	70 seconds
☑	Email marketing	2,629	2.93%	77	7.79%	6	63.37%	51 seconds
☑	Other campaigns	11,095	0.35%	39	7.69%	3	98.3%	4 seconds
	Total	161,967	1.54%	2,501	3.4%	85	79.57%	60 seconds

Figure 11.31 – Traffic Analytics

Furthermore, since marketers' KPIs are now being more commonly tied to revenue, a report such as that shown in *Figure 11.32* shows which sources brought the most revenue. This helps inform marketers of where their budget should be spent. The following report shows that **Organic search** accounted for almost $314,000 in revenue for this marketing team, which reinforces the earlier assumption that more budget should be placed on SEO.

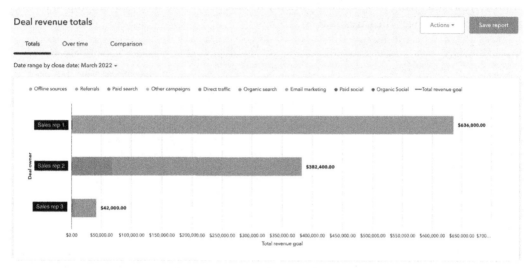

Figure 11.32 – Deal revenue by source

The preceding examples are related to the types of information and questions management teams ask of their marketers in order to justify the spending on marketing activities. However, if you are having difficulties even generating enough leads and ensuring they are converting to relevant opportunities, the insights you would need from your reports are slightly different.

For example, most marketers are challenged by which campaigns would bring them not just the most leads but the most qualified leads. Therefore, you would want to possibly pay attention to your funnel report to ensure that the conversion rates from leads to MQLs, then SQLs, and finally the **Opportunity** stage are improving over time. If for any reason these rates are dropping between the different life cycle stages, then it is a signal to either improve your nurturing programs or possibly use more specific retargeting campaigns to get those contacts over the threshold.

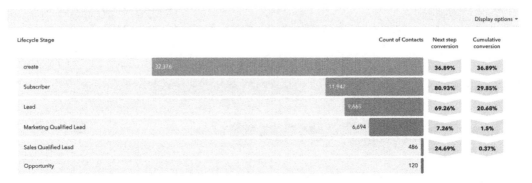

Figure 11.33 – Contact funnel report

The main message of this section is that it is not enough to be able to build the reports but it is important to be able to interpret these reports for sufficient insights in order to inform your marketing plan.

However, it's important to note that sometimes, there are other reports or manipulations that you would like to do to get a more complete picture of your customer's journey to find ways to improve your company's revenue. In the next section, we will take a look at some third-party tools that work seamlessly with HubSpot to give you more flexibility in reporting.

Exploring third-party tools that can give further insights into your reports

Although the HubSpot reporting tool is quite robust and can definitely meet most of the reporting needs of any marketing and sales team, sometimes there is a preference to combine data from other sources to get a complete outlook of the performance of your marketing and sales efforts. An example of such cases is sometimes a **software as a service (SaaS)** company has its own platform where the activity of the user takes place and, therefore, in order to measure things such as usage of their product or churn rates, they will need to combine this data related to sales information or even to measure which lead sources bring better customers. Another requirement of dashboards could be the ability to manipulate the layout data, where a user can add a report from HubSpot but also next to it add a report from Google Analytics if needed.

There are a host of platforms that give you the ability to satisfy your reporting needs. Here are a few of them, all of which have native integrations with HubSpot.

Supermetrics

Users who are interested in exporting their data to Excel, Google Data Studio, or other databases or data warehouses might consider Supermetrics. With HubSpot, not all of the data points are easily integrated into other platforms, but with Supermetrics, you are able to collect any data point from HubSpot and manipulate it as you wish. One of the most popular use cases that Supermetrics can offer is the ability to combine all your HubSpot data with other platforms so you can measure the true journey and conversion of your contacts to leads and customers. Learn more about the Supermetrics connector with HubSpot at this link: `https://supermetrics.com/connectors/hubspot`.

Databox

Databox is essentially HubSpot for reporting needs. Agencies tend to be the most popular customers of this platform simply because it allows the user to combine many different HubSpot portals into one reporting tool so you can easily switch between dashboards to show each client their performance. Similar to Supermetrics, you can also combine reports from different data sources, giving you a more complete view of your marketing efforts, and have them displayed on multiple platforms such as mobile, desktop, TV display, and Apple. Learn more about this platform and its integration with HubSpot at this link: `https://databox.com/integration/hubspot`.

Mixpanel

Mixpanel is the go-to reporting platform for SaaS companies using HubSpot in order to measure user behavior and user engagement of their platforms. This reporting platform can integrate directly with the reporting tool in custom-built SaaS applications to capture mostly the post-free-trial or post-purchase customer behavior on the platform. To learn more about this integration, visit `https://ecosystem.hubspot.com/marketplace/apps/marketing/analytics-data/mixpanel-data-sync`.

Dealtale

This platform is probably one of the easiest platforms to use for manipulating reporting data. Its biggest superpower is that there is no coding needed to integrate this platform with HubSpot or any other data source, and once the data is in, you can slice and dice it in multiple ways, which allows you to gain insights and information that is not always obvious. To learn more about this reporting platform, visit this site: `https://dealtale.com/welcome-to-dealtale/#`.

Dear Lucy

I came across this platform on the recommendation of one of my clients and I must say, I was pretty impressed. The less intimidating name takes away the feeling of being overwhelmed when preparing reports. It really allows SaaS companies to track key **annual recurring revenue (ARR)** and **managed recurring revenue (MRR)** metrics, churn, and growth. To learn more about this reporting platform, visit `https://www.dearlucy.co/hubspot`.

The platforms mentioned here are simply the tip of the iceberg of what's available. To choose the right platforms, you first need to understand what exactly you are trying to measure or which insights you are missing in your current reports. There are also more sophisticated reporting tools that **business intelligence (BI)** teams within medium-sized and enterprise companies often make use of, such as Tableau and Sisense, among others. So, don't get overwhelmed, but my suggestion is to start with HubSpot and then explore the different tools that exist to see which best fits the gaps in your reporting.

Summary

Reporting is essential to every type of business, as data is essential to make better, more informed decisions. That being said, once you understand what you need, it is easy to work backward and build the foundation needed to support the expected flow of data and information.

However, it isn't always easy to decipher which reports are needed early in a project. The main goal of building an effective reporting system is to focus on revenue reporting. Whenever in doubt, try to ensure your reports either directly contribute to revenue goals or, at the very least, tell the story of how they contribute.

In the next chapter, we will take a look at the evolution of inbound marketing and understand which is really more effective, inbound or outbound marketing.

Questions

Understanding that reports are the bottom line for every decision made within a company, it would be remiss of me if you leave this chapter without ensuring certain principles have been understood. Here are a few questions to help you verify your understanding:

1. When preparing a reporting dashboard for your management team, which five reports would you include in this dashboard?

2. If you had to choose three marketing reports, which would you include to track how your efforts are contributing to deals?

3. How would you measure your contributions to the sales team's efforts?

Further reading

- *How to Build and Analyze Marketing Reports [Examples & Templates]*: https://blog.hubspot.com/marketing/running-marketing-reports-ht

- *How to Calculate ROI in Marketing [Free Excel Templates]*: https://blog.hubspot.com/marketing/how-to-prove-the-roi-of-your-marketing-slideshare

- *How to Create a Funnel Report [Quick Guide]*: https://blog.hubspot.com/marketing/funnel-reporting

- *6 Simple HubSpot Reports Your Dashboard Needs*: https://blog.hubspot.com/customers/6-simple-hubspot-reports-your-dashboard-needs

- *Building Custom Reports in HubSpot*: https://academy.hubspot.com/courses/building-custom-reports-in-hubspot?library=true&library=true&q=reports

Part 3:
Is HubSpot Right
for Your Business?

The HubSpot platform was initially built upon the foundation of the inbound methodology, when its co-founders, Brian Halligan and Dharmesh Shah, realized that consumers were quickly gaining purchasing power and businesses needed a way to match the way they sell to how consumers were buying. However, after more than 20 years and with the myriad of platforms available, all competing for consumers' attention, the inbound methodology has evolved significantly from the funnel approach to the flywheel and now the latest RevOps. In this part, we help you understand each of these approaches and how HubSpot is even more relevant for your business in these rapidly changing times.

This part contains the following chapters:

12

Inbound or Outbound – Which Is Better for Your Business?

The concept of inbound and outbound marketing is, by now, quite a familiar concept among businesses. However, most businesses struggle with the decision of which is better, which tactic to use for their type of business, or how to implement either of these methodologies correctly to impact their business successfully. Before we get into answering any of these questions, let's first understand the difference between the two.

In the most basic terms to identify the difference between the two methodologies, think about who initiated the sale. If it was the company, then it's outbound; if it was the buyer, then it's inbound.

Some popular examples of outbound tactics include TV ads, billboards, trade shows, and more recently, email blasts to purchased lists, cold calling, and even paid ads. While inbound tactics include content marketing (websites and blogging), **search engine optimization (SEO)**, or social media, the key difference once again is that outbound marketing uses "push" tactics while inbound marketing uses "pull" tactics.

So which is better?

Truthfully, there is no clear-cut answer to this question. It is becoming more and more apparent that most businesses need a combination of both because after all, we are selling to humans. As Neil Patel, co-founder of Crazy Egg and Kissmetrics, described it, some people wait on others to suggest what they want while some will go out of their way in search of what they need. And, as a business, you don't want to miss out on either type of customer.

In the end, neither is better nor worse but you do need to understand when to use either concept.

In this chapter, we will explore the following topics:

- Implementing inbound marketing for your business
- Converting traffic to customers using inbound marketing
- Businesses thriving best with the inbound marketing
- Scaling your marketing with inbound marketing
- Increasing sales with Inbound Marketing

By the end of the chapter, you will get a firm understanding of inbound and outbound marketing and if the two can co-exist for today's businesses.

Implementing inbound marketing for your business

Most times, businesses are hesitant to implement inbound marketing strategies as they think it will take too much time. If you are in the early stages of your business, it's difficult to compete with millions of websites all vying for the attention of the same audience. How do you get noticed? How do you drive that audience to your business instead of your competitor's? And, if you are in the later stages of your business, you have most likely gained success using some of the outbound tactics mentioned previously so you may not have been that convinced that you needed it…until the year 2020 came around.

Given the global pandemic we all faced, it is now quite apparent that regardless of the type of business you run or whether you are an early-stage start-up or a more advanced company, some form of inbound marketing is needed. The struggle sometimes lies within where you should begin and what you should do and when.

The goal is to start now. Start where you are. Start with the resources you have. Don't try to go too big too soon because it can get overwhelming, not to mention costly.

But, what exactly does that mean?

Building awareness with inbound marketing for a new product launch

Well, let's say you've started a new start-up. Your product is ready for the world and you desperately need to get in front of your audience. What do you do? The first place to begin is to understand that at this stage, you normally need to achieve two goals – build awareness and generate leads. Fortunately, today, a website becomes the first thing most businesses create so that's one inbound tactic checked.

Another inbound tactic to consider is probably creating a social media campaign that includes a contest or free giveaways in order to spread the word. One popular way some brands often use is to get their followers to leave a comment on a question asked or to tag people who they would love to show some appreciation to, and the person with the most likes gets a prize.

Sometimes, even partnering with another company that complements your business to send out an email blast to their database about your new product is used to generate new leads for your business or product.

But, these tactics, although great, are often not sufficient to generate real business. We need to consider how we convert this traffic into actual paying customers.

Converting traffic to customers using inbound marketing

We now understand what it takes to generate interest for your product, but how do we take it to the next level and convert this traffic to paying customers? Let's take a look at how the entire process can look. For your new product or service launch, hosting a webinar is a good tactic to generate leads (inbound tactic), and promoting that webinar on LinkedIn (inbound tactic) will get you brand awareness as your existing followers will see those posts. And, even though they may not all choose to register, some may share it or tag people they know might be interested. But, *after* the webinar, we need to also be on top of how we nurture those leads (inbound tactic) until they convert to a sales opportunity.

The point is that the second phase of inbound marketing, engage, is just as important as the first, attract, and for companies who fail at inbound marketing, the reason is usually that they did not plan for the entire customer journey. They tend to focus on just one part of the funnel and have no plan for what should happen to those leads once they enter the funnel.

For more established businesses who have been successful to date using more traditional methods such as billboards or television advertisements, but now are also considering including inbound strategies, the challenge may still exist of where to begin. Again, it depends on your ultimate goal. Do you need more leads or do you wish to penetrate new markets?

If generating more leads is the priority, then the quickest win may lie within your existing network or customers, which is the third phase of inbound marketing, delight. Creating an email referral campaign (inbound tactic) that offers them incentives to recommend your business to their network can be one tactic to use. Or, having them give testimonials or case studies about your business or service that you can then use on your website or other sales collateral is also useful as it can be used as part of the *engage* stage in your inbound marketing strategy.

There are many opportunities for businesses to successfully implement inbound marketing but the challenge is being able to plan for every stage of your customer's journey. In the next section, we discuss which types of businesses thrive best with inbound marketing.

Businesses that thrive best with inbound marketing

For some businesses, it can feel that inbound marketing is not right for them. It's either that they don't see their audience hanging out on social media (for example, government officials) or their business model is dependent on walk-in visitors (for example, car distributors) or they simply don't see the need for it because they think their target audience is relatively small (for example, the neighborhood florist).

The good news is that every type of business can benefit from inbound marketing because the reality is – whether you are selling **business to business (B2B)**, **business to consumer (B2C)**, or **business to government (B2G)** – at the end of the day, who you are really selling to is **business to human (B2H)**. Behind each of these companies are human beings and if you focus on how to connect with them, 80% of your work is done. So, let's dive right in to see how you can reach each of these types of consumers through inbound marketing.

First, let's take a look at B2B marketing. Most businesses that focus on B2B audiences are selling complex products that only other businesses can appreciate the need for, as they are the ones providing the solution to improve the customer experience for the end customers. For example, a data science platform that helps credit card companies analyze a huge number of transactions in real time in order to prevent fraudulent activity will not focus on targeting shoppers, but instead, will need to attract CIOs, head of data scientists, and fraud experts in these relevant companies. Another example is a company providing technology that allows dairy farmers to monitor the health of their cows in real time, which won't be interesting for the end consumers, but will most certainly intrigue farmers who would like to ensure the quality of milk and meat they provide as suppliers is of the highest standard and not risk the population's health. However, even with all these incredible benefits, the challenge is making these businesses aware of your solution and then turning them into customers.

The inbound methodology is one of the more successful marketing strategies that B2B businesses can implement as often, for their clients, the process of deciding which technology to implement within their existing framework is a long process with a lot of decision-makers involved. Therefore, inbound marketing allows you to first get found (*attract*), then stay on top of their mind as the clients continue internal discussions (*engage*), and finally, deliver such an amazing product and customer experience that they are happy to continue working with you and eventually refer you (*delight*).

For B2C businesses, the experience is a bit different as the reality is that you are often dealing with a product that has a relatively short sales cycle. Therefore, it can be thought that inbound marketing is not that relevant for these types of businesses. To some extent, that may be true since if you think of goods and services that have a relatively low price point and are deemed as essentials, people will purchase them either way. An example of such a type of business is supermarkets. But then, some goods may still fit into this category and inbound marketing can be very relevant to them, for example, a hairdresser or florist.

In this case, as a B2C business, you want to make sure you use inbound marketing to educate your customers about what makes you different from the competition. Note that this does not have to become a soapbox where you simply brag about yourself, but instead, take the opportunity to educate them about something they may not be necessarily aware of. For example, if you are a hairdresser, writing blogs about how to take care of your scalp for more healthy hair growth or creating videos on Instagram that show the results of the before and after haircuts of your clients is an inbound method you can easily implement to attract more clients.

Another group of B2C clients that can benefit from inbound marketing is those clients that sell more expensive products, such as car dealerships. Most consumers don't decide to purchase a car right away; they have a process similar to the audience of B2B companies, which means the sales cycle is a bit longer than the typical B2C purchase. Therefore, building a process where you can attract prospective customers, engage them by providing a trickle of information at every point of engagement, and then convert them to be a customer is very much akin to the inbound process.

On the other hand, B2G businesses trying to implement the inbound methodology might face the biggest challenge, since reaching government officials on online channels such as social media or expecting them to attend your webinar might be against their protocol. But, as mentioned earlier, the goal is to remember that, at the end of the day, these are still human beings and they will interact with online channels in some way, they simply may just avoid putting themselves out there publicly. So, don't expect them to like your LinkedIn or Facebook post or to sign up for your webinar, but do expect that just like the other 98% of people, they are searching for solutions to their challenges on search engines. So, optimizing your content to be found when relevant keywords are searched or ensuring there are ways to capture their details once they land on your content are essential inbound tactics that, if implemented correctly, can help you reach this specific target audience.

Now that you understand how inbound marketing can most likely benefit your business, let's look at how you can use it to scale your marketing, increase your sales, and delight your customers.

Scaling your marketing with inbound marketing

In order to use the inbound methodology to scale your marketing, you must first understand that there are five fundamentals of inbound marketing: **buyer personas**, **content**, **buyer's journey**, **contacts**, and **setting goals**. Each of them plays a crucial part in your inbound strategy and, when combined, allows you to attract, engage, and delight your customers by empowering them to reach their goals at any stage.

The HubSpot CRM software is built upon this methodology. Unlike other CRM platforms such as Salesforce, Zoho, or Pipedrive, HubSpot is built with the intention of personalizing your interactions with a prospect even when this interaction happens at scale. Therefore, to successfully implement HubSpot and see ROI, you must be willing to think about your entire customer journey and find the best way to keep track of it in HubSpot. But, where do you begin? How do you create a successful inbound strategy? The answer lies in the flywheel.

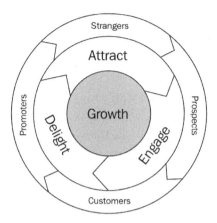

Figure 12.1 – The flywheel

The flywheel depicts the momentum a business can generate when they do the following:

- **Attract** the right people using relevant and valuable content that establishes the business as a trusted advisor in their niche.

- **Engage** with them further by continuously providing insight and solutions for their pain points and challenges.

- **Delight** them by giving them the necessary support to see success with the services. The goal is to keep the flywheel spinning faster and faster, as this represents the ability to invest in the right strategies to acquire and retain customers.

But, how exactly do you attract visitors, turn them into leads, and eventually nurture them into customers at a faster rate so your flywheel gains momentum? Let's find out:

- **Buyer persona**: The first step is to understand exactly who you wish to sell to, and who your ideal customer is. What are their challenges and goals, where do they go when they need information, and who are their trusted sources? Taking the time to develop this first pillar of your inbound strategy – your buyer persona – will allow you to develop the necessary content that will position you as their trusted advisor.

- **Content**: This brings us to the next important pillar of the inbound strategy: creating content. Content creation is usually one of the most daunting aspects of implementing an inbound strategy as it often feels like an overwhelming task to create enough content to feed the beast. But, the point is – it doesn't have to be as often, as you can repurpose a lot of the content that already exists. So, your goal should be to first run a content audit by mapping out all the website pages, sales collateral, blogs or articles, or anything else that might have been created in the past. Then, decide on which pieces can be repurposed/rewritten for the different stages of your buyer's journey.

- **Buyer's journey**: This is the next pillar to understand within the inbound framework. How do you capture the path a prospect generally takes before becoming your customer? Generally, there are three stages a buyer goes through before purchasing any product or service: **awareness**, **consideration**, and **decision**.

  Therefore, you may want to begin with your version of how you think people are made aware of your solution, what drives them to consider your business as a viable option, and finally, what made them choose you from all other options that exist. One important piece of advice, though, is that you should verify your hypothesis by asking your customers these questions directly at some point in your engagement with them. You will be surprised to hear what their actual journey was, and this could provide some valuable insights into existing opportunities for further marketing your business.

- **Contacts**: The next pillar, and probably the most important, but one that is not always maintained to a high standard, is contacts. The main, if not the only, reason for implementing an inbound strategy is to gain contacts. But, most times, the gathering of the information about these contacts and its maintenance isn't properly thought through. This is why HubSpot's CRM is an integral part of its ecosystem, as it allows you to gather and store the information in a systematic way, giving full transparency to your marketing, sales, and service department. It is, therefore, important to consider what the most important pieces of information are that you need to collect about your contacts, so this can be included in your inbound marketing strategy.

Taking the time to map out these four pillars allows you to set better goals and expectations within your organization, as you will now have a clearer picture of what is possible given your audience and the available resources. You can actively map out the number of contacts you need at each stage of the buyer's journey in order to reach the business revenue goals. And, you can set a content plan to determine the mix of content needed to keep your contacts engaged at different points of their journey. The point is that setting these goals will allow you to understand not just which tactic to use but how to blend them to achieve your desired goals.

Generally, the decision to use any of the myriads of tactics at your disposal depends on what you are trying to achieve – more brand awareness, an increase in leads, or converting more prospects to sales-qualified leads.

To achieve more brand awareness content marketing, some of the tactics you can begin with are SEO, social media marketing, social selling, and targeted paid advertising. Content marketing paired with SEO allows you to get in front of your target so that when they search for relevant keywords, they can find your business. But, the reality is that SEO takes some time to see meaningful results, typically about 6 to 9 months, and it usually demands that you create content consistently. If you wish to see faster results, then targeted paid advertising can be an option. With paid advertising, you can amplify your reach to a wider audience in a shorter amount of time and with less commitment of resources. It is even sometimes sufficient to use an existing website page or repurpose a piece of evergreen content for this purpose. The goal is to remember to optimize these pages so they can also be used as a tactic to generate leads.

This brings us to the next goal, which is the real reason any company invests in inbound marketing – to generate more leads. As HubSpot depicted in one of its blogs, *How to Create and Execute a Successful Lead Gen Strategy* (`https://blog.hubspot.com/marketing/lead-generation-strategy`), there are four Ls to every lead generation strategy:

- **Lead capture**: In its simplest form, this requires two basic principles – a **call-to-action (CTA)** and a form. Visitors must be prompted to take action in some way, so the use of active language such as "Register Here" or "Download Now" is the first prompt to direct a user to fill out a form in exchange for something. This brings us to the next point, lead magnets.

- **Lead magnets**: In order to generate more leads, you must have something of value for which your prospect is willing to give up their email address. Some examples of popular lead magnets are e-books, webinars, free trials, checklists, and bonus tips. However, gone are the days when people were excited to sign up for everything. Now, thanks to us marketers, users hesitate a great deal before they decide to make this move for fear of being spammed. So, this brings us to the next important part of a lead generation – understanding how to improve conversions.

- **Landing page conversion techniques**: Landing pages became an essential part of helping businesses convert visitors to leads. As visitors got bombarded with more and more information, it is necessary to help them to focus. And, this is what a landing page essentially does: focus on one piece of content and one action you wish your visitors to take in exchange for that valuable information.

- **Lead scoring**: Now that you have the leads pouring in, you must be able to help your sales teams prioritize their efforts. It must be clear for them which leads are almost ready to buy. So, this is where lead scoring comes in. It is a technique that helps to quantify the characteristics of your prospects and the interactions they have with your content by assigning points for different types of engagement. For example, leads with a specific job title may get 10 points, or leads that sign up for a free trial may be assigned 30 points. The goal is to accumulate these scores and those contacts that pass a certain threshold, such as 70 and above out of 100, should be flagged to the sales team for immediate follow-up.

The final component of the inbound strategy of converting these leads into customers depends on using tactics such as **email marketing** for nurturing the leads and ensuring marketing and sales are aligned so there is proper follow-through of the leads brought in. Emails are one of the oldest and most effective lead generation tactics as they can be used at any point in the inbound journey.

Increasing sales with inbound marketing

The inbound methodology is not just for marketing. In recent times, sales teams also recognized that they needed to transform the way they sell to the consumers as the buyer's journey changed. It is no longer sufficient to just sell products. Instead, there is a need to guide buyers into making a decision that is best for them. There is a need to prioritize the needs, challenges, goals, and interests of the buyer instead of simply focusing on making the sale. So, how do you achieve this turnaround? How do you get your salespeople to adopt a more inbound approach in order to increase sales?

The first step is to understand the buyer's journey. Every purchase decision generally goes through three phases: awareness, consideration, and decision. The buyer generally becomes aware they have a problem, they then consider various options as possible solutions to the problem, and finally, decide on a specific solution.

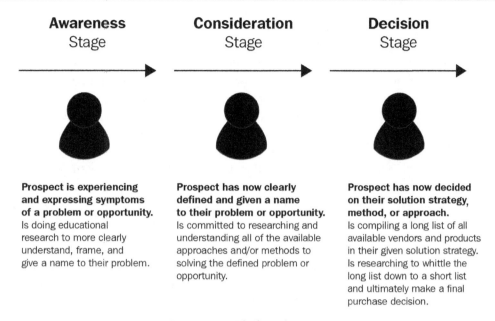

Awareness Stage

Consideration Stage

Decision Stage

Prospect is experiencing and expressing symptoms of a problem or opportunity. Is doing educational research to more clearly understand, frame, and give a name to their problem.

Prospect has now clearly defined and given a name to their problem or opportunity. Is committed to researching and understanding all of the available approaches and/or methods to solving the defined problem or opportunity.

Prospect has now decided on their solution strategy, method, or approach. Is compiling a long list of all available vendors and products in their given solution strategy. Is researching to whittle the long list down to a short list and ultimately make a final purchase decision.

Figure 12.2 – The buyer's journey

The next phase of transforming to an inbound sales methodology relies on the ability to develop a sales process that will support buyers. This involves understanding what your salespeople can do to support the customer through each of the stages of the buying process. In most cases, the stages in this sales process will look something like this – identify, connect, explore, and advise.

It, therefore, means that inbound sales teams will identify people who are already in the buying process instead of pursuing buyers who may not be interested or relevant. Once they've identified such buyers, they will attempt to connect with them by communicating with them through online conversations that are personalized and built on the buyer's interest, not just through cold outreach using a generic elevator pitch.

Once the buyer expresses interest, an inbound salesperson will explore their prospect's goals and challenges to decide whether their offering is a good fit for their customer's needs. They won't just dive into presentation mode delivering a speech. And, once the prospect seems to be a good fit, the salesperson will then advise on how their product/solution is uniquely positioned to satisfy their needs.

One great example of the inbound sales methodology in full effect is demonstrated by a company called BarkBox. BarkBox is a monthly subscription service that provides a surprise box of toys and treats for man's best friend – dogs. In order to choose the right combination of treats for its customers, BarkBox sales teams identify their customers as they subscribe to their online programs that give prospects an idea of the types of treats to try for their dogs. They then connect with them by calling each individual prospect to find out more about their dogs. They are often heard asking prospects about the breed of dogs they have, their usual habits, what they enjoy eating, and even sharing some of their personal dog stories in this exchange. They then do further exploration by suggesting some of the goodies they can possibly send as part of the surprise box and even advise what other solutions might be appealing to their canine customers. It is no surprise that this company is now serving over 1 million dogs per month and exceeding yearly revenue of $365 million as of 2020.

So, whether it's for your marketing or your sales, the inbound methodology has proven time and time again that you can't expect great results without putting your customers' needs first.

Summary

Inbound marketing has become a cornerstone methodology that digital marketers have come to rely upon to consistently bring in relevant leads, as it ensures people at least show interest in what you have to offer before you begin to pitch to them. When done correctly, meaning by implementing the pillars discussed in this chapter, you can definitely scale your marketing, increase your sales and revenue, and eventually, use this momentum to improve and expand your business, regardless of your type of business, size, and stage.

In the next chapter, we will look further at the marketing funnel. We will examine how the funnel, the flywheel, and now RevOps have contributed to the evolution of inbound marketing and how businesses can adopt these methods to increase sales by putting the customer at the center.

Questions

To help you remember some key concepts and tips discussed in this chapter, here are a few review questions to consider:

1. What is the difference between inbound marketing and outbound marketing?

2. What are the three phases of the customer journey?

3. Can you suggest one tactic in each phase of the customer journey that your business can implement in the next 30 days?

Further reading

- *Inbound Marketing, Revised and Updated: Attract, Engage, and Delight* by Brian Halligan and Dharmesh Shah: `https://www.amazon.com/Inbound-Marketing-Revised-Updated-Customers/dp/1118896653/ref=sr_1_1?crid=3BL8PCXCZZLKK&keywords=inbound+marketing+brian+halligan&qid=1638723261&sprefix=inbound%2Caps%2C691&sr=8-1`

- *What Is Inbound Marketing?*: `https://www.hubspot.com/inbound-marketing`

- *Inbound Marketing vs. Outbound Marketing*: `https://blog.hubspot.com/blog/tabid/6307/bid/2989/inbound-marketing-vs-outbound-marketing.aspx`

13

Leveraging the Benefits of the Marketing Flywheel

From the funnel to the flywheel to revenue operations (**RevOps**), what does it really mean for businesses and—more specifically—for marketing, sales, and service teams?

Before we dive into the tactics, we must first understand the fundamental differences between these three (marketing, sales, and service) concepts. The funnel was the initial concept of how marketing and sales teams attracted and acquired customers. It was a more linear approach to track how many prospects came in from the top and eventually channeled their way to the bottom of the funnel until they became customers.

As customers became more empowered and knowledgeable and the flow of information became easier and more transparent, it became increasingly important for businesses to pay attention to how customers were treated as this eventually impacted their growth. Word of mouth could never beat any other marketing tactic to generate more customers. Therefore, the flywheel concept was born as it placed customers at the forefront of all business decisions. The funnel produces customers while the flywheel ensures those customers help you grow.

Finally, RevOps emerged as a solution to help manage technical challenges that inevitably arise when companies grow. With both the funnel and the flywheel, it is important to ensure that everything works and there is a smooth handover from marketing to sales to customer success and customer service. The goal is to reduce friction and ensure customers and prospects have a seamless experience when interacting with your company, and this is the role RevOps plays.

Now that we have understood each of these concepts, let's explore how the flywheel and RevOps can contribute to your company's further growth and improved experience for your customers. In this chapter, we will explore the following topics:

- Achieving faster growth and increasing profit with the flywheel
- Aligning marketing and sales using HubSpot properties
- Using RevOps to boost business sales

Let's dive right in.

Technical requirements

To get the most out of this chapter, you will need the following:

- HubSpot Marketing Professional
- Super admin access to your HubSpot portal
- Admin access to each of your business's social media ad platforms (LinkedIn, Facebook, and Google AdWords)

Achieving faster growth and increasing profit with the flywheel

Two words—customer experience. This is what every business today should be focused on in order to ensure **business continuity (BC)** and growth. As Brian Halligan, Chairman of HubSpot, succinctly put it, "*It used to be what you sell that really matters, now it's how you sell that really matters.*" Flywheel is a term derived from mechanical engineering. It describes a circular object whereby once an additional force is applied to it, more energy is produced, causing the object to rotate faster.

This concept was then adopted in marketing in the last decade as it became clearer that for companies to generate a continuous supply of leads and prospects, they must rely on their customers to produce that momentum for them. Therefore, any friction that interferes with a good customer experience will automatically slow this momentum, resulting in fewer leads and—eventually—sales.

It is therefore important for all **business units** (**BUs**)—marketing, sales, product, and service—to be aligned to one goal: outstanding customer experience. But how does a company actually achieve this?

Aligning teams for outstanding customer experience

First, it would be to ensure that from the very first interaction with your company, a prospect feels heard and understood. Your offer should match their needs and meet them at the exact time they are looking for a solution to their current challenge. This is where the concept of inbound marketing comes into play. As a marketer, your intention should be to create a blog post, e-book, or other marketing assets with the goal of attracting your target prospects to educate them on why this challenge exists and provide possible solutions to this problem. With this action, you are taking the first step in providing relevant information. It then becomes timely because you have optimized this piece of content using **search engine optimization** (**SEO**) techniques, so once a user searches for these specific keywords, your piece of content shows up for them in the search engine results. You didn't just take out a TV ad and show it to 1 million random people, interrupting their favorite TV show or sports game.

The next step would be to engage qualified prospects using tactics such as email nurtures, free trials, or webinar events to get them to speak to your sales reps or try out your product before purchasing. At this stage, marketing and sales teams are working very closely together to ensure prospects understand the benefit of using your product instead of the competitor's so that they can finally convert these leads to customers. For most companies operating under the funnel method, this is where the process usually stopped. Once a customer is gained, the goal has been achieved, and it is assumed that marketing would start the process all over again.

Implementing systems and processes to facilitate a RevOps strategy

It was soon discovered, though, that focusing on delighting customers and ensuring they have a smooth onboarding experience and have gained the promised benefits of your product or service would eventually bring your company future leads. But for this process to happen, many more departments had to be involved and processes put into place to have overall transparency of information about the customer. This is where RevOps plays an important role as it now includes connectivity of the various systems each department uses and how they each reflect the information needed. Having these systems and processes in place is critical for delivering an outstanding customer experience.

One example of a system that facilitates a RevOps strategy is a **customer relationship management (CRM)** system such as HubSpot that connects the entire customer life cycle—marketing, sales, and service—in one view in order to drive predictable results. Take, for example, HubSpot's CRM that allows you to see on one screen the marketing details of a customer—for example, which channel brought them in, such as direct traffic—then, on the same screen, you can see details of conversations with your sales reps, and on the customer service side, issues they are currently trying to solve with your service team. This is all in one view, as seen in the following screenshot:

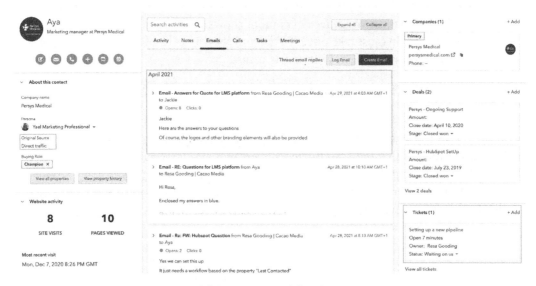

Figure 13.1 – HubSpot customer lifecycle view per contact

An example of a process that needs to be in place is an agreement on specific metrics that each team should be responsible for attaining and measuring. For instance, marketing teams may be responsible for website traffic and—more specifically—net new monthly visitors and visitor-to-submission rate to ensure the quality of traffic is qualified. Sales teams are responsible for the number of calls completed per month and the number of deals closed per month, while customer success teams are responsible for keeping their eye on the churn rate of customers within 1 year.

Implementing all these strategies just described successfully leads to a delightful customer experience that in turn leads to the ultimate goal of having a faster-turning flywheel. No longer are you concerned about the linear relationship the funnel provides to your bottom line, but now, you are focused on creating momentum with your customers so that they can in turn be the force within your flywheel that increases revenue and ensures predictable growth.

Now, let's look deeper into exactly how we can leverage the flywheel concept to match the way we sell to the way buyers purchase.

Aligning marketing and sales using HubSpot properties

One of the most misunderstood—and, therefore, misused—properties in HubSpot is lifecycle stages. Up until writing this chapter, HubSpot lifecycle stages were predefined and could not be changed. However, in recent times, HubSpot now allows companies to define their own lifecycle stages to fit their organization's needs.

Lifecycle stages in HubSpot consist of seven stages—Subscriber, Lead, **Marketing Qualified Lead (MQL)**, **Sales Qualified Lead (SQL)**, Opportunity, Customer, Evangelist, and more. This property is meant to highlight at what stage a prospect is in their journey with your business; therefore, it combines the activities of marketing, sales, and customer service. It generally isn't a field that should be manually managed; the more effective way to use it is to build conditions that will automatically update these lifecycle stages through workflows.

One such way to build these conditions is through another field called Lead Status. Lead Status exists to help sales reps understand what is the present situation with a contact and what should be done with that contact now. Unlike lifecycle stages, you can update this field to your preferred statuses. HubSpot offers default options such as New, Open, In Progress, Attempted to Contact, Unqualified, Connected, Open Deal, and Bad Timing. It is important to note that these statuses are different from the actual deal stages in HubSpot that were discussed in *Chapter 3, Using HubSpot for Managing Sales Processes Effectively*. To understand the difference, remember that lead statuses help you identify which contacts need to be worked on or followed up on, while deal stages let us know which contacts are an active opportunity and which part of the sales process they are in currently.

So, how do you actually use HubSpot to match the way you sell to the way buyers purchase? There are several methods used, but here, we will focus on two of the most popular methods, as follows:

- **Sales-focused approach**: This method is very popular among new companies or start-ups that need to show traction quickly. The goal is to get as many customers as possible quickly, and therefore the sales teams will reach out to every qualified contact that comes into the funnel. This does not necessarily mean they have to request a meeting with sales or sign up for a free trial, but they have certain characteristics—for instance, the right company size, the right job title, the right industry—and this is sufficient to deem them qualified. With this approach, you will align lead statuses to lifecycle stages, which will be explained further shortly.

- **Buyer-focused approach**: On the other hand, more mature companies that have already gained traction in the market or are pursuing a very targeted or niche audience will prefer this method. Here, the sales teams would not pursue a contact until they have raised their hands and requested a demo or signed up for a free trial. Therefore, marketing is required to set up very tailored paths to nurture and engage these prospects so that they will take this action. With this approach, you will align actions the buyers take to lifecycle stages, which we will explain further.

In the following sections, we will discuss each of these approaches in depth.

Setting up HubSpot using a sales-focused approach

As mentioned previously, if you are a company looking for traction quickly, you will need your sales teams to be on top of all leads that come into the CRM. However, you will need to set this process up in such a way that every single contact is accounted for, and it can be clearly understood which part of the funnel they are in and what is the status of your engagement with them. The following diagram illustrates how this alignment might look:

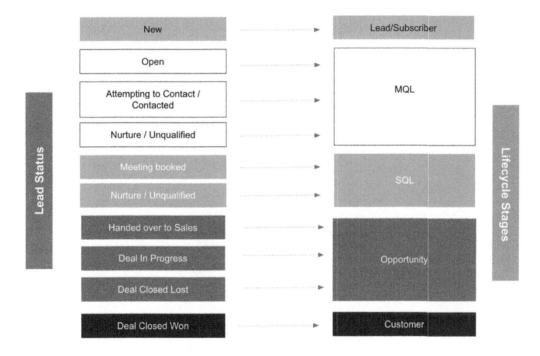

Figure 13.2 – Aligning lead status to lifecycle stages

Remember that lead statuses can be changed to match your internal sales process and lifecycle stages. In the preceding example, when each of the lead statuses is updated, the lifecycle stage should be updated to the corresponding value, as seen in *Figure 13.2*. Note that most of these actions can be automated using HubSpot workflows.

For instance, every new contact that enters your database can be automatically updated to a **New** status by setting the enrollment trigger of a workflow to **Create date is after DD/MM/YY**, **Lead status is unknown**, and **Lifecycle stage is unknown**, as shown in the following screenshot:

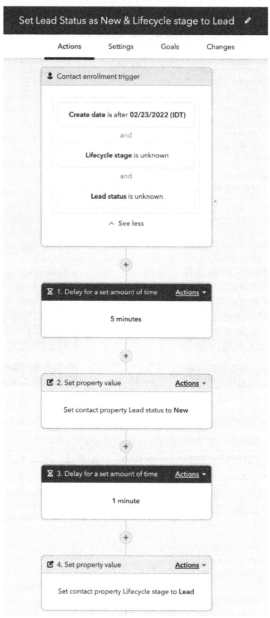

Figure 13.3 – Enrollment triggers for workflow when setting contacts as New

Then, in the same workflow, you can set the lifecycle stage to **Lead** and lead status to **New**. The following screenshot shows a graphical representation of what this workflow will look like in HubSpot:

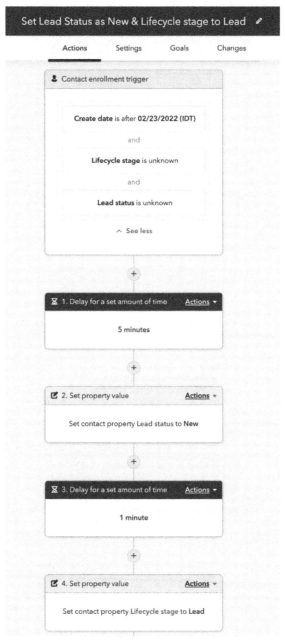

Figure 13.4 – Setting property values in workflows

Similarly, instead of having sales reps manually update the lead status each time a contact responds to their emails or they complete a phone call, another workflow can be triggered where the enrollment criterion is **Recent sales replied email date is known** or **Call outcome is any of Connected** with all the preceding values for lead status and lifecycle stages, as seen in the following screenshot:

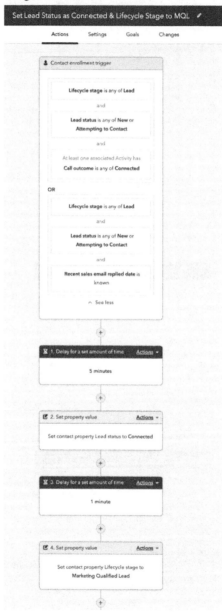

Figure 13.5 – Enrollment triggers for a workflow updating lead status to Connected

Then, you can add steps to set the **Lead status** property value to **Connected** and the **Lifecycle stage** property value to **Marketing Qualified Lead**, as shown in the following screenshot:

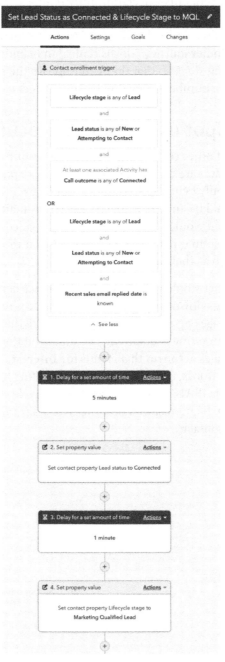

Figure 13.6 – Setting Lead status to Connected and Lifecycle stage to Marketing Qualified Lead

The goal is to automate as many of these statuses as possible so that as the sales teams do their daily tasks, the lead statuses and lifecycle stages would be automatically updated according to the actions taken. This will significantly reduce the time sales reps will spend maintaining the CRM. Setting up this process has the added benefit of reducing friction between marketing and sales teams as marketing teams will finally have clarity on where each contact is in the customer journey. This is critical in helping them to understand where customers are getting stuck so that they can improve the experience in that part of the funnel and increase the number of qualified leads that get to sales teams.

Setting up HubSpot using a buyer-focused approach

Another common method other companies use when pursuing a more targeted persona or wanting to ensure contacts are qualified sufficiently before passing them on to sales is a contact's lifecycle stage only being updated if they took specific marketing actions. For example, a subscriber would be anyone who left only their email address when signing up for a newsletter, while a lead would be anyone who downloaded at least one piece of top of the funnel content—such as an e-book—and submitted a bit more information in addition to their email address, such as their name and job title.

On the other hand, a contact would only be updated to a marketing qualified lead if they took several actions, such as downloading at least three pieces of content and visiting at least three other website pages besides the asset pages where they downloaded the content. Usually in this method, marketing is qualifying a contact's actions using the **IBANT** methodology, which is a sales acronym that stands for **Interest, Budget, Authority, Need, and Time**. In other words, depending on the marketing actions a prospect takes, they are qualified using this IBANT method and their lifecycle stages are updated accordingly. The following diagram shows how lifecycle stages are mapped to the qualification criteria of a contact:

Different lifecycle stages and their qualification criteria

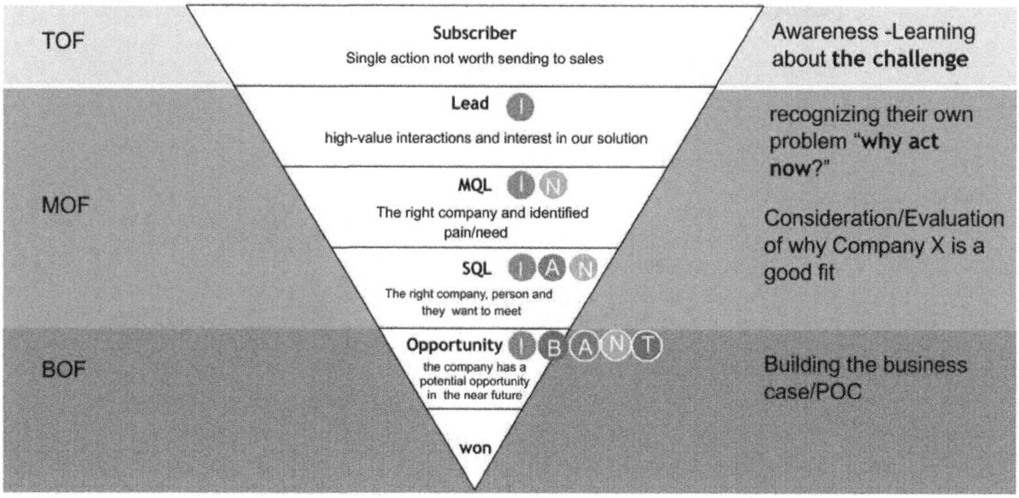

Figure 13.7 – Lifecycle stages mapped to the IBANT methodology

To set up these processes in HubSpot, you can also use workflows so that the lifecycle stages would be updated accordingly. For instance, according to this diagram, a contact would only be updated to SQL when the person has shown interest—that is, they have visited a few key pages on the website—as well as being the right authority—that is, their job title includes the words **senior** or **VP** or **Head** or **Director**. Then—most importantly— they have requested a meeting, which could take the form of filling out a demo form or a **Contact us** form.

The workflow will therefore have the following criteria as its enrollment trigger:

1.   Contact has filled out demo form or **Contact us** form

2.   Contact's job title contains any of **VP**, **Director**, or **Head**

3.   Contact has visited pages with **Uniform Resource Locators** (**URLs**), pricing page, and **About us** page

4.   Update the lifecycle stage to **Sales Qualified Lead**

The following screenshot shows what the workflow will now look like:

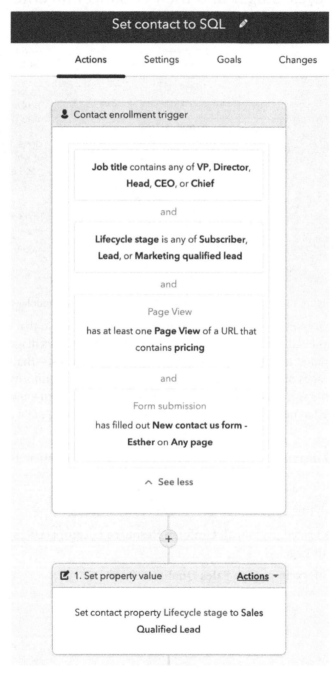

Figure 13.8 – Workflow for updating a contact to Sales Qualified Lead using a buyer-focused approach

Notice in each of the previous workflow examples shown that the previous possible lifecycle stages of the contacts are added to the enrollment trigger. This prevents the workflow from moving a contact that is already in a more advanced stage backward. You would never want to move a contact that is a current opportunity back to a marketing qualified lead or lead, even if the opportunity falls through. Moving contacts backward distorts the results of your funnel and does not give a true representation of your conversion rates from lead to MQL and SQL, and so on. So, if a deal falls through, there are other ways to update the contact's status—for example, updating the deal stage to **Closed Lost**—but the lifecycle stage would always stay as **Opportunity**. This allows the marketing team to nurture these contacts differently in order to re-engage them at a future date.

Using RevOps to boost business sales

In order to fully understand how to build a RevOps strategy, it is important to first understand which challenges existed to birth this new category. RevOps came into being to solve three core issues for companies, as follows:

- To get all systems in a company connected so that information can be shared in a secure but cohesive manner
- To improve misalignment between marketing, sales, and service
- To drastically improve the customer experience so that it will be more personalized at scale

So, developing a RevOps strategy would mean you are solving one of these core issues. Let's take a look at each of them and see how most companies are tackling these issues.

Connectivity and security strategy

This challenge became more prominent as the marketing and sales technology stack began to grow exponentially. Just take a minute to count how many different systems your marketing and sales teams use today. Most likely, there is a website built on WordPress or Wix that is being optimized using SEMRush to improve organic rankings. Then, there is a need for a platform such as Mailchimp or ActiveCampaign for sending emails, multiple social media accounts, and paid ad platforms such as Google Ads or LinkedIn Ads. On top of that, you may be using a landing page platform such as Leadpages or Unbounce and planning an **account-based marketing** (**ABM**) campaign using Demandbase or Terminus. Then, because your analytics are not connected to each of these platforms, you may be considering an analytics platform such as Google Data Studio or Databox to unify all analytics coming from different sources. And that was just marketing.

Sales teams today are also using a host of tools such as Outreach or Salesloft for prospecting to new leads, LinkedIn Sales Navigator or ZoomInfo for sourcing new leads, Gong for tracking calls, Bombora or Clearbit for sales intelligence, and so on. In the end, most companies are stuck trying to get all these systems talking to each other and mostly talking to their main system—the CRM—so that all these insights can be captured.

The challenge, however, is that generally, these systems weren't necessarily built with the foresight of having to connect to your bespoke systems, therefore connecting them all requires developers to consider creating **application programming interfaces** (**APIs**) to facilitate such integrations. So, how does a RevOps team begin solving this challenge?

The first task is to understand exactly which information is needed in order to accurately predict future revenue and track current revenue. You then need to consider what are the options for transferring data from one platform to another without losing information and—more—importantly security. With the rise of the **General Data Protection Regulation** (**GDPR**) and consumer protection laws, businesses must be ever more cognizant of data falling into the wrong hands or being misused in any way. The systems being considered therefore must have very strict security parameters.

Once these requirements are clearly outlined, then an exploration of which tools are best suited for the job can be done. This is how you make an informed decision on the systems your company needs and ensure information can be distributed in a secure and timely manner.

Unifying communication between marketing, sales, and service

Historically, marketing and sales teams always had different opinions on the lead quality of the prospects they were handing over. One of the more regular occurrences was that service teams were also finding themselves in difficulties with the customer as sales reps would often promise certain features, capabilities, or even pricing during the sales process to close the sale. Then, once the customer had made a purchase, these options were not quite available.

RevOps teams thus had to step in as the overarching layer to glue these teams together and get them responsible for each other's **key performance indicators (KPIs)**. For example, marketing teams were no longer just responsible for increasing website traffic as their main KPI for some organizations; it was necessary to extend this KPI to the number of qualified meetings booked. Similarly, sales teams were no longer responsible for just the number of customers closed each month, but their KPI also included keeping low the number of customers that churn after 3 months or 6 months. Likewise, customer success teams were no longer just being measured by the number of customers that successfully completed the onboarding process but by how many of them they were able to upsell or get to extend their existing contracts.

So, when considering implementing a strategy for this part of your organization, you need to analyze which part of the funnel is leaky or contributing to the most friction in your flywheel and implement systems and processes to reduce this friction. Adding further KPIs or success measures to each department is one strategy that helps unify these teams.

Personalization at scale to improve customer experience

Customer experience, as we have already established, is the foundation of an organization's success in this new connected world. Customers expect you to know their needs sufficiently enough in order to address them, sometimes even before they indicate they have an issue. Therefore, to meet this need, organizations are employing RevOps teams to be the gatekeeper of the experience customers receive, as their KPIs are tied directly to revenue impact.

For companies to earn their customers' trust and—at the same time—provide the personalized experience they are expecting, teams must have visibility across the entire customer journey so that they can provide a timely response.

Testing the impact of the flywheel

At the time of this writing, there is no benchmark of measurement your flywheel should achieve in order for you to know if your organization is performing well or not. The goal is simply to get it turning faster, and this is usually seen in the growth that is achieved month on month, quarter on quarter, and year on year. The higher these growth metrics, the faster your flywheel is spinning. But if you wish to have a more overarching picture of how well your flywheel is performing, check if your marketing team can take a vacation for 1 month and if your business will still gain new prospects and qualified leads for your sales teams to close.

As well as this measurement, here are some more formidable metrics that can also be used to track activity on each part of the flywheel:

- **Attract**: How much website traffic are you gaining from month to month? Note that you would want to look at net new visitors primarily as this would generally lead to more new customers.

- **Engage**: There are usually two phases of this metric. The first phase measures intent to purchase. For example, for software companies with a free or trial version of their product, you would want to track how many free/trial users are signing up each month; for e-commerce businesses, you would probably want to track how many people click the link to purchase; and for tech companies, you would want to track how many people sign up for demos. The more of these types of users you have, the more momentum your flywheel gains.

  The second phase measures actual purchase—that is, how many of these qualified leads that signed up for a free trial or booked a demo, or clicked the link to purchase, actually turned into customers. And then, you would want to track how many of these customers churn. The more customers churn, the more your flywheel loses momentum.

- **Delight**: Understanding how many of your customers would recommend your business is a great metric to measure delight. You will know this by sending out your **Net Promoter Score (NPS)** surveys to existing customers. A higher score with more customers answering the survey generates more momentum for your flywheel, while a low promoter score with fewer customers responding will result in your flywheel losing momentum.

Measuring these KPIs allows you to understand how well your flywheel is performing and gives you the opportunity to identify gaps and areas of friction.

Summary

Today, the flywheel has become the cornerstone of most business operations as it puts the customer at the forefront. However, this is not to say that the funnel is totally irrelevant. For some business use cases, the funnel still has value, but when combined with the flywheel, the force that is expended from customer satisfaction keeps the wheel spinning, allowing your teams to produce regenerative business without too much effort.

So, by now, you should be considering two options: either sending your marketing team on a 1-month sabbatical or realizing that if your customers are not the center of every conversation in your business, it's time to consider implementing a RevOps strategy to ensure BC. In the next chapter, you'll learn how to use HubSpot for every type of business.

Questions

Have a go at answering the following questions:

1. What is the difference between the funnel, the flywheel, and RevOps?

2. How does implementing a RevOps strategy improve alignment between marketing and sales?

3. Which metrics can you use to measure the speed of your flywheel?

References

*   *The Flywheel*: https://www.hubspot.com/flywheel

*   *How the Flywheel Killed HubSpot's Funnel*: `https://blog.hubspot.com/marketing/our-flywheel?_ga=2.227119064.430926925.1652084970-1769221773.1652084970`

*   *Growing Your Business With a Flywheel Model*: `https://academy.hubspot.com/lessons/flywheel?hsCtaTracking=12bfc6bc-820a-4ce1-b29a-e5e21549b948%7C1d137fed-f7d5-4d10-b7d7-9e0e0d0b920f`

*   *RevOps: The Modern Operating Model for Fast-Forward Organizations*: `https://www.gartner.com/en/articles/revops-the-modern-operating-model-for-fast-forward-organizations`

*   *What Is Revenue Operations (RevOps)? A Complete Guide*: `https://www.salesforce.com/resources/articles/what-is-revenue-operations/`

14
Using HubSpot for All Types of Businesses

So far, you have understood the value of having a **Customer Relationship Management (CRM)** platform in your business and are probably evaluating your options. In this chapter, we will provide some insights into how various types of businesses use HubSpot.

In this chapter, we will cover the following topics:

- Is HubSpot right for your business and team?
- HubSpot for B2B technology companies
- HubSpot for SaaS companies
- HubSpot for manufacturing companies
- HubSpot for e-commerce businesses
- HubSpot for healthcare companies
- HubSpot for automotive companies
- HubSpot for insurance companies

By the end of this chapter, you will have a clear understanding of which tools within HubSpot can provide the most benefit to your company and which portals (or Hubs) you would most likely need to invest in.

Is HubSpot right for your business and team?

As a manager or business owner, one of the most crucial decisions you are required to make is about which CRM system to invest in. And to do that successfully, there are five key areas you must consider:

- **Ease of use**: How easy would it be for you and your team to use and, more importantly, maintain the system? Would you require a developer or a systems administrator to execute minor changes? Or would your VP sales or VP marketing team be able to manage the system on their own? For agile businesses or companies with smaller teams, the system must be managed by a non-tech person so that the changes that are needed in the CRM systems can be made with relative ease to facilitate their growth. HubSpot is one of the few CRM systems – if not the only one – that has been relatively easy for marketers and sales professionals to manage on their own. To use most of the functions outlined in this book, a developer isn't needed and no coding knowledge is required.

- **Budget**: What investment is needed to set up and keep the system? This investment should include the cost of the CRM system, support, extra personnel to manage the system, and flexibility within all these costs to manage fluctuations within your business. HubSpot is generally quite favorable in all of these areas as the cost of the system is broken up by the different Hubs you wish to invest in.

  Firstly, the CRM is free, so to manage your ongoing sales activities, even without paying for HubSpot, you have access to a system that can facilitate this for you. The cost begins once you upgrade to the Marketing Hub. It costs 45 USD at the time of writing this book. To access more features, the price increases to 800 USD per month for the first 2,000 contacts and 50 USD per month for every additional 1,000 contacts. In addition, there is a built-in feature called Marketing and Non-marketing contacts that helps you manage the number of contacts you wish to pay for during your billing period. It allows you to be more flexible with managing your costs. Users who choose HubSpot as their preferred CRM also have the option to upgrade to Sales Hub, which also starts at 45 USD per month. Sales Hub offers additional sales tools that can enhance the efficiency of a sales rep. You can read more about it in *Chapter 4, Empowering Your Sales Team Through HubSpot*.

When it comes to customer support, HubSpot offers free support to all its customers in the form of the **HubSpot Academy**, its **Community**, as well as chat, email, and phone for those within the professional packages. It also does not require a dedicated resource to manage the platform as this can often be done by the marketing or sales team.

- **Adoption**: Ensuring your sales and marketing teams use the system you've invested in is always the most critical part of choosing a CRM system. Even though a system may check all the requirements for management in terms of cost and features, the project can still fail if no one uses the system. In my experience, there is always going to be some level of resistance from team members when implementing a new CRM. However, the key to success is facilitating the onboarding in such a way that users feel that their needs and requirements will be addressed in this new system and that the system won't make them do *extra work*. When it comes to onboarding your team to any CRM, it is important to have the necessary support and understanding. This is why HubSpot is one of the more chosen platforms because, besides its rich library of online support, it has a vast network of partners worldwide that can always assist in setting up the system, as well as training your team. This significantly helps in increasing the level of adoption throughout your team.

- **Scalability**: When choosing a CRM, the ability for your business to grow with that platform and have your processes adapt to the changes within your organization is imperative. HubSpot is a very modular platform that continuously invests in new features that match the changes in the environment where businesses operate. As your business grows, you can add more features and capabilities to amplify your marketing and sales processes.

- **Alignment**: In today's world, businesses can no longer afford to operate in a fragmented way. Internal departments need to be aligned to improve the customer experience. This is because customers have come to expect a certain level of attention and preparation from the very first interaction. CRM systems help you achieve this as they offer transparency and help systemize the way your teams should work. HubSpot, in particular, being the only CRM system that offers an all-in-one marketing, sales, and service platform, facilitates one shared source of truth within an organization, which translates to more transparent **revenue operations (RevOps)**. Complex integrations or tools that are cobbled together are no longer an issue as the information can easily be transferred between departments.

Now that we have a clear understanding of whether HubSpot is the right fit for your business and team, let's dive a bit deeper and get more specific regarding your particular industry and how your business can benefit from using HubSpot.

HubSpot for B2B technology companies

If your business falls into this category, it is more than likely that HubSpot can be a good option for your business. Here are the reasons why:

- B2B tech businesses generally have a long sales cycle (**SALES**)

- The process of gaining customers demands a lot of education (**MARKETING**)

To effectively manage your sales process, you must have a clearly defined procedure regarding how a deal progresses. In other words, you must have clear steps in your pipeline that indicate the part of the sales process where a prospect exists. This is even more important for a B2B tech company where the sales cycle is much longer. Imagine being able to recall why a prospect is in a specific stage 6 months after your last call with them. This can be difficult. Therefore, the ability to build specific stages that can be answered with either *yes* or *no* ensures each stage is unbiased, reviewable, and buyer-centric.

The main challenge with working with sales reps is ensuring that they update the data in the system. Having the pipeline created is only the beginning of the process. Ensuring that they put in additional data, such as the close date, the amount on the deal, or even associating the contact they are speaking to as it relates to the deal, is the bigger challenge. This is the power of HubSpot.

Here's what the HubSpot pipeline looks like:

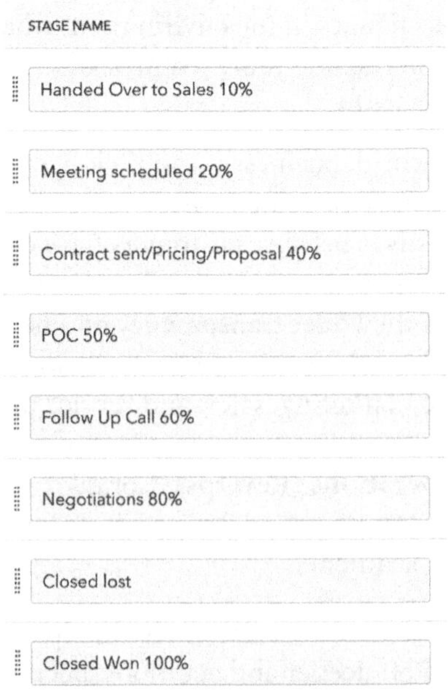

Figure 14.1 – HubSpot pipeline

By using features such as **UPDATE STAGE PROPERTIES**, certain alerts can be put in place to remind the sales reps to update these fields. Without these pre-conditions being fulfilled, the reps would be unable to move the deal to a more advanced deal stage. The following screenshot shows the pipeline with conditions:

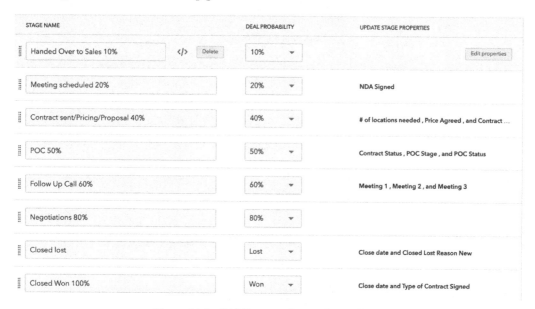

Figure 14.2 – HubSpot pipeline with conditions

There is also the option to build workflows that will send reminder emails or alerts to the owners of the contacts or deals if something is missing. On the other hand, you also don't want to give your sales reps too much administrative work to complete in the system as this is often the top pain point that renders most CRMs unused. So, using workflows also helps automate some of the actions in the system.

For example, if you need to have the lead status of a contact updated when the sales rep has made contact with them, you can build a workflow that will be triggered when the sales rep sends an email to the contact. This workflow will change the lead status from **New to Attempting to Contact** to **Contact replied to email** when the enrollment trigger is set.

The following screenshot shows how easily this workflow can be built:

Figure 14.3 – Building a workflow to update lead status

HubSpot can tell if a sales rep has reached out to a prospect by email or phone as they can connect both their emails and telephones to HubSpot and log every email and call.

Marketing for B2B technology companies

To accelerate their marketing, B2B tech companies can make the most use of HubSpot's features, such as the ads tool to set up paid ad campaigns on social platforms such as LinkedIn or Facebook, to attract their ideal prospect.

In addition, tools such as email marketing and workflows allow them to create drip campaigns for various segments of their database to improve conversion rates. From lead (someone that has shown interest) to sales qualified lead (someone that has indicated they would like to speak to sales or see a demo and have the ideal characteristics, such as a relevant job title, company size, and so on) ensures the marketing team is increasing the pipeline for the sales team. B2B tech companies that manage to successfully use HubSpot see a considerable amount of improvement in the number and quality of leads they attract, as well as the conversion rate of these leads to opportunities and customers.

HubSpot for SaaS companies

Most marketers tend to approach **Software-as-a-Service (SaaS)** marketing as they would B2B marketing. However, some important differences must be considered as it often impacts the CRM that's chosen to manage their sales and marketing. These differences are as follows:

- **The product is intangible**: Due to the intangible nature of SaaS products, since they are mostly technological products, they do not exist physically, whereas some B2B products can be tangible. Generally, for SaaS products, you are selling a service, not a brand or product.

- **Recurring payments**: SaaS products often demand the user to sign up for a monthly or yearly subscription. This facilitates the process of automatically taking payments from the customer, so long as they use the product. This is unlike a typical B2B product, which usually involves a one-time purchase.

- **SaaS buyers tend to be expert users**: As there are usually other competitors in the market, most SaaS product buyers conduct research on various platforms before selecting one.

- **SaaS products offer free trials versus proof of concepts (PoCs)**: Traditional B2B tech companies tend to have very complex projects that take a lot of resource investment to set up and deploy. Therefore, their version of a *free trial* often comes in the form of a POC, which can last anywhere between 6 weeks to 1 year. On the other hand, SaaS products are more sign-up-and-play until you need to pay to play.

- **Shorter sales cycle**: SaaS products tend to have relatively shorter sales cycles. They last between 6 to 18 months. On the other hand, a B2B company's sales cycle can be anywhere between 6 months to 3 years.

- **Higher churn rates**: Due to the ease of purchase, SaaS customers tend to have the ability to churn faster. This is because no long-term commitment is required or no crazy investment was spent upfront to install the product.

Sales management for SaaS companies

For better sales management, HubSpot allows SaaS companies to build multiple pipelines to track free trials, new prospects, and renewing customers. This is particularly necessary for companies that need a sales conversation with a prospect before converting them into a customer. This is typical for sales with enterprise companies, where their needs and use of the service would be exponentially larger and sometimes more complex than smaller companies. This can be seen in the following table:

Suggested Deal Stages for SaaS companies
(Free Trials / New Customers / Renewal Customers)

Free Trials & New Customers	Renewals
Demo Scheduled	Renewal Consideration
Demo Completed	Verbal Commit
Free Trial	Contracting
Review post free trial	Closed Won
Contract Sent	Lost (Churn)
Closed Won	
Closed Lost	

Figure 14.4 – Suggested deal stages for SaaS companies

The preceding table shows some of the stages that can typically be taken into consideration when building such a pipeline.

Marketing for SaaS companies

When it comes to marketing, the customer journey that a prospect for a SaaS product takes can be quite a zig-zag since these clients often come in at different stages. Therefore, a cocktail of marketing tactics must be used to capture these leads at the right time. Every SaaS marketing strategy uses some combination of channels and tactics such as email, paid ads, organic social media, **search engine optimization** (**SEO**), and webinars, to name a few.

Therefore, the CRM you choose must be able to do four main things:

- Be flexible enough to cater to the different levels of awareness so that campaigns can be created to capture leads in the various stages of awareness, consideration, and decision-making.

- Capture the source of each lead and track their progress until they become a customer.

- Segment the database from prospects and customers so that communication can be streamlined accurately.

- Produce meaningful reports so that the marketing and sales teams can make more data-oriented decisions.

Customer service for SaaS companies

With the ability to host both marketing and sales activities on one platform, SaaS companies enjoy a holistic view of the customer journey, which allows them to measure the **return on investment** (**ROI**) of their efforts. But HubSpot also has the added advantage of its Service Hub. This Hub serves two main purposes:

- The customer success teams can onboard new customers.

- The customer service teams can handle any inquiries promptly.

This gives both teams the ability to see every interaction a customer had with your company from the moment they showed interest in your product to the time they eventually became a customer.

Within the Service Hub, it is possible to build a customer success pipeline to track each stage of the onboarding process to ensure a smooth post-sales customer experience. The following screenshot shows an example of what such a pipeline may look like:

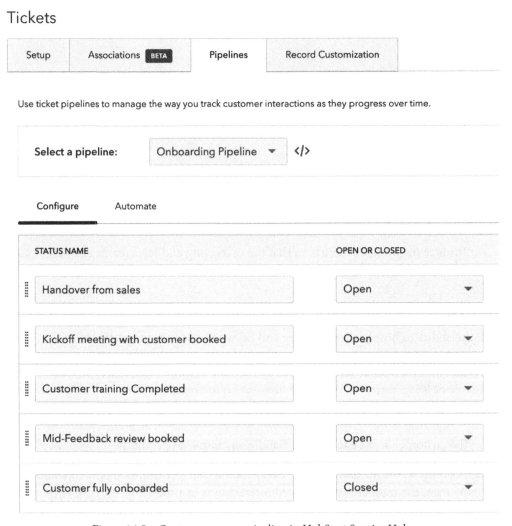

Figure 14.5 – Customer success pipeline in HubSpot Service Hub

Once the onboarding process has been completed, SaaS customers typically access a support team for answers to questions that may have arisen. Therefore, having a very clear, transparent path of how each customer's request is received, handled, and resolved is important to ensure the customer leaves with a positive experience.

HubSpot's Service Hub also allows you to build such a pipeline for the customer service or support teams, as shown in the following screenshot:

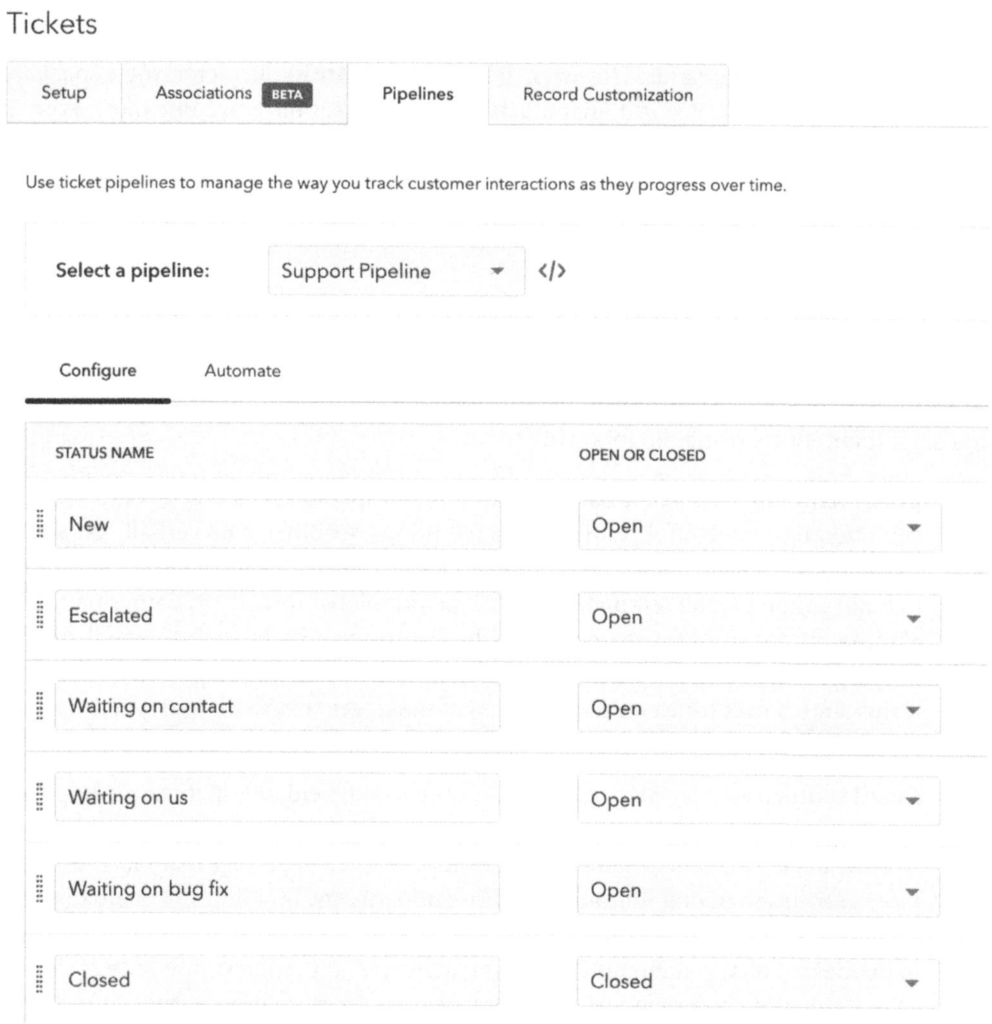

Tickets

Setup	Associations **BETA**	Pipelines	Record Customization

Use ticket pipelines to manage the way you track customer interactions as they progress over time.

Select a pipeline: Support Pipeline   ▾   </>

Configure   Automate

STATUS NAME	OPEN OR CLOSED
New	Open ▾
Escalated	Open ▾
Waiting on contact	Open ▾
Waiting on us	Open ▾
Waiting on bug fix	Open ▾
Closed	Closed ▾

Figure 14.6 – Customer support pipeline in HubSpot Service Hub

It is important to note that using Service Hub to manage customer success and customer support is more practical than trying to use the sales pipeline. Service Hub offers additional features such as feedback surveys and a knowledge base, which are not available in Sales Hub. These tools are essential to capturing relevant feedback from customers, as well as lightening the load from your customer support teams by redirecting users to online articles where they may already find the answers to their questions.

HubSpot for manufacturing companies

Traditionally, manufacturing businesses have relied on distributors or their direct sales team to generate business. Additionally, since they were serving multiple regions, this approach worked well in the past, as it meant they often had *boots on the ground* to fulfill their local customers' demands. However, as global competition is increasing, especially today in a post-COVID-19 world, manufacturing businesses have become more exposed and realized the need to redefine their sales processes and go digital as much as possible.

Fortunately, HubSpot is the solution that has helped many manufacturing businesses pivot to a digital model. Here is a preview of how various HubSpot sales tools can assist manufacturing businesses.

Sales for manufacturing companies

HubSpot can help the sales teams of manufacturing companies improve their efficiency and scale their efforts using the following tools:

- **Email templates**: As a field sales rep (or any salesperson, as a matter of fact), you often find yourself repeating the same things, whether it be verbally or while writing to prospects. HubSpot's templates are the perfect solution to allow you to build canned email templates that can be populated directly to your email, eliminating the need for searching for the last time you sent such an email and then copying and pasting it. Moreover, these templates can be shared across your sales teams so that everyone can see the types of messages that work best when trying to reach out to a prospect.

- **Email sequences**: For sales reps that must be in the field, often, it is near impossible to keep up with emails. Moreover, during COVID-19, when travel was prohibited worldwide, it forced field sales reps to transition their meetings from face-to-face meetings to digital interactions. This suddenly meant an influx of emails and follow-ups, which can be difficult to keep up with. HubSpot sequences allow you to queue personalized emails that can be delivered at predetermined intervals. This automatically frees up time for sales reps to do more prospecting, as well as ensuring nothing falls through the cracks.

- **Email tracking**: A common problem all sales reps experience is not knowing if a prospect has opened their email. HubSpot's email tracking tool allows you to know how many times your email has been opened and when it was last opened. This then allows the sales team to reach out to these prospects in a more timely fashion and increase their response rates.

These are just a few of the sales tools that can help reps be more efficient. In *Chapter 4, Empowering Your Sales Team Through HubSpot*, we discussed many more tools, such as Documents, Meetings, Prospect Tool, and others, all of which are very handy, regardless of whether you are on the road or stuck at home and having to ensure business continuity.

Marketing for manufacturing companies

On the marketing side, HubSpot also has a few tools that enhance the manufacturing marketer's ability to attract qualified prospects before handing them off to sales. It is a popular complaint that sales teams are often frustrated with the quality of the leads that are brought in by marketing. Therefore, these tools can make a huge difference in how the marketing team assesses lead quality before giving them to sales. Here is a breakdown of some of these tools:

- **Progressive forms**: HubSpot has a feature that allows marketers to ask different questions to visitors that are returning to their website. So, instead of seeing fields such as name, email, and company, a user (upon their second visit) will see these fields replaced with fields that ask questions such as *What is your timeline for making a decision? 3 mths, 6mths, 1 year, other* or *Which role best describes you? Director, Manager, End User, Administrator.*

- **Lead scoring**: The target customers for manufacturing companies tend to be very big companies with multiple people showing interest in the product or solution. Therefore, to help the sales team prioritize which leads they should focus on, you can use lead scoring. By assigning points based on demographic attributes, such as the size of the company and job title, as well as behavioral attributes, such as the number of times the prospect has visited the website in the last 3 months or which forms they filled out, sales reps can pay attention to contacts with higher points as it indicates that they are more sales-ready.

HubSpot for e-commerce businesses

e-commerce businesses mainly target B2C customers, although they may attract some B2B interest as well. However, unlike some of the other segments we've discussed so far, e-commerce businesses are heavily judged based on their customer experience. Now, of course, all businesses should pay attention to customer service, but e-commerce businesses in particular need to provide a frictionless customer experience; otherwise, they lose customers in large quantities. This is why HubSpot plays a pivotal role in their success.

HubSpot offers all the necessary features to manage the customer journey from pre-sale (Marketing Hub), sale (CRM), and post-sale (Service Hub). In this section, however, we will primarily focus on Service Hub since the marketing and sales tools have been thoroughly discussed throughout this book.

Service for e-commerce companies

HubSpot's Service Hub showcases the following tools to help e-commerce businesses deliver a seamless customer experience:

- **Ticketing**: A customer can be assured of a speedy response to their query once they submit a question via chat, email, or a form on the website. Submitting a query automatically generates a ticket that can be sent to the respective sales rep in various forms, such as email, Slack, or text message, so that it can be dealt with immediately. Moreover, it allows the sales reps to manage the problem internally as they can add more people to the ticket if they need to escalate it or reassign it to someone else. It also allows the customer service team to manage the process by updating the progress of the ticket as it moves through the ticketing pipeline. The following screenshot shows the HubSpot ticketing pipeline:

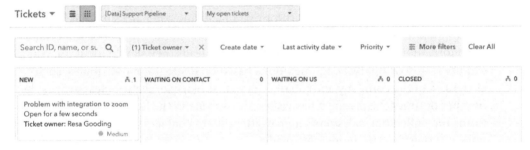

Figure 14.7 – HubSpot's ticketing pipeline

- **Chatflow**: Another useful feature in Service Hub is the business's ability to use the live chat or chatbot to communicate with the customer in real time. This is often critical for e-commerce businesses as customers generally want an immediate response when they have a concern or question.

- **Customer Feedback**: e-commerce businesses tend to want to keep their fingers on the pulse to understand where customer satisfaction lies as this is often the engine for future growth. Therefore, the need to deliver **net promoter score** (**NPS**) surveys or other types of feedback surveys helps them keep abreast of this.

- **Knowledge Base**: As we discussed in terms of SaaS companies, e-commerce businesses also need to have a knowledge base to answer the most frequently asked questions by prospects and customers. It saves the sales reps a lot of time in answering every query individually. It is quite easy to build such knowledge bases within HubSpot. The following screenshot shows an example of what building a knowledge base in HubSpot would typically look like:

Figure 14.8 – An example knowledge base setup and statistics

- **Integrations**: Last but not least, as most e-commerce businesses work with other platforms such as **Shopify** and **WooCommerce**, they must integrate seamlessly with these platforms. HubSpot has native integrations for these popular choices as well as some others, such as **BigCommerce**, **Magento**, and **WIX**, to name a few. The following screenshot shows what HubSpot's App Marketplace looks like:

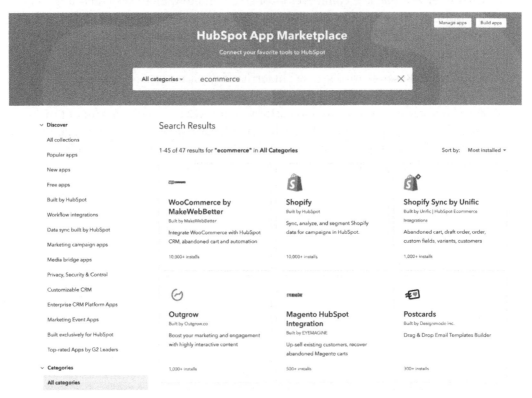

Figure 14.9 – HubSpot Marketplace – e-commerce integrations

So, just when you thought HubSpot was mainly for B2B clients, it is clear that B2C companies can also benefit from its use. This is especially true for businesses operating in the e-commerce space as it combines the core operations of their business – marketing, sales, and service.

HubSpot for healthcare companies

For all the reasons mentioned so far, such as marketing, sales, and service, healthcare companies can strongly benefit from HubSpot. However, one of the biggest benefits HubSpot can provide for such companies is the CMS hub, which allows such companies to build customer-centric websites. The main benefit is the ability to personalize the web experience using HubSpot's smart content feature. This feature allows marketers to change the customer experience for different segments of their database based on factors such as location, stage in the funnel, or even membership list.

Smart content can also be used on landing pages and emails within HubSpot so that different segments can also receive more personalized messages. However, the steps for each of these marketing tactics are the same. To use smart content in emails, follow these steps:

1. Create a marketing email by going to **Marketing | Email** via the top menu and selecting regular email or automated email, depending on how you wish to send the email. Remember that a regular email is sent once, whereas an automated email is used in a workflow.

2. Create lists that represent the segment of contacts you wish to send an email to. To do so, go to **Contacts | Lists**, click on **Create list**, and choose the appropriate filter(s). In this example, we created a list of nurses and surgeons.

3. Once the email content has been created, click on the text module and select **More | Add smart rule**:

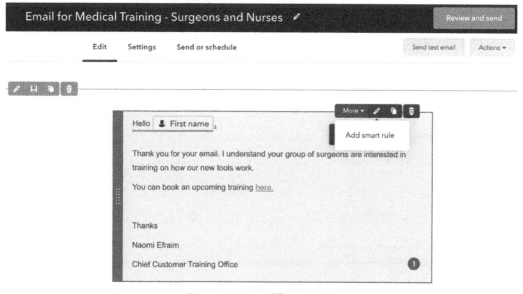

Figure 14.10 – Add smart rule

4.   A pop-up box will then appear, prompting you to choose one of two options – **Contact list membership** or **Contact lifecycle stage**. In this case, as we wish to send the email to various contacts located in the lists we prepared in the previous step, we will choose **Contact list membership**.

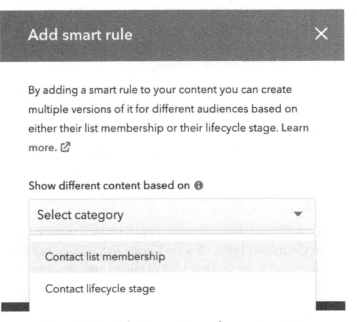

Figure 14.11 – Selecting a category for smart content

5.   Once you have selected **Contact list membership**, you can choose one of the lists that was previously built. In this case, we chose **Surgeons**:

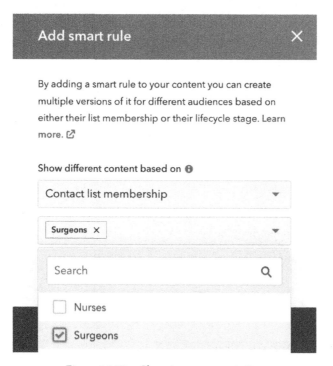

Figure 14.12 – Choosing a segmentation

6. Click **Create** once you have selected a list:

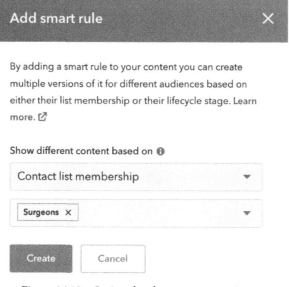

Figure 14.13 – Saving the chosen segmentation

7. You will notice a section on the left that will alert you of the smart rule variation you have created. There is the **Default** option and your list selection, which in this case is **Surgeon**:

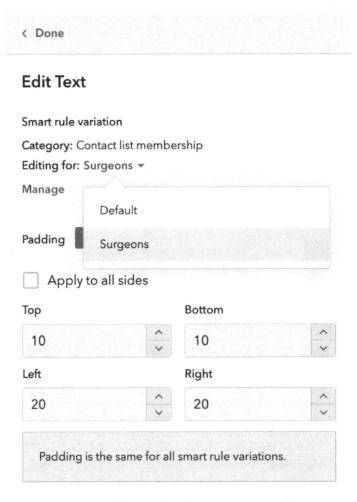

Figure 14.14 – Selecting the relevant category to edit text

8. You can add as many options as you would like by clicking on **Manage** and then repeating *Steps 4* and *5* to add additional segmentations. This can be seen in the following screenshot:

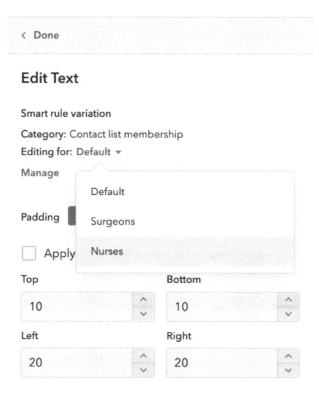

Figure 14.15 – Adding additional segmentations

9. Once you have defined your smart rule lists, you can edit the content you would like either of these contacts to receive by switching between the **Editing for** option found in the left module.

10. The following screenshot shows what the content for **Surgeons** may look like:

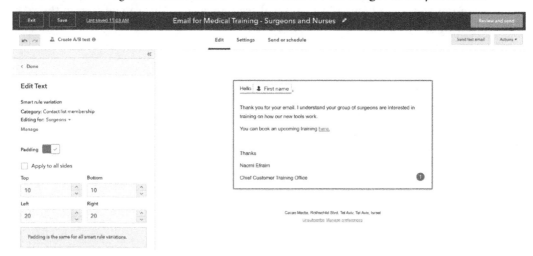

Figure 14.16 – Editing text for surgeons

11. The following screenshot shows what the alternative text for another segmentation, such as **Nurses**, may look like:

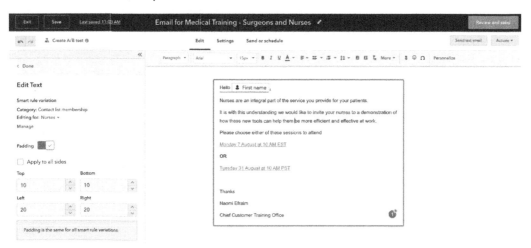

Figure 14.17 – Editing the text for Nurses

12. Once you have edited the text, you can click on **Settings** and add subject lines for each of the segments:

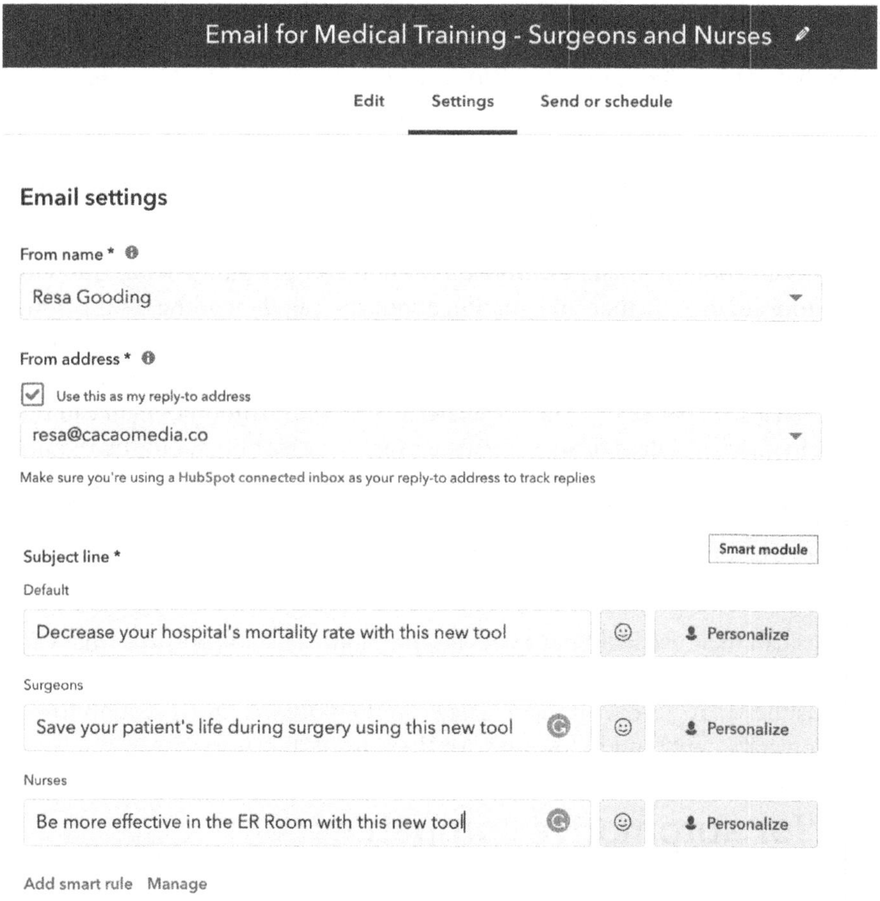

Figure 14.18 – Creating subject lines for each segmentation

This is just one of many examples of how HubSpot can be used in the healthcare industry.

HubSpot for automotive companies

Typically, automotive companies have relied on in-person interactions to sell their products and services. From cars to car parts to car services, **original equipment manufacturers (OEMs)**, car dealers, and car service providers, they all typically need to invest in brick and mortar locations and outbound marketing techniques such as flyers, TV ads, radio ads, or billboards to attract their target audience. Today, even though most have made the shift to incorporate digital assets in their portfolio in the form of websites and email marketing, there is still room for improvement.

Sales for automotive companies

Some ways that automotive companies can consider using a tool such as HubSpot to boost their sales is, for example, adding both a live chat and a chatbot to their websites to ensure there is constant communication between sales reps and prospective customers, regardless of whether the reps are working or not. A chatbot can be built to answer questions about the specs of the car, its availability, and its financing options, or even to book a test drive.

Visitors of this chatbot can then be enrolled into nurture workflows using HubSpot's automation tools to drip further information about the car, depending on the options the users selected. For instance, if a visitor was mostly interested in understanding the available financing options, a series of emails could be set up to be sent to them over time explaining the various banks that the car dealer works with. Another email can then be set up to go out in another 3 days or so to provide more information about the requirements needed to access the financing. And if the visitor doesn't get in touch with the sales rep after this, a third email can be sent with testimonials from happy drivers who got their card financed. The call-to-action in each email would be to book a call with the sales rep to learn more.

The sales reps can then use HubSpot's CRM to maintain a list of prospects that came through the website or chat tool to store important information that's collected from any conversations they may have with them. They can then use the **Deals** section to keep track of more serious prospects and follow up with them until they purchase.

Service for automotive companies

Once the customer has purchased a vehicle, the car dealership can use HubSpot's service tools to manage their continued service. For instance, HubSpot's Service Hub can be used to build a customized ticket pipeline to manage the yearly service of the customer's car or any issues that may arise after purchase. From the moment the customer purchases the car, they can be enrolled into an automated workflow that will send a series of emails to the customer 3 months before their service date, reminding them of such. They can also use the survey tool to conduct reviews that can be used to attract more customers.

The automotive industry now has the opportunity to stay in contact with customers throughout their journey. They no longer need to depend on walk-ins or tactics that are difficult to measure in terms of ROI and can use HubSpot to assist in this regard.

HubSpot for insurance companies

Insurance is one of the longest-existing industries and the most challenging to adopt digital practices in. One of the reasons for their slow adoption is mainly due to the legacy systems they typically use – they are generally on-premises and not in the cloud.

This is because of the financial regulations around customer privacy and data protection. However, there is still an opportunity for this industry to use marketing automation systems to conduct more personalized marketing campaigns and then integrate these systems into their CRMs to manage the customers post-sale.

Marketing for insurance companies

Most insurance companies are finding it difficult to attract the younger generation. One way to attract this audience is by educating them about why insurance is important. They can do so by using digital ads, which can be promoted on the social media channels they frequently use. Once they click on these ads, it can lead them to a conversion page where they can put in an email address to access a checklist or infographic that describes life with and without insurance. It is expected that the majority of visitors won't automatically want to purchase insurance just from this one interaction, but here is where retargeting comes in.

Using HubSpot's ads tool, you can build complementary ads that will continue to pop up in the feeds of those who initially clicked on the ad to show them further insurance information. These complementary ads can show a breakdown of the expected payout after 20 years if a certain amount is invested. Alternatively, these ads can show the different types of insurance since most young people only think of car insurance when they hear the word insurance. So, educating them about life insurance, health insurance, travel insurance, or property insurance can open them up to the possibilities of securing their future and assets.

And of course, using the workflow properties in HubSpot, as discussed previously, can help insurance companies to nurture these prospects further. The point is that even though some industries may think of themselves as too complicated or traditional to change to stay relevant, they must find ways to connect with their current audience using more current methods.

Summary

By now, it should be quite apparent that HubSpot can be – and has been – successfully implemented across a slew of industries. Its compact and comprehensive solutions allow companies to set up their marketing, sales, and services on one platform instead of cobbling together a host of disjointed platforms. Furthermore, the added benefit to link the entire customer journey from marketing to sales to customer service differentiates it further from its competitors. As a business operating post-COVID-19, the ability to gain deeper insights into what's working and what's not and make the pivot faster than you would have initially is imperative to your survival.

This brings us to the end of this book, but note it is only the beginning of the many ways you can use the HubSpot CRM platform for scaling your business. Our primary goal throughout this book was to give you the foundation needed to build the necessary processes and campaigns to help attract the right customers and reduce friction in your sales process. We showed you the technicalities of setting up some of the features, gaining quick wins, and then expanded your view on how the system can be deployed across various business processes and industries. As HubSpot continues to grow and expand its platform there are many other functions we did not touch upon. Some of them are Operations Hub that allows you to expand the functionality of the system by helping you integrate to other systems or CMS Hub that allows you to build a website that personalizes and deepens the relationship with your contacts. That being said, we hope you got value from this book and left with a better understanding of exactly how the HubSpot CRM system can help you achieve your business goals.

Question

Try answering this question: What are some factors you can consider to determine whether HubSpot is right for your business?

Further reading

To learn more about the topics that were covered in this chapter, take a look at the following resources:

- *HubSpot for e-commerce*: https://www.hubspot.com/e-commerce-marketing

- *The Ultimate Guide to e-commerce*: https://blog.hubspot.com/marketing/e-commerce

- *Why HubSpot is a game-changer for healthcare marketing*: https://www.riverbedmarketing.com/why-hubspot-is-a-game-changer-for-healthcare-marketing/

- *Creating a successful inbound marketing strategy in the healthcare sector*: https://www.hubspot.com/case-studies/fatebenefratelli

Assessments

This section contains the answers to the questions from all of the chapters.

Chapter 1, Overview of HubSpot – What You MUST Know

1. HubSpot is another content management platform in addition to a CMS platform (such as WordPress) that hosts your website. Therefore, you cannot use your regular domain, www.yourwebsite.com, to host these additional pages in HubSpot but must instead use a prefix, such as info.yourwebsite.com or pages.yourwebsite.com.

2. HubSpot uses Google Analytics to populate some of the information seen in the *Analytics* section. However, unlike Google Analytics, HubSpot can give you a further breakdown of exactly *who* came to your website and not just generic numbers.

3. You can visit the **Projects** tool in your portal. This is found by clicking your company name in the top-right corner of your portal and then choosing **Projects** in the dropdown menu.

Chapter 2, Generating Quick Wins with HubSpot in the First 30 Days

1. Analyze the top pages (besides your home page) that bring traffic to your website. Then, do a keyword search and optimize one or two pages with two to three keywords that have high search volume but low SEO difficulty.

2. Give part of something away that is valuable to your audience but invite them to contact you to get the rest of the information. Or, offer a free consultation instead of just inviting them to contact you.

3. Use progressive forms that will change the fields being asked each time a prospect revisits your website.

Chapter 3, Using HubSpot for Managing Sales Processes Effectively

1. Any of the following works:

   - What does the rep need to do to help the prospect move forward?

   - What indicates that the rep has completed their role in that phase of the buying process?

   - Is there any specific information they need to collect from the prospect?

   - Are there certain commitments they need to secure?

2. If you answer yes to any of the following questions:

   - Do you sell multiple products to various segments of your audience?

   - Do you sell across verticals?

   - Is your sales cycle drastically different from one territory to another or one type of customer to another?

   - Do you have distinct funnels?

3. To update other properties as deals progress through the pipeline, or to send internal email notifications for important updates so you don't have to spend time updating colleagues.

Chapter 4, Empowering Your Sales Team through HubSpot

1. Sequences.

2. Yes.

3. Using the **Document** tool allows you to see statistics on the engagement of the document, for example, how many pages the recipient read and how long they stayed on each page. In addition, if they try to forward the document to someone else on their team and you have turned on the GDPR options for the document, the second recipient will not be able to access the document without first entering their email address. This would then alert the sender that another person has accessed the document.

Chapter 5, Increasing Your Online Visibility Using HubSpot's SEO Tool

1. Change the country filter to your desired country.

2. HubSpot's SEO tool allows you to build a pillar and subtopics relational diagram that helps show you gaps in your content and SEO opportunities to maximize. You can then create content for topics or keywords that are frequently being searched for.

3. Semrush, Ubersuggest, and Moz.

Chapter 6, Getting Known through Social Media on HubSpot

1. LinkedIn and Facebook.

2. You should try to connect as many team members' profiles as they give their permission, as this helps increase the reach of your organic profile posts.

3. Lead source to deal conversion.

Chapter 7, Expanding Your Reach with Paid Ads Managed on HubSpot

1. Super Admin in HubSpot and Admin in the Ad accounts.

2. No. Only individual Ad accounts can be connected to HubSpot.

3. At least 300.

Chapter 8, Conducting a Portal Audit

1. A portal audit helps you to identify issues or gaps in the maintenance of data or the current structure of the portal in terms of naming conventions and your inability to find important information.

    You should first check that your website is connected to HubSpot. This sometimes gets disconnected if there was a recent website redesign or upgrade. To fix this, you would need to reconnect the domains to HubSpot.

You should start with understanding the missing gaps in your data. In other words, what information is needed for the report to be generated but isn't currently being collected? Also, looking at how properties are built. If most properties are single-line text and not drop-down, then it is harder to pull the information in reports, so these properties would need to be rebuilt.

Chapter 9, Converting Your Visitors to Customers

1. ReCAPTCHA and GDPR in the **Form** tool.

2. Top-performing landing pages usually have the following five features:

- A headline text.

- An explanatory subtext.

- A form.

- An image or video.

- And, in most cases, there is no navigation bar.

3. By turning off the re-enrollment button found in the enrollment trigger of the workflow.

Chapter 10, Revive Your Database with HubSpot Email Marketing Tools

1. Here are the elements needed to build an effective email strategy:

- Your goals

- Your audience

- Content

- Schedule of sending

- Reporting

2. Yes, using the integration with Canva

3. Any of the following can work:

- Pay attention to the subject lines and ensure they are short but click-worthy.

- Keep the content short. Any email that is over 60 words must offer great value and not just be a long-winded sales pitch.

- Use personalization wherever possible – in the subject line, in the preview of the text, in the body of the email, and, of course, in the salutation.

- Try not to add too many links to the email that take users to different content.

- Ensure the links are relevant to the action you want the contacts to take.

Chapter 11, Proving That Your Efforts Worked Using the Reports

1. Management typically cares about these five reports:

- Revenue forecast

- Deal time spent in each stage

- Number of opportunities created

- Deal velocity

- Deal revenue by source

2. Three reports that show marketing influence on deals are as follows:

- Opportunities by Original Source

- Deals Won by Source

- Lead to Opportunity Rate

3. The number of opportunities marketing helped generate for them or the number of deals won that were influenced by marketing efforts.

Chapter 12, Inbound or Outbound – Which Is Better for Your Business?

1. Inbound marketing is when the buyer finds the seller through their own efforts and initiates contact. Examples of inbound tactics are SEO and social media. Outbound is when the seller initiates the sale with the buyer. Examples include billboards, and TV or radio advertisements.

2. Attract, Engage, Delight.

3. A typical answer can include the following:

- Attract: Promote an offer on social media.

- Engage: Build an email nurture to further engage those who converted from the offer.

- Delight: Follow up with customers to get a testimonial from them that can be used on your website

Chapter 13, Leveraging the Benefits of the Marketing Flywheel

1. The funnel is a more linear approach to tracking how many prospects came in from the top and eventually channeled their way to the bottom of the funnel until they became customers. The Flywheel uses the energy of the interactions with customers to generate more customers. RevOps reduces friction and ensures the customers and prospects have a seamless experience when interacting with your company by ensuring all technical and foundational aspects for each team are well connected and transparent.

2. It facilitates the connectivity of the various systems each department uses and how they each reflect the information needed in order to deliver an outstanding customer experience

3. Some metrics to measure the speed of the Flywheel are as follows:

- Website traffic

- Intent to purchase

- Actual purchase

- CSAT score

Chapter 14, Using Hubspot for All Types of Businesses

Some factors to consider before implementing any CRM system are as follows:

- Ease of use
- Adoption
- Budget
- Connectivity
- Scalability

Index

`Packt.com`

Subscribe to our online digital library for full access to over 7,000 books and videos, as well as industry leading tools to help you plan your personal development and advance your career. For more information, please visit our website.

Why subscribe?

- Spend less time learning and more time coding with practical eBooks and Videos from over 4,000 industry professionals

- Improve your learning with Skill Plans built especially for you

- Get a free eBook or video every month

- Fully searchable for easy access to vital information

- Copy and paste, print, and bookmark content

Did you know that Packt offers eBook versions of every book published, with PDF and ePub files available? You can upgrade to the eBook version at `packt.com` and as a print book customer, you are entitled to a discount on the eBook copy. Get in touch with us at `customercare@packtpub.com` for more details.

At `www.packt.com`, you can also read a collection of free technical articles, sign up for a range of free newsletters, and receive exclusive discounts and offers on Packt books and eBooks.

Other Books You May Enjoy

If you enjoyed this book, you may be interested in these other books by Packt:

Digital Marketing with Drupal

José Fernandes

ISBN: 9781801071895

- Explore the most successful digital marketing techniques
- Create your digital marketing plan with the help of Drupal's digital marketing checklist
- Set up, manage, and administer all the marketing components of a Drupal website
- Discover how to increase the traffic to your Drupal website
- Develop and implement an e-commerce marketing strategy for your Drupal Commerce store

- Manage your daily marketing activities using Drupal
- Get started with customizing your consumers' digital experience
- Find out what's next for Drupal and digital marketing

Salesforce for Beginners

Sharif Shaalan

ISBN: 9781838986094

- Understand the difference between Salesforce Lightning and Salesforce Classic
- Create and manage leads in Salesforce
- Explore business development with accounts and contacts in Salesforce
- Find out how stages and sales processes help you manage your opportunity pipeline
- Achieve marketing goals using Salesforce campaigns
- Perform business analysis using reports and dashboards
- Gain a high-level overview of the items in the administration section
- Grasp the different aspects needed to build an effective and flexible Salesforce security model

Packt is searching for authors like you

If you're interested in becoming an author for Packt, please visit `authors.packtpub.com` and apply today. We have worked with thousands of developers and tech professionals, just like you, to help them share their insight with the global tech community. You can make a general application, apply for a specific hot topic that we are recruiting an author for, or submit your own idea.

Share Your Thoughts

Now you've finished *Empowering Marketing and Sales with HubSpot*, we'd love to hear your thoughts! Scan the QR code below to go straight to the Amazon review page for this book and share your feedback or leave a review on the site that you purchased it from.

`https://packt.link/r/1838987142`

Your review is important to us and the tech community and will help us make sure we're delivering excellent quality content.

Made in the USA
Middletown, DE
26 January 2023

23086279R00265